The Politics of Multi-faith

Political and Public Theologies

COMPARISONS – COALITIONS – CRITIQUES

VOLUME 5

The titles published in this series are listed at *brill.com/ppt*

The Politics of Multi-faith

The Limits of Legible Religion in Europe

By

Ryszard Bobrowicz

BRILL

LEIDEN | BOSTON

Lund University Open Access Fund (Year of funding: 2024)

Cover illustration: Photo of the Prayer Room at the Airport Chopin in Warsaw, Poland. Used with kind permission by the author.

The Library of Congress Cataloging-in-Publication Data is available online at https://catalog.loc.gov
LC record available at https://lccn.loc.gov/2024043746

Typeface for the Latin, Greek, and Cyrillic scripts: "Brill". See and download: brill.com/brill-typeface.

ISSN 2666-9218
ISBN 978-90-04-71435-9 (paperback)
ISBN 978-90-04-71436-6 (e-book)
DOI 10.1163/9789004714366

This book is printed on acid-free paper and produced in a sustainable manner.

Contents

Acknowledgments

This book has been a result of multiple years of research and would not be possible without the support of my family, friends, and colleagues, even if the responsibility for the presented ideas is entirely mine. I would like to express sincere gratitude to all of them.

First, I would like to thank my wife, Katarzyna Bobrowicz. It would be hard to account for all of her impact on my development. Her academic career allowed me to pursue my interest in religion and was a reason for our moves, first to Scandinavia, and then to Benelux, where I worked on the book. Her organizational skills helped me improve my working habits and structure my activities. Her writing prowess helped me improve my English writing. Finally, her unceasing support helped me continue the work even in challenging moments.

I would also like to thank my doctoral supervisors: Stephan Borgehammar, Johanna Gustafsson Lundberg, Ulrich Schmiedel, Mika Vähäkangas, and Terry Biddington. All had a significant impact on this book, and I am grateful for that. I am grateful to Stephan for supporting my writing skills with his excellent editing and for introducing me to different fields of practical theology during the reading courses. I am grateful to Johanna for expanding my perspective on issues such as religious literacy or Scandinavian creation theology, her positive energy, and her willingness to turn good ideas into concrete projects. I am grateful to Ulrich for his detailed feedback on my drafts, his engaged outlook on public theology, and his impressive knowledge of multiple fields necessary to tackle the challenging questions of this book. I am grateful to Mika for his unique perspective on interreligious relations, his global outlook, and the friendly research environment he built. I am grateful to Terry for his vast expert knowledge of multi-faith spaces, impressive active engagement as Dean of Spiritual Life, and his generosity as a host during my visit to Winchester. Furthermore, I would like to thank the opponent at my final seminar, Dan-Erik Andersson, for providing extensive comments on the first draft of this book.

I would also like to thank all my colleagues at the Centre for Theology and Religious Studies at Lund University which created a supportive research environment where most of the book has been prepared. I am also grateful to the broader environment provided by Lund University, including especially those from the Joint Faculties of Humanities and Theology.

I would also like to thank people from other research organizations. I would like to thank those who hosted me for Erasmus+ exchanges at the University of Winchester (Terry Biddington), University of Edinburgh (Ulrich Schmiedel), Theological University of Apeldoorn (Herman Selderhuis), and the Trinity

College Dublin (Fáinche Ryan, Cornelius Casey, and Michael Kirwan). I am grateful to colleagues from external research units with which I collaborated at different stages of my doctoral studies: Political and Public Theologies Lab at the University of Edinburgh, the Chair of Canon Law at the University of Bonn, Judith Hahn, and the Research Unit for Systematic Theology at KU Leuven, which hosted me during the final stages of the book writing, with special thanks to Judith Gruber as my host. Finally, I am thankful to colleagues from the networks with which CTR collaborates, such as EARS, EUARE, the Hamburg-Basel-Lund Group, LERU, the Scandinavian Network for Theology and Practice, and the Scandinavian Creation Theology Group.

Finally, I would like to thank the whole team behind A World of Neighbours. Interfaith Praxis for Peace, the project led by the Church of Sweden, which allowed me to gather practical experience and test my theories in practice. First, I would like to express my gratitude to Dirk Ficca, whose sudden passing in December 2021 left a gap that cannot be filled. Our close collaboration, his friendly advice, and his feedback on my theoretical ideas profoundly impacted my life during my doctoral studies. I would also like to thank Anna Hjälm for being a great leader, colleague, and visionary. I am also grateful to the rest of the team that developed and still develops the Practitioners' Network as a standalone organization. Their collective experience was an immense source of knowledge and inspiration for my work.

I would like to acknowledge all of the funders that supported my research during my doctoral studies: Centre for Theology and Religious Studies, Centre for European Studies, and Joint Faculties of Humanities and Theology at Lund University, European Academy of Religion, Erasmus+, *Stiftelsen Landshövding Per Westlings minnesfond, Innovationskontor Syd*, Institute of Catholic Theology at Hamburg University, *Andreas Rydelius stiftelse, Oscar and Signe Krookska Fonden*, CEMES at the University of Copenhagen, *Lunds Missionssällskap*, and Royal Society of Edinburgh. I want to thank Lund University Library Book Fund for open access funding for this book.

I would like to thank Ulrich Schmiedel again for his role as the editor of Brill's series on Political and Public Theologies which published this book, as well as the two anonymous reviewers whose comments helped significantly improve the original manuscript.

I also thank my grandparents, my siblings, and my parents for accompanying and supporting me on my path. I also thank my broader and extended family for all the formative experiences we went through together. I would not be the person I am today without them.

Finally, I would like to thank all the animals that accompanied me in my daily struggle with research and writing, especially during the long, lonely days of the pandemic: Ina, Timmy, Filemon, Stefan, Dilmah, Penny, Kira, Lilly, Snow, and Gustaw.

Figures

INTRODUCTION

A Mismatch between the Promise and the Practice

Imagine a small room with white walls and gray wall-to-wall carpeting. A modest IKEA drawer unit stands in the corner. A few books might be on the shelf, a small rectangular carpet hidden inside the drawer. Everything is lit with two fluorescent tubes. The only indication of the room's primary purpose is an inconspicuous sign on the door: "MULTI-FAITH AND CONTEMPLATION ROOM."[1]

Take a moment to scan this room. Think about how it affects your senses. How would you feel in such a room? What sensations would you experience? Would it make you feel comfortable? Would it incline you towards contemplation? Would you want to spend time there? Would you spend part of your lunch break visiting it? Would it be a place for you to de-stress or deal with a crisis? Moreover, if you are a believer, would that be adequate space for you to pray?

If you like the aesthetics of minimalism or brutalism, you might enjoy that kind of space. If you are under a lot of pressure or overstimulated, you might appreciate the emptiness of the space. And, if you consider yourself religious or spiritual but do not rely on any external manifestations of your belief, you might find the lack of visual stimulation an advantage, allowing you to focus on your internal experience, although the glaring cold light might disturb you a little.

However, for those who prefer, or even need, a specific ambiance, use artifacts, or rely on specific features in their environment, this room will be purposeless at best. At worst, it can prove to be the source of tensions, as was the case, for example, in the United Kingdom, where Muslim students at some universities protested in the street, requesting dedicated rooms,[2] in Denmark, where the matter was taken up to the level of the Danish parliament, with a debate on whether to forbid such places altogether,[3] or in Germany, where

1 The example is based on the Tate Modern multi-faith room as described by Andrew Crompton, "The Tate Modern multi-faith room: where sacred space and art space converge and merge," LSE Blog "Religion in the Public Sphere", 2016, accessed 17th of March, 2022, http://eprints.lse.ac.uk/id/eprint/76477.

2 Poonam Taneja, "Prayer facility row at university," *BBC News*, 1st of April 2010, http://news.bbc.co.uk/2/hi/8598455.stm.

3 Christoffer Zieler, "Parliament split in debate over prayer rooms," *University Post*, 23rd of February, 2017, https://uniavisen.dk/en/parliament-split-in-debate-over-prayer-rooms/.

three universities closed down their multi-faith spaces because of rising conflicts.[4]

The reasons for these tensions might be difficult to imagine—how can a bland space be the reason for any reaction, let alone a stark opposition? One might say that if someone does not find these spaces appealing, they could simply not use them. However, there is a caveat there. That could be the case if these spaces played a supplementary role. Unfortunately, this is not always the case. For example, for those whose religious observance requires regular practice at set times of the day, using a faraway religious temple is not a possibility. And, as in many institutions of Western Europe, if institutional policy, either directly or indirectly, forbids religious practice in places other than multi-faith spaces, this poses a significant problem.

While such spaces exist worldwide, in Europe they take a peculiar position, and thus tell us something about how we approach religion here. In their intra-institutional form, multi-faith spaces are remarkably alike in countries as disparate as Poland and Sweden, with the minimalist design described above.[5] They seem to be filled with meaning and cause particular problems in a way that is not that common outside of Europe, provoking contradictory reactions—for example, in the Danish context, they were accused of both being "really Islamic"[6] and fulfilling elements of political correctness more understandable to atheists than Muslims,[7] while in a questionnaire by the Danish Ministry of Education their use was associated more often with Christians than Muslims.[8] In this sense, they operate as vehicles for particular ways

4 Raphael Warnke, "No space for Allah as German unis close prayer rooms," *The Local Germany*, 11th of March 2016, https://www.thelocal.de/20160311/no-place-for-allah-as-german-unis-close-prayer-rooms/.

5 Andrew Crompton, "The Architecture of Multi-faith Spaces: God Leaves the Building," *The Journal of Architecture* 18 (2013), https://doi.org/10.1080/13602365.2013.821149.

6 Marie Krarup in a Facebook post, quoted, among others, in Jens Haag, "Marie Krarups Kritik Af Retræterummet På KUA Er Vanvittig Forfejlet," *Uniavisen*, 15th of December 2016, https://uniavisen.dk/marie-krarups-kritik-af-retraeterummet-paa-kua-er-vanvittig-forfejlet/.

7 Christian Langballe and Bertel Haarder, "§ 20-Spørgsmål S 242 Om Religionsneutrale Bederum På Hospitalerne." 18th of November. Copenhagen: Folketingen, 2016. https://www.ft.dk/samling/20161/spoergsmaal/s242/index.htm.

8 Undervisnings Ministeriet, Information vedr. aktindsigt i undersøgelse om bederum på offentlige uddannelsesinstitutioner, fra undervisningsministeren. Bilag 2, (Copenhagen: Undervisnings Ministeriet, 2017). For more, see Ryszard Bobrowicz and Emil Bjørn Hilton Saggau, "The Organisation of Prayer Rooms in Educational Institutions in Denmark—Moderate Secularism Between Perception and Practice," *Nordic Journal of Religion and Society* 35, no. 2 (2022), https://doi.org/10.18261/njrs.35.2.3.

of thinking and are subject to contestation based on them. In other words, they exemplify the European approach to the politics of multi-faith.

This book aims to analyze and provide tools for understanding the contradictory responses to multi-faith spaces by critically examining the visions of religion behind, in, and around them. The main research questions guiding this analysis are as follows: What are the underlying tendencies in thinking about religion behind multi-faith spaces? Are there any ideas inherent in the materiality of the spaces that condition specific approaches to them? What is the context in which such spaces operate? What are the basic assumptions shared by all those engaging in the discourses about these spaces? Are there any specific problems in thinking about religion that the conflicts around multi-faith spaces highlight?

This book's central argument is that there exists a tendency to think about religion that reduces it only to the features relevant from the perspective of the state—what I call "legible religion" throughout the book. Such a tendency, focusing on either the utility or the threatening character of the affected phenomena, influences how most multi-faith spaces are designed and function, limiting the types of religiosities accepted within them. This results in a clash between what they promise and what they provide. While such spaces promise that they cater to everyone and allow for freedom of religion or belief, they reduce the scope of what is allowable to particular understandings of religiosity. As a result, that understanding is subject to contestation between different groups trying to impose their vision of religiosity.[9] While not unique to Europe, this tendency is more common in European countries than in other parts of the world because of historical developments. And because of those historical developments, this tendency has a hegemonic status that makes it difficult for alternatives to emerge.

Thus, this book covers three issues. First, it offers an approach to intellectual history that could provide insight into the development of such a tendency and its main features. It is a proposal for an alternative view of secularization, in which religion does not decline or disappear but is, at least in some of its forms, turned banal because of a reductive approach. In this approach, the return of religion, as increasingly advocated by numerous scholars, does not

9 As discussed more extensively in the first part of the book, I understand "religion" as a constructed term, used to artificially differentiate a certain group of phenomena from other categories of phenomena, often to ascribe specific traits to it, for example, especially violent character or special public utility, and to make it manipulable. I take a pragmatic approach to this term. I study how it is employed in public discourse in Europe. I discern between religion as a differentiating category, and religiosity as a particular form of expressing believing, belonging, and behaving.

mean a revival of religion but a sudden increase in the presence of "unbanal" religiosity. The response to that return is a struggle between different groups that are gatekeeping what is considered either "good" or "bad" religiosity. Second, this book analyses how such a tendency is translated into practice based on the history, materiality, and context of multi-faith spaces. Based on the analysis of concrete multi-faith spaces, I will show how the architecture and policies surrounding multi-faith spaces differentiate between religions and religiosities, providing mechanisms to control "bad" religion and utilize "good" religion. Third, this book reflects on how to move beyond some fallacies of this tendency to match the promise with the practice. I will highlight why administrative reductions are problematic and, referring to notions such as subsidiarity, conflict transformation, and intergroup contact theory, I will discuss possible directions for solving these problems.

With this, the book aims to contribute to the rapidly growing field of public theology, which I understand following E. Harold Brietenberg Jr.'s as a "theologically informed public discourse about public issues addressed to [religious bodies], as well as the larger public or publics, argued in ways that can be evaluated and judged by publicly available warrants and criteria."[10] While the field has systematically begun to include different types of publics and engagement,[11] the administrative angles in question remain understudied. This book hopes to begin filling this gap.

1 The Assumptions behind the Book

Several assumptions accompany me throughout the book. First and foremost, the book starts from a critical interest in going beyond the level of explicit meanings, and an attempt to understand what the underlying assumptions of our everyday thinking and infrastructure are and where they come from.

---

10 E. Harold Brietenberg Jr. , "To Tell the Turth: Will the Real Public Theology Please Stand Up," *Journal of the Society of Christian Ethics* 23, no. 2 (2003), https://doi.org/10.5840/jsce20032325.

11 See for example Katie Day and Sebastian Kim, "Introduction," in *A Companion to Public Theology*, ed. Katie Day and Sebastian Kim (Leiden: Brill, 2017); Ulrich Schmiedel, "'Take Up Your Cross': Public Theology between Populism and Pluralism in the Post-Migrant Context," *International Journal of Public Theology* 13, no. 2 (2019), https://doi.org/10.1163/15697320-12341569; Ulrich Schmiedel, "The legacy of theological liberalism. A ghost in public theology," in *T&T Clark Handbook of Public Theology*, ed. Christoph Hübenthal and Christiane Alpers (London: T&T Clark, 2022); David Tracy, "Three Kinds of Publicness in Public Theology," *International Journal of Public Theology* 8, no. 3 (2014), https://doi.org/10.1163/15697320-12341354.

More precisely, I am interested in reviewing and tracing the formation of the contemporary *épistémè*.[12] That is the reason why the book not only describes contemporary multi-faith spaces and notions that shape them, but also looks at the historical lineages of these notions, as I investigate how institutions such as law and arrangements concerning, for example, spatial design and materiality, are constitutive of social reality.[13] Thus, the first part of the book combines historical and contemporary perspectives.

More concretely, I am interested not in the contemporary *épistémè* as such, but as it pertains to the assumptions underlying the imagined transformation of Europe from a predominantly Christian society into a religiously diverse one (even if the historical unity of Christianity tends to be overestimated and the historical presence of non-Christians tends to be underestimated). In the British context, Adam Dinham refers to this as the "multi-faith paradigm," a renewed consciousness of religious diversity followed by an intense policy interest in it.[14] The notion of paradigm refers to the scientific methodological considerations proposed by Thomas Kuhn in *The Structure of Scientific Revolutions.* In his work, Kuhn describes the development of science as a sequence of periods of normal science and revolutions. Normal science follows a set of fixed assumptions based on a paradigm, an exemplary scientific achievement, which defines legitimate questions and methods. A revolution replaces the old paradigm with a new one, reframing both the questions and the methods.

Unlike Dinham, Kuhn referrs to science rather than policy or social consciousness. Thus, the application of the term to the latter cannot strictly follow Kuhn's definition. Within the context of this work then, I define "multi-faith paradigm" in much less rigorous and exclusive terms, as a set of loose boundaries and conceptual structures that influence how different phenomena are understood, interpreted, and how challenges are resolved; a conceptual scheme or system that is dominant in a given social context and accepted as normal. However, similarly to Kuhn, I am interested in finding exemplary thinkers. Again, in the context of policy their work holds a certain level of influence that impacts why some ways of thinking prevail over others, but they do not

12 Michel Foucault, *The Archaeology of Knowledge* (London: Routledge, 1992).

13 For more on that see Clifford Geertz, *Local Knowledge: Further Essays in Interpretative Anthropology* (New York: Basic Books, 1983), 24; Talal Asad, *Formations of the Secular: Christianity, Islam, Modernity* (Stanford, Stanford University Press, 2003); Austin Sarat and Jonathan Simon, "Beyond Legal Realism: Cultural Analysis, Cultural Studies, and the Situation of Legal Scholarship," *Yale Journal of Law & the Humanities* 13, no. 3 (2001).

14 Adam Dinham, "The Multi-Faith Paradigm in Policy and Practice: Problems, Challenges, Directions," *Social Policy and Society* 11, no. 4 (2012): 577. https://doi.org/10.1017/S1474746412000255.

dominate the scene to the extent that no other ideas can emerge without a revolution. Thus, in the theoretical chapters, I attempt to identify several pairs of such exemplary thinkers: Auguste Comte and Karl Marx, Max Weber and Émile Durkheim, as well as Samuel Huntington and Jürgen Habermas.

In conceptual terms, the investigation focuses on religion, secularity, and religious diversity. I do not treat them as ahistorical, natural phenomena, but rather constructed and contingent outcomes of social negotiations and power relations.[15] I am interested in the category of religion in three main senses: first, as a separate category, a precondition for any specific tendencies in approaching it; second, as a category contrasted with the notion of the secular; and, third, as making possible the distinction between, and within, different religions, and thereby differentiating between "good" and "bad" religion, as well as "good" and "bad" religiosity.

The differentiation between the religious and the secular leads me to an interest in secularity, an underlying, dichotomous conceptualization of the public sphere. As recent research made abundantly clear, while secularity began as a Western concept, and was imposed on other cultures in often colonial arrangements, particular secularities have been locally negotiated "against the backdrop of their specific cultural imprints."[16] It is not possible, then, to speak of just one secularity. Nonetheless, colonial relationships underpinning it mean that particular secularities have often been overshadowed by a universalizing tendency, which treats the differentiation between the religious and the secular as more or less the same around the world. In this sense, secularity is different from secularism. Christoph Kleine and Monika Wohlrab-Sahr note that while secularity refers to "institutionally as well as symbolically embedded forms and arrangements for distinguishing between religion and other societal areas, practices, and interpretations," secularism concerns "institutional arrangements for separating politics and religion, and to their ideological legitimisation."[17] I discuss both terms further in chapter 2.

15 Saba Mahmood, *Politics of Piety: The Islamic Revival and the Feminist Subject* (Princeton: Princeton University Press, 2005); Saba Mahmood, *Religious Difference in a Secular Age: A Minority Report* (Princeton: Princeton University Press, 2015); Asad, *Formations of the Secular*; Talal Asad, *Genealogies of Religion: Discipline and Reasons of Power in Christianity and Islam* (Baltimore: Johns Hopkins University Press, 1993); Elizabeth Shakman Hurd, *The Politics of Secularism in International Relations* (Princeton and Oxford: Princeton University Press, 2008); Brent Nongbri, *Before Religion. A History of a Modern Concept* (New Haven and London: Yale University Press, 2013).

16 Christoph Kleine and Monika Wohlrab-Sahr, "Research Programme of the HCAS "Multiple Secularities—Beyond the West, Beyond Modernities"," (2016). https://www.multiple-secularities.de/media/multiple_secularities_research_programme.pdf.

17 Kleine and Wohlrab-Sahr, "Research Programme of the HCAS "Multiple Secularities—Beyond the West, Beyond Modernities"," 3.

The contingent character of notions of religion and secularity is shared by the notion of religious diversity, especially concerning the principles underlying how distinct religions are differentiated. The way in which boundaries between religions are categorized both mirrors the existing power relations and establishes new ones, stratifying society and limiting the meanings and discourses that are admitted in the public space.[18] Like with notions of religion and secularity, they operate as if they were natural and given. And yet they differ both in time and space, and, again, like secularity, can be reviewed at different levels. I discuss it further in Chapter 1.

Thus, the arrangements concerning religion, secularity, and religious diversity can be studied at different levels of particularity. Here, I take a middle position. I want to nuance the notion of Western secularity and its understanding of religious diversity by discussing the tendencies of the organization of the religious and the secular in different European countries. In that sense, I remain somewhere in-between the generalizing notion of Western secularity and the study of particular arrangements in a given country or locality. I am interested in how certain features of secularity in Europe result in similar features of secularisms across European countries that, in turn, are embodied in the shape of and approach to multi-faith spaces. Thus, I study the commonalities between different European countries, policies, thinkers, and debates while attending to differences when they are needed to understand the particular context.

While the interest in the "multi-faith paradigm" instructs the theoretical considerations in this book, actual multi-faith spaces are my empirical concern. Part 2 discusses their different aspects. It must be underlined that this book is not meant to be a comprehensive study of such spaces. Other good studies have attempted to do that.[19] Rather, I am interested in multi-faith

---

18 For more see Marian Burchardt, *Regulating Difference* (Rutgers University Press, 2020). https://doi.org/10.36019/9781978809635.

19 Ralf Gregor Brand, Andrew Crompton, and Chris Hewson, "Multi-faith Spaces—Symptoms and Agents of Religious and Social Change," University of Manchester and University of Liverpool, 2012, accessed 17 September 2021, http://cargocollective.com/wwwmulti-faith-spacesorg; Karla Johanson and Peter Laurence, "Multi-Faith Religious Spaces on College and University Campuses," *Religion & Education* 39, no. 1 (2012), https://doi.org/10.1080/15507394.2012.648579; Terry Biddington, "Towards a Theological Reading of Multi-faith Spaces," *International Journal of Public Theology* 7, no. 3 (2013), https://doi.org/10.1163/15697320-12341293; Crompton, "The Architecture of Multi-faith."; Andrew Crompton and Chris Hewson, "Designing Equality: Multi-Faith Space as Social Intervention," in *Religion, Equalities, and Inequalities* (London and New York: Routledge, 2016); Jonathan D. Smith, "Multi-faith spaces at UK universities display two very different visions of public religion," *Religion and Global Society*, 12th of August 2016, https://blogs.lse.ac.uk/religionglobalsociety/2016/08/multi-faith-spaces-at-uk-universities-display-two-very-different-visions-of-public-religion/; H. R. Christensen et al., "Rooms of Silence at Three

spaces as vehicles for particular ways of thinking. Thus, in my choice of examples, I look for overarching patterns in shaping and approaching such spaces. In accordance with the theoretical part, I am especially interested in historical spaces that impact the formation of future spaces, as well as in establishing what different contemporary spaces have in common.

There are three main ways in which these spaces are analyzed here: first, from the perspective of their history and development, asking about the processes that led to their formation; second, from the perspective of their materiality, asking what forms of religious/contemplative practice they are adapted to; and third, from the perspective of their context, both institutional and political, asking what kind of perception of these spaces is suggested by them. In short, I am interested in the concept of religion behind, in, and around such spaces.

In this sense, multi-faith spaces operate in my analysis as "texts," which I interpret historically and hermeneutically. Dominick LaCapra points out in "Intellectual History and Its Ways" that texts operate as events in their own right that do not only mirror reality but also modify it.[20] Similarly, multi-faith spaces contribute to existing discourses, affirming, changing, or disrupting them.[21] Because of that, I start by studying their background, following up with the study of their particular shape, their place in the larger whole, and the relation between them.

However, I consciously omit the question of the intention behind the construction of such spaces. Here, I follow the methodology of legal studies, which highlights the elusiveness of intention behind legal texts, despite the extent to which such a process is documented.[22] Rather, legal scholars aim to understand the law due to the influence of different contemporary stakeholders and interest groups.[23] While multi-faith spaces sometimes have a leading founder, they still result from complex intra- and extra-institutional dynamics

---

Universities in Scandinavia," *Sociology of Religion* 80, no. 3 (2018), https://doi.org/10.1093/socrel/sry040; Terry Biddington, *Multi-faith Space: History, Development, Design and Practice* (London: Jessica Kingsley Publishers, 2020).

20 Dominick LaCapra, "Intellectual History and Its Ways," *The American Historical Review* 97, no. 2 (1992), https://doi.org/10.2307/2165726.

21 Quentin Skinner, *Visions of Politics: Regarding Method*, vol. 1 (Cambridge: Cambridge University Press, 2002).

22 Marcin Matczak, "A Theory That Beats the Theory? Lineages, the Growth of Signs, and Dynamic Legal Interpretation," *Social Science Research Network* (2015), https://dx.doi.org/10.2139/ssrn.2595519.

23 Robert W. Gordon, "Critical Legal Histories," *Stanford Law Review* 36, no. 1/2 (1984), https://doi.org/10.2307/1228681.

and constellations of stakeholders. These stakeholders and groups of interest, rather than the intention behind them, are of primary importance for my analysis of the context of multi-faith spaces.

2 The Structure of the Book

This book comprises six chapters divided into two parts. Part 1 offers an explanatory theoretical framework that presents the preconditions, formation, and emergence of contemporary tendencies in approaching religion in Europe, which I call "legible religion."

Chapter 1 investigates the main assumptions needed for the emergence of legible religion and its main interests. It discusses the way in which religion emerged as a distinct category, separate from the state, and how it began to be used also in the plural, as religions, laying the foundations for thinking in terms of religious diversity. It also shows how the relation between the state and religion evolved into a model in which the state could not only govern, but also manipulate religion. This allowed the state to start thinking about religion in two concrete ways: either functionally, as a potential utility, or essentially, as a threat. As I argue in this chapter, all these developments led to the emergence of legible religion, that is, a central-level reductive framework that limited the understanding of religion only to those features that seemed relevant from the perspective of increasingly centralizing state bureaucracies.

Chapter 2 looks at how legible religion turned from a postulate into a neutral baseline. It starts by discussing the two initial engines of legible religion, namely, secularization as the justifying narrative, and secularism as the programmatic agenda. It then shows how their interaction led to what I call the "secularizing cycle of legible religion," in which state policies impacted individual and collective behavior, and how the modern consensus emerged out of that. Finally, it shows how this consensus impacted the emerging alternatives, summed up under the notion of the "return of religion," leading them to inherit most of the original assumptions of legible religion.

Chapter 3 is concerned with the adaptation of legible religion to the narrative of the return of religion. The chapter examines the construction of dividing lines between "good" and "bad" religions and their policy implementations. It shows the emergence of a division between the types of religiosity that are considered beneficial to social cohesion and those that are constantly supervised and strictly controlled as a potential danger; between those that can be translated, as epitomized in the thinking of Jürgen Habermas, and those that should be fought by all means possible as a threat to our civilization, as epitomized in the thinking of Samuel Huntington.

Part 2 looks at the implementation of the abovementioned ideas in practice, thus focusing on the questions: How are the normative assumptions behind the tendencies in approaching religion, described in Part 1, translated into action? And what can we do to overcome the challenges they pose? Chapter 4 traces the development of multi-faith spaces and their materiality, and the formulation of different directions in their design. It examines the importance of chaplaincy in this process and its relation to both the ideas of secularization and the return of religion. As argued in this chapter, multi-faith spaces, especially in their intra-institutional versions, embody notions inherent in the multi-faith paradigm. They promote specific versions of religion, either as a basis for desired social actions or as strictly controlled and regulated activity, promoting a version of religiosity that is individual, private, iconoclastic, cognitive, and, to some extent, syncretic.

Chapter 5 looks beyond the internal arrangements of these spaces at their broader placement and context. Focusing on the broadly publicized "problematic" cases of university spaces, it analyzes the role that naming, institutional context, and the broader environment play in the perception of these places that often operate as "closets for religion." It examines the attempts to control religion both by implicit and explicit policies and the impositions of certain perceptions in political discourse. It also demonstrates the difference between policies that enforce the framework of legible religion and policies that try to move away from it.

Chapter 6 starts by investigating what is problematic in the operations of legible religion. It refers to the work of James C. Scott and Hartmut Rosa, showing that administrative reductions often deprive the phenomena they influence of the features that made them valuable in the first place. These reductions also repress the creation of local, practical solutions, making the task of solving problems extremely difficult. Devised centrally, the solutions must work in all situations; they cannot just satisfy the needs of any particular situation. Finally, they turn "mute" relationships into the default, reifying relationships and turning individuals into clusters of neatly identified identities. In response, I propose three directions for thinking about possible solutions: subsidiarity, a reconceptualization of conflict, and encounter. In regard to subsidiarity, the chapter discusses the importance of resigning from the strictly top-down approach to religion, which results either in the strict imposition of secularity on the public sphere or the often arbitrary gatekeeping between different forms of religiosity. Instead, it advocates for a greater embrace of local negotiation, engagement of a greater number of stakeholders in decision processes, and the relegation of not only responsibility but also agency to levels as grounded as possible. As a countermeasure to the association of religion with conflict, this chapter discusses the need for a reevaluation of conflict. Instead of conflict avoidance, or even conflict management, it proposes conflict transformation and the re-conceptualization of religion, peace, and conflict studies. Finally, in place of the functionalist and utilitarian approach to religion, I follow the ideas of encounter, coalition-building, and inter-faith praxis as a possible basis for social action that is not reductive. However, I argue that individual change is not sufficient, but that structural change must follow.

PART 1

Legibility Theorized

CHAPTER 1

The Foundations of Legible Religion

Europeans are used to the operations of the modern welfare state and its benefits, such as broad access to education, healthcare, or roads. They are so commonly perceived as a given that we rarely marvel at their resounding success in increasing levels of literacy, the longevity of people, or the ability to drive at previously unimaginable speeds on public motorways. But these and other elements of the functioning of a modern state are a result of remarkable changes throughout the centuries. The fact that the state works in an orderly way and operates so successfully in a vast number of fields that go beyond mere power, from education and healthcare to public administration and agriculture, is a result of the emergence of complex ways in which modern states, through their administrative representatives and institutional settings, make the reality under their jurisdiction governable, much of which emerged only in the nineteenth century and onwards.

This turn in modern statecraft is described in detail in James C. Scott's *Seeing Like a State: How Certain Schemes to Improve the Human Condition Have Failed*. Scott sets out by analyzing the pervasiveness of state efforts at sedentarization, or, in other words, why states have been hostile to "people who move around."[1] His investigation leads him to a broader pattern of the development of modern statecraft—that every state wants to make a society "legible—and hence manipulable—from above and from the center" for the purpose of governing.[2] As Scott puts it, states aim to "arrange the population in ways that simplif[y] the classic state functions of taxation, conscription, and prevention of rebellion."[3]

Scott argues that pre-modern states were "imperfect" in lacking in-depth knowledge about their subjects, control tools, and standardized measures. This situation changed significantly in early modernity.

> Much of early modern European statecraft seemed similarly devoted to rationalizing and standardizing what was a social hieroglyph into a legible and administratively more convenient format. The social simplifications

1 James C. Scott, *Seeing like a State: How Certain Schemes to Improve the Human Condition Have Failed* (New Haven: Yale University Press, 1999), 2.

2 Scott, *Seeing like a State*, 2.

3 Scott, *Seeing like a State*, 2.

 | DOI:10.1163/9789004714366_003

> thus introduced not only permitted a more finely tuned system of taxation and conscription but also greatly enhanced state capacity. They made possible quite discriminating interventions of every kind, such as public-health measures, political surveillance, and relief for the poor.[4]

To substantiate this thesis, Scott offers a whole array of examples concerning forestry, weights, measures, population registers, language, law, and even the design of whole cities, the collectivization of property, or humanitarian aid.[5] Each of these phenomena was, at a certain point, made legible in an effort to make reality more governable by administratively reducing it to only the features deemed relevant by state representatives. That reduction, however, came at a cost. It did not stop at the analytical level but reshaped the phenomena in question. Scott continues:

> These state simplifications, the basic givens of modern statecraft were, I began to realize, rather like abridged maps. They did not successfully represent the actual activity of the society they depicted, nor were they intended to; they represented only that slice of it that interested the official observer. They were, moreover, not just maps. Rather, they were maps that, when allied with state power, would enable much of the reality they depicted to be remade.[6]

Such changes were especially dangerous where they affected reality in a too robust and muscular fashion. This was especially true when they were supported by an ideological

> self-confidence about scientific and technical progress, the expansion of production, the growing satisfaction of human needs, the mastery of nature (including human nature), and, above all, the rational design of social order commensurate with the scientific understanding of natural laws.[7]

Reductions in favor of legibility, in other words, despite their extreme benefits to the state's capacity, create a danger of missing the crucial features of

4 Scott, *Seeing like a State*, 3.

5 See also James Vincent, *Beyond Measure: The Hidden History of Measurement* (London: Faber & Faber, 2023).

6 Scott, *Seeing like a State*, 3.

7 Scott, *Seeing like a State*, 4.

reality that support the very vitality of the phenomena under the state's jurisdiction. Supported by state coercion, they can suffocate these phenomena, leading to their decline or even disappearance. Nineteenth-century German forestry exemplifies this well. At that time there was a concerted effort to make forests more legible—in this case, referring to the creation of standardized forests with a reliable yield of timber per square meter. The old forests were cut down in favor of new, legible forests, in which same-age, same-species trees were arranged in linear alleys with the underbrush cleaned. In the beginning, these new forests were a resounding success. The forests returned a reliable yield in their first generation. Over time, however, something began to malfunction. Subsequent generations of stripped-down forests observed a gradual drop in timber class because of the disruption of the nutrient cycle. Low water retention began to pose a significant problem and the vast areas of same-specie trees were prone to quickly spreading diseases. The worst-case scenarios led to the death of entire plantations. As Scott points out, "A new term, *Waldsterben* (forest death), entered the German vocabulary to describe the worst cases."[8]

The reader might wonder, what does it all have to do with multi-faith spaces? Scott, after all, never considers religion in his book. I would argue that Scott's idea that states struggle to make reality under their jurisdiction legible has large explanatory power with regard to the phenomena defined as religious. It can help us understand why multi-faith spaces exist and why they lead to so many different reactions. But it can also explain why we find it so hard to assess their problems and discuss them. The effects of legibility in the context of religion are magnified because, unlike natural phenomena like forests, religion refers to a socially constructed category, in the definition of which states take an active role. The continuous process of creating *legible religion*, then, can not only remake the phenomena it is interested in but also redefine what religion is and should be in ways that will not allow us to fully assess how these phenomena are affected. While in the case of forests, their death is a clear indication that something went wrong, in the case of phenomena defined as religious the situation is significantly more ambiguous. The protests of Muslim students, for instance, can be categorized as cultural incompatibility, not a challenge to the way religion is approached in the public sphere. The gradual increase in the number of 'nones' can be viewed simply as a result of progress and, naturally accompanying it, secularization.

That is why this book begins with a genealogical exercise. The sign "MULTI-FAITH AND CONTEMPLATION ROOM" does not make much sense unless we

8 Scott, *Seeing like a State*, 20.

understand the vast web of significations that hide behind it. And without that sign, the room does not necessarily give us clues as to what it should be used for—the largely empty white-walled room could as well be simply a break room, a closet, a space for small workshops, or whatever else someone could imagine. Multi-faith paradigm needs to be set in the context of the state's attempts at making religion legible. Thus, the following chapter is an attempt at defining and describing the main components that influenced the ways in which European states attempted to make religion legible. First, I will discuss the necessary assumptions that had to emerge in order for legible religion to be even possible: the analytical distinction of 'religion' and 'religions,' and the notion that they can be governed and manipulated by the state. Second, I will discuss two main understandings of legible religion that became important to the state: religion as a utility and religion as a danger.

1 Prerequisites of Legible Religion

1.1 *Religion Is a Distinct Category That Can be Used in the Plural*

The term 'religion' does not have a clear referent. Up until today, scholars struggle to find a definition that would be neither too narrow, missing some of the phenomena that are customarily considered religious, or too broad, including phenomena that would not be considered religious in common sense.[9] This conundrum might be partly due to the fact that the term is a peculiar European invention. Historically and globally, to define such a separate sphere of life could be considered rather bizarre.

The exact etymology of the term is uncertain, but it is quite clear that the Roman use of its Latin predecessor, *religio*, was quite different from our modern understanding. Around the beginning of the current era, Romans did not separate any sphere of life as religious but were interested in how someone conducted themselves as a member of society. *Religio* permeated all spheres of life with the notion of sacred obligations that one had to uphold.[10] Lack of regard for these obligations moved someone beyond the boundaries of acceptability and put them in the dangerous space of *superstitio*. In the words of a stoic Roman philosopher, Seneca, "*religio* honors the gods, *superstitio* wrongs

9 For a review of different approaches, see Daniel L. Pals, *Nine Theories of Religion* (Oxford: Oxford University Press, 2015).

10 Mary Beard, John North, and Simon Price, *Religions of Rome. A History*, vol. 1 (Cambridge: Cambridge University Press, 1998), 216.

them."[11] *Religio* included a broad range of traditional cults, not only those later considered as pagan, but, for example, practices of Judaism, highly respected for their ancient character.[12]

The focus on conduct began to change with the increasing establishment of Christianity following the Edict of Milan in 313. Public interest moved *religio* from something that was understood in terms of conduct to something that was understood in terms of belief. The notion of orthodoxy started to play an increasing role in defining what was required from the members of the Roman public, moving to the North with the reformulation of the Western Empire and the coronation of Charlemagne in 800. And yet, even at that time the understanding of religion as a separate category of life would be an anachronism. Even the analytical distinction between the church and state would take a millennium to mature, to which we will return in the next section.

But the term religion would take modern shape and significance as it would begin to function not only in the singular but also in the plural form. The notion of 'religions,' understood as distinct sets of beliefs that can be analytically separated, would be possible thanks to the redefinition of *religio* by Christianity. As Jörg Rüpke argues, "it was Christianity ... —with its stress on belief and its wish to drive out 'heretics'—that came to create 'religion' as something different from social life and 'religions' as the plurality of its illegitimate forms."[13] The dichotomy of *religio* and *superstitio* would be replaced by a variety of mutually exclusive religions. Marianne Moyaert refers to this process of co-dependent selfing and othering through religious difference as "religionization."[14]

Building on the work of scholars such as Tomoko Masuzawa,[15] Brent Nongbri, the author of *Before Religion: A History of a Modern Concept*, argues that the

11 Beard, North, and Price, *Religions of Rome. A History*, 1, 216.

12 See, for example, Tessa Rajak, "Was there a Roman charter for the Jews," in *The Jewish Dialogue with Greece and Rome* (Leiden: Brill, 2001).

13 Jorg Rüpke, "Religious Pluralism," in *The Oxford Handbook of Roman Studies* (Oxford: Oxford University Press, 2012), 1. Whether that is indeed the case may of course be disputed. As for example Roger Beck shows, doctrine, understood by him as "that which within the given religious group is negotiated (or negotiable) concerning legitimate representations," was not "invented" by Christians, but was a common feature of other cults as well, for example, Mithraism. Unlike Mithraism, however, as Beck argued, Christianity did not have a constantly contested fluid doctrine, but reified and sanctified its doctrine over time. See Roger Beck, *The Religion of the Mithras Cult in the Roman Empire* (Oxford: Oxford University Press, 2006), 90.

14 Marianne Moyaert, *Christian Imaginations of the Religious Other: A History of Religionization* (Hoboken, NJ and Chichester: Wiley, 2024), 3.

15 Tomoko Masuzawa, *The invention of world religions, or, How European universalism was preserved in the language of pluralism* (Chicago: Chicago University Press, 2005).

term played a significant role in the process of European colonization—both in space and time. With the expansion of European empires, different rites and beliefs of conquered natives were categorized as separate religions. With the archeological and historical conquest, ancient rites and beliefs followed the same fate.[16] The fact that we can distinguish easily between paganism and Christianity, Judaism and Islam, Shintoism and Buddhism is rarely contested in public debates. Quite the opposite, their analytical distinction is often accompanied by a description of its essential character. In its most banal manifestation, it allows a politician like the Dutch leader of the Party for Freedom, Geert Wilders, to write on Twitter: "islam is evil. And barbaric and violent by nature. It wants all non-muslims to submit [sic]."[17]

The distinction of religion as a separate category and religions as its plural form constitutes the first necessary component in laying the foundation for the legible religion of modern European states. Without it, the state interventions would lack a subject to manipulate. But the fact that religion can be analytically separated does not necessarily mean that it should be of interest to the state or that it can be manipulated. Thus, we need to take a closer look at where this belief comes from.

1.2 *Religion Can be Governed by the State*

Every large social organism requires discernment between what is and what is not allowable. In other words, governability requires boundary-making. The distinction between *religio* and *superstitio* and the focus on conduct was a way in which Romans tried to order their society. The rapidly expanding Roman empire was largely respectful of the traditional cults they encountered during conquests.[18] The rules of the *interpretatio Romana* allowed for translating such foreign cults into a common Roman framework, thus laying a foundation for

---

16 Brent Nongbri, *Before Religion. A History of a Modern Concept* (New Haven and London: Yale University Press, 2013), 24–25; 129–131.

17 https://twitter.com/geertwilderspvv/status/866282919412678657?lang=en.

18 See John North, "Religious Toleration in Republican Rome," *The Cambridge Classical Journal* 25 (1979), https://doi.org/10.1017/S0068673500004144; Perez Zagorin, *How the Idea of Religious Toleration Came to the West* (Princeton, NJ: Princeton University Press, 2003); John Scheid, "Religions in Contact," in *Ancient Religions*, ed. Sara Iles Johnston (Boston, MA: The Belknap Press of Harvard University Press, 2007). However, it should not be mistaken with the contemporary understanding of tolerance, that is, freedom to choose what one believes in. For example, Zagorin noted that "At nearly all stages of their history the Romans were willing to accept foreign cults and practices; this de-facto religious pluralism is entirely attributable to the polytheistic character of Roman religion and had nothing to do with principles or values sanctioning religious toleration, a concept unknown to Roman society or law and never debated by Roman philosophers or political writers" 4.

unity in the encountered diversity.[19] Common participation in civic rituals set the boundaries for religious diversity. The excessive, problematic devotion or the refusal to participate in the cult of the emperor without an ancient precedent could lead to localized persecutions, as was the case concerning, for example, the Bacchic cult and Christianity, although blanket condemnation of a given group would not happen until Diocletian's edict against Christians from 303.[20] Romans were more interested in banning concrete practices and gatherings than cults altogether.

As already mentioned, a significant change in understanding of religious diversity came with Christianity. The provision of legal status to Christianity in the 313 Edict of Milan began what some describe in strong terms as the "Constantinian shift,"[21] an interweaving of the Christian churches with the imperial government. Following the Edict of Milan, the Roman system gradually "converted" into a Christian understanding, reflected in laws proclaimed by subsequent emperors. Under the rule of Theodosius I, Christianity was turned from a *religio licita* into a *religio regalis*, becoming the de facto state religion of the Roman Empire. This change is well exemplified by the Book XVI of the *Codex Theodosianus*, the first Roman codification from 438. There, Roman society was arranged according to a strict stratification based on adherence to

---

19 See Clifford Ando, "Interpretatio Romana," *Classical Philology* 100, no. 1 (2005), https://doi.org/10.1086/431429.

20 Gervase Phillips, "Deviance, Persecution and the Roman Creation of Christianity," *Journal of Historical Sociology* 29, no. 2 (2016), https://doi.org/10.1111/johs.12071.

21 The term was popularized by John H. Yoder, who wrote that: "The most impressive transitory change underlying our common experience, one that some thought was a permanent lunge forward in salvation history, was the so-called Constantinian shift. The Renaissance, the Enlightenment, the Industrial Revolution, and numerous important changes since then have changed our immediate agenda, but without setting aside the foundational challenge of the confusion between the Good News and the establishment for which the son of Constantius Chlorus and a Serbian barmaid was partly the agent, partly the beneficiary, and mostly the symbol. Our unending concern to reassure ourselves that what we are about 'has a future' is constitutive for our cultural style, formed as it is by the way in which our common Western story has taught us to identify socio-political flourishing with validation." John H. Yoder, "Is There Such a Thing as Being Ready for Another Millenium?," in *The Future of Theology: Essays in Honor of Jürgen Moltmann*, ed. Miroslav Volf, Carmen Krieg, and Thomas Kucharz (Grand Rapids, MI and Cambridge, U.K.: William B. Eerdmans Publishing Company, 1996), 65. The idea of the Constantinian shift has been widely disputed, see, for example, Peter J. Leithart, *Defending Constantine: The Twilight of an Empire and the Dawn of Christendom* (Downers Grove, IL: IVP Academic, 2010). John D. Roth, ed., *Constantine Revisited: Leithart, Yoder, and the Constantinian Debate* (Eugene, OR: Pickwick Publications, 2013). Simon P. Schmidt, *Church and World: Eusebius's, Augustine's, and Yoder's Interpretations of the Constantinian Shift* (Eugene, OR: Pickwick Publications, 2020), 127–36.

the correct creed and association with the right leaders. At the same time, the proper practice was relegated to a further place—with "orthodox" Christians at the top, pagans and Jews in the middle, and heretics and apostates at the bottom.[22] Boundary-making, as well as selfing and othering, moved towards religonization, even if the focus was still largely on orthodoxy and heresies, rather than religions in the plural.[23]

The Constantinian shift meant that Christianity and the state became nearly equivocal, which did not mean that the structure of authority remained clear. For example, the increasingly political nature of diocesan and monastic appointments led to significant tension erupting in the so-called Investiture Struggle—the question of who has the ultimate say in such appointments, and, in turn, whose authority is superior—the pope's or the emperor's. While the answer to this question would fluctuate over time, the Investiture Struggle would lay the foundations for the separation of the state and church as a byproduct. In an attempt to establish his supremacy, Pope Gregory VII issued *Dictatus Papae* in 1075, a compilation of 27 statements that discussed the relationship between the church and the world. The pope situated himself as the highest authority to princes,[24] bishops,[25] and emperors[26]. He assumed complete immunity[27] and infallibility,[28] the only right to appoint bishops,[29] adjudicate over them[30] and over more significant cases of every church,[31] or call for General Synods.[32] He assumed legislative and administrative power over the internal organization of the church.[33] With the subsequent expansion of canon law and the enforcement of the hierarchical administrative diocesan and monastic structures under the papal leadership, the church began to constitute a parallel, international structure *alongside* the states, not necessarily *within* them.

---

22 Ryszard Bobrowicz, "The Inverted Relationship: Constitutive Theory of Law and the Enforcement of Orthodoxy in Book XVI of the Theodosian Code," in *Law, Religion and Tradition*, ed. Jessica Giles, Andrea Pin, and Frank S. Ravitch,(Cham: Springer Nature Switzerland AG, 2018).

23 Moyaert, *Christian Imaginations of the Religious Other: A History of Religionization*, 3.

24 *Dictatus Papae* §9.

25 *Dictatus Papae* §4 & §13.

26 *Dictatus Papae* §12.

27 *Dictatus Papae* §19.

28 *Dictatus Papae* §22.

29 *Dictatus Papae* §3.

30 *Dictatus Papae* §4.

31 *Dictatus Papae* §21.

32 *Dictatus Papae* §16.

33 *Dictatus Papae* §7 & §14.

Between the beginning of the current era and early modernity, the foundations for what religious diversity means and how the relationship between church and state is organized were laid out. First, at the time of early Christianity, understanding diversity in terms of creedal adherence came to the forefront. While the distinction in some form between the sacred and the secular already operated in early Christianity, it was not translated into strict political terms until the second millennium.[34] Then, during the eleventh century, the Papal Revolution laid the grounds for the separation of the secular from the ecclesial, creating conditions in which one could influence the other.[35]

Thus, subsequent centuries observed changing models of the relationship between the two. In 1302, the bull *Unam sanctam* described the papal approach to the subject. The pope differentiated two distinct types of power, described as two swords: a spiritual and a temporal. Both types of power belonged to the church but were exercised by different authorities. Spiritual power was exercised *by* the church directly, while temporal power was exercised by secular authorities *on behalf of* the church and at the church's will. The church, at least in principle, was able to manipulate the state.

In practice, though, the so-called doctrine of two swords did not have much success as the papacy was significantly weakened with both the move to Avignon and the Western Schism. Although reaffirmed two centuries later by Pope Leo X at the Fifth Lateran Council, it was considered not much more than mere fiction and was soon overshadowed by the Reformation.[36] During the sixteenth century, the religious dominance of Catholic authorities was broken, and with it the political obedience of some local rulers. Reformers like Martin Luther[37] or John Calvin[38] replaced the doctrine of the two swords with the doctrine of the two kingdoms, which assumed the need to separate the spiritual and the temporal. Although in practice the level of interference between the two remained subject to disputes between different Protestant groups and localities, the idea that church and state should be, at least to a degree, separated, retained a significant presence in political thinking ever since.

34 Larry Siedentop, *Inventing the Individual. The Origins of Western Liberalism* (Cambridge, MA: Belknap Press, 2017), 199.

35 See Harold J. Berman, *Law and Revolution. The Formation of the Western Legal Tradition* (Cambridge, MA and London, England: Harvard University Press, 1983), 32.

36 Matthew J. Tuininga, *Calvin's Political Theology and the Public Engagement of the Church. Christ's Two Kingdoms* (Cambridge, MA: Cambridge University Press, 2017), 30–31.

37 Martin Luther, "Temporal Authority: To What Extent it Should Be Obeyed (1523)," in *Martin Luther's Basic Theological Writings*, ed. Timothy F. Lull (Minneapolis: Fortress Press, 1989), 664–65.

38 Tuininga, *Calvin's Political Theology*, 59.

The confusion that followed from the emergence of multiple churches and rivaling models of governing led to the gradual dissolution of Christendom and paved the way for rethinking the relationship between state and church altogether. New approaches abandoned the ideal of complete uniformity on behalf of a more territorial approach. First, the new rule of governance, summed up by the Latin phrase *cuius regio, eius religio*, was established in the Peace of Augsburg in 1555, allowing for the coexistence of multiple Christianities within the Holy Roman Empire, depending on the religion of the ruler.[39] While it still upheld the ideal of uniformity within a single state, those who did not share the beliefs of the prince could, at least in principle, move to a territory where their creed was established.

The principle of *cuius regio* was somewhat limited in scope, not only geographically but also denominationally—for example, it did not include Reformed Christians. They were included only about a century later in what some view as the turning point for the creation of modern states, international relations, and, not the least, approaches to religion—the Peace of Westphalia.

The early modern period observed the struggle between competing conceptions of the relationship between the secular and the ecclesial domain. Out of the dispute between the two swords and the two kingdoms, the former placing the secular under the control of the ecclesial, and the latter separating the two, a third option emerged, which turned the former on its head and argued for the supremacy of the political over the religious. While still advocating for uniformity, early notions of what would evolve into religious tolerance provided a space for individual dissent. Dissociating religious dissent from other civic matters allowed for a personalized and individualized understanding of religion as a category of its own. By that time, then, not only religion and religions functioned as analytically distinct categories, but the principle of *cuius regio* relegated the matters of religion under the authority of the prince, paving the way not only to governability, but also manipulability.

1.3 *Religion Can be Manipulated by the State*

By now we have observed two crucial developments in the understanding of the notion "religion" that had to occur in order to allow for the emergence of legible religion—that religion can be analytically distinguished as a separate

39 For more, see for example, Robert von Friedeburg, "Cuius regio, eius religio: The Ambivalent Meanings of State Building in Protestant Germany, 1555–1655," in *Diversity and Dissent: Negotiating Religious Difference in Central Europe, 1500–1800*, ed. Howard Louthan, Gary B. Cohen, and Franz A. J. Szabo, Austrian and Habsburg Studies (Oxford, NY: Berghahn Books, 2011).

area of life and that it can be used in the singular as well as the plural; and that religion can be separated from the state and that it can be governed by it. But there is one more assumption that had to occur for religion to become a subject of attempts at legibility. States had to assume not only that they could govern religion, but also that they could manipulate it.

This distinction might seem subtle. But it means a difference between simple boundary-making, in which the state chooses the established religion or limits allowable practices, and a more significant level of interference, in which the state adapts religion to its primary goals. This analytical distinction helps us understand a significant change in the thinking that followed from the emergence of modern statecraft. While in the past, this type of interference would also occur, it would be made by the rulers as religious leaders. With the advance of modern statecraft though, the state would consciously distance itself from religion, and yet retain the right not only to govern but also to manipulate it.

The starkest early example of such manipulability would take place during the French Revolution. At that time, all previous developments in thinking about religion and statecraft would converge, establishing a standard for future, central-level attempts at transforming religion. As René Rémond puts it, the decisions "taken at the time … inaugurated a new era—our own."[40] Despite of the changes described above, before the Revolution, all countries remained confessional. Religion was not yet fully distinguished from other social phenomena, even if the first attempts at that had already occurred. Religion was present in all significant aspects of social life, from political legitimation, through the guidance of collective engagement, to the instruction of each individual's private life.

The French Revolution changed these conditions significantly. The territoriality and drive for autonomy that gradually emerged earlier, influenced Enlightenment ideas,[41] were translated into the modern notion of national sovereignty. Nations, rather than monarchy, aristocracy, or clergy, would become

40 René Rémond, *Religion and Society in Modern Europe*, ed. Jacques Le Goff, The Making of Europe, (Oxford: Blackwell Publishers, 1999), 8.

41 Scholars seem divided on the decisive character of the French Revolution. Some have argued that it was a class revolution, while other see it as either an intellectual or a cultural one, in which the ideas of the Enlightenment played a decisive role. As T. C. W. Blanning pointed out, however, these two takes are not necessarily mutually exclusive, and all these aspects probably had at least some impact. For more on that see: Roger Chartier, *The Cultural Origins of the French Revolution*, trans. Lydia G. Cochrane (Durham and London: Duke University Press, 1991); T. C. W. Blanning, *The French Revolution. Class War or Culture Clash* (London: Macmillan Press, 1998), 5.

the main source of authority.[42] The idea of the "approval of the nation" became the primary means of political legitimization—even Napoleon took steps to establish himself as a hereditary emperor through plebiscites between 1799 and 1804.

These changes significantly transformed public reasoning and reformulated ideas of the private and the public sphere. Roger Chartier argues that "it was precisely that newly conquered autonomy that made it possible and conceivable to constitute a new 'public' founded on the communication established between 'private' persons freed of their duties to the ruler."[43] A newly-found equality characterized this new public sphere—regardless of the participant's status in the social hierarchy, everyone was supposed to be an equal partner in the discussion within this newly-founded public sphere.[44] The focus was on the quality and coherence of their arguments. The public sphere was constituted as an instance of a higher degree than the established authorities and was supposed to be the final judge of all arguments.[45]

This created a specific approach to public reasoning. The new principle of rationality became one of the cornerstones of the Revolution. Discussion was viewed as the primary way of resolving social disputes. The ideas of the Enlightenment were implemented in practice. William Doyle points out that there was a "wider commitment of the men of 1789 to promoting rationality in human affairs. The collapse of the old regime, they thought, presented them with an opportunity to take control of their circumstances and remold them according to a conscious plan or set of principles."[46]

The principles of the public sphere and rationality were embraced in the Declaration of the Rights of Man and of the Citizen, which, in article 10, reads: "No one may be disturbed on account of his opinions, even religious ones, as long as the manifestation of such opinions does not interfere with the established Law and Order."[47] Rémond points out that this resulted in two

---

42 William Doyle, *The French Revolution: A Very Short Introduction* (Oxford: Oxford University Press, 2019), 83.

43 Chartier, *The Cultural Origins*, 21.

44 Habermas wrote about the emergence of a "bourgeois public sphere" (*bürgerliche Öffentlichkeit*) at that time. For more, see Jürgen Habermas, *The Structural Transformation of the Public Sphere: An Inquiry Into a Category of Bourgeois Society* (Cambridge, Massachusetts: MIT Press, 1998), xv.

45 Chartier, *The Cultural Origins*, 21.

46 Doyle, *The French Revolution*, 97.

47 "Declaration of Human and Civic Rights Of 26 August 1789," Conseil Constitutionnel, 2021, accessed 8 March 2021, https://www.conseil-constitutionnel.fr/en/declaration-of-human-and-civic-rights-of-26-august-1789.

significant breakthroughs. First, it equalized theological opinions with ordinary ones, allowing the former the same liberty as the latter. Second, as a result, it uncoupled the bonds between citizenship and Catholic affiliation, rejecting confessional uniformity as the basis for national unity.[48]

However, while the declaration significantly transformed the approach to religion, religion remained an essential part of the social constellation for decades to come. In the wake of the declaration, common religious bonds were still considered fundamental for national unity, and religious figures remained important, for example, during the national ceremonies following the Revolution. Moreover, the dispossession of the clergy from their land, followed by remunerations in return, created an ecclesiastical budget and turned priests into state officials.

In this context, the republicans followed the earlier traditions of regalism, the notion that the kings have a right to lord over the church on their territory. Implementing the idea of a broad overhaul of all institutions, the Constituent Assembly unilaterally moved on to reform the church in the Civil Constitution on the Clergy of 1790. Without overt attention to historical precedent, the whole organization of the French church was upended, as ancient diocesan lines were replaced by the newly defined departments.[49] New clergy and bishops were supposed to be chosen during elections. The bishops of neighboring districts were supposed to consecrate those elected. Finally, the Holy See was supposed to receive nothing more than a notification.

While some of these actions were not without precedent in French history, the overall interference in ecclesiastical matters was exceptional and unacceptable to Rome. After a prolonged silence, Pope Pius VI condemned the 1790 Constitution in the encyclical *Quod aliquantum* issued in 1791.[50] The pope condemned the institutional reorganization and the underlying assumptions concerning equality (contrasting it with divinely instituted power structures) and liberty (contrasting it with Catholic obedience), accusing the Assembly of following in Luther and Calvin's footsteps.

This put French Catholics, especially the clergy, in an impossible position. They were torn between loyalty to France and adherence to the pope. Just as the pope required obedience to Rome, the French Assembly viewed it imperative

48 Rémond, *Religion and Society*, 39–40.

49 Rémond, *Religion and Society*, 43.

50 Pius VI, *Breve Quod Aliquantum* (Rome: San Pietro, 1791). For more on the subject see, for example, André Latreille and Joseph E. Cunneen, "The Catholic Church and the Secular State: The Church and the Secularization of Modern Societies," *Cross Currents* 13, no. 2 (1963): 220–21.

to remain loyal to the state that paid clergy their salaries. As Rémond points out, the situation escalated further when the Assembly acted on behalf of the constitutional church and persecuted those loyal to Rome.[51]

The repressions were accompanied by a series of measures that secularized France in a more "modern" fashion. The Assembly instituted a secular civil registry and civil marriages to free these institutions from clerical involvement. They abolished celibacy and invalidated monastic vows as incompatible with the principles of liberty. They dispersed monastic orders as socially useless. Finally, and, in Rémond's view, most significantly, they introduced a radical break between religion and society by legalizing the behavior that was directly incompatible with the church's teaching—divorce.[52]

However, while formally significant, the practice was less congruent. Chartier noted that the move away from the "old" religion did not result in the abandonment of all sacrality. On the contrary, 54% of priests, vicars, and parish assistants swore an oath to the Civil Constitution, constituting a large group of the "public ecclesiastical functionaries."[53] Instead, Chartier argues, there was a systematic attempt at translating Christianity into the language of the new civil religion oriented towards such ideals as virtue, humankind, the regeneration of the human species, or the transformation of society. He writes:

> Massive and profound, for all its anomalies and contrasts, the secularization that transformed France during the last third of the eighteenth century should not be understood as a desacralization. Although it marked a distance taken—or imposed—from acts that manifested the submission of behavior to the norms and injunctions of reformed Catholicism, secularization did not, by that same token, signify that all reference to religion was eliminated, not even outside the bastions of traditional faith. Violently dechristianizing in the short term, on a deeper level the Revolution doubtless constituted the manifest culmination of a "transfer of sacrality" that, even before it rose to the surface, had silently shifted to new family-oriented, civic, and patriotic values the affect and emotion formerly invested in Christian representations.[54]

To summarize, the French Revolution took the first steps towards adopting the principle of manipulation—a central-level transformation—as an

51 Rémond, *Religion and Society*, 44.
52 Rémond, *Religion and Society*, 46.
53 Chartier, *The Cultural Origins*, 106.
54 Chartier, *The Cultural Origins*, 109.

underlying paradigm for state policies towards religion. It introduced the idea of sovereignty as based on the assent of the nation, a new principle of public rationality, and it severed the ties between confessional uniformity and national unity. In the conflict with the pope, Catholicism was set against the Enlightenment principles of liberty and equality, creating a dichotomy between Catholicism and modernity, which would last well into the twentieth century. However, by severing the ties with ancient traditions, translating the sacred into the language of a new civil religion, and adopting rationality in designing the new institutional order of religion, the Revolution also opened the road to the principles of state legibility and rational planning that characterized the modernism of the nineteenth century: the focus on religion either as utility or as a threat.

2 The Focus of Legible Religion

2.1 *Religion Has Utility*

Some suggest that the very idea behind the Constantinian shift was to unite the empire around a new cultic practice.[55] Similarly, the success of the Reformation is sometimes attributed partly to the opportunism of princes, who saw benefits in taking over ecclesial possessions.[56] We might never know what motivated the conversion of either, but these kinds of conceptualizations definitely testify to our modern awareness of religion being able to fulfil a function or provide utility to the state. A full appreciation of this, however, requires several steps in analytical development described in the section above. Only when the state separated religion and viewed it as both governable and manipulable, it could try to turn it into a functional tool.

The earliest examples of functional thinking can be traced back to the aftermath of the Reformation. At that time, French lawyer and humanist Jean Bodin proposed that religion could function as a stabilizing force if disputes around

55 For a discussion of the topic see, e.g., R. Ross Holloway, *Constantine & Rome* (New Haven: Yale University Press, 2004); K. L. Noethlichs, "Revolution from the top? 'Orthodoxy' and the persecution of heretics in imperial legislation from Constantine to Justinian," in *Religion and Law in Classical and Christian Rome*, ed. Clifford Ando and J. Rüpke (Stuttgart: Franz Steiner Verlag, 2006); Charles Odahl, *Constantine and the Christian empire* (New York: Routledge, 2010); Robert Louis Wilken, *The First Thousand Years: A Global History of Christianity* (New Haven and London: Yale University Press, 2012).

56 For a discussion see, e.g., Scott H. Hendrix, "Loyalty, Piety, or Opportunism: German Princes and the Reformation," *Journal of Interdisciplinary History* XXV, no. 2 (1994), https://doi.org/10.2307/206343.

it were appropriately guided. On the one hand, Bodin maintained that uniformity in this respect should be the state's primary goal. On the other, Bodin postulated that those who would not want to keep to uniform beliefs should be allowed to live according to their distinct faith.[57]

According to Nongbri, these notions of plurality and tolerance constituted a fundamental change in approach, allowing for the differentiation of religion from civic matters, as expressed, among others, in the *cuius regio* principle. Rather than attempting society-wide religious cohesion, it required the emergence of the "personalized notion of religion as focused on the salvation of the individual soul."[58] While Bodin's approach was unusual at the end of the sixteenth century, it gathered significance in the seventeenth century. In Nongbri's view, this approach was solidified by *A Letter Concerning Toleration* by John Locke, which set the standard for religious tolerance in the centuries to come. As Nongbri points out, Locke redefined the church from an unchallengeable holy body with divine authority to a voluntary association for the public worship of God and individual salvation.[59] Locke also redefined religious differentiation, with belonging to a particular religion based on accepting the same "Rule of Faith and Worship."[60]

These different developments culminated during the French Revolution, allowing for a full embrace of the functionalist thinking about religion. While the Napoleonic rule broke with the progressive de-Christianisation of the French Revolution, it followed in its footsteps in several other ways. The secularized lands remained firmly in the hands of the Napoleonic state. While the importance of Catholicism as a majority religion was recognized again, the struggle for uniformity of affiliation was no longer as intense. The relative freedom of conscience, including major Christian denominations and Jews, was largely retained, although religious cults and structures were carefully controlled. The possibility of worship was closely regulated and could be rescinded by the local mayor if deemed threatening to public peace. Both Catholic and Protestant clergy received salaries from the state, and, from 1808 onwards, rabbis were included too.[61] Several other centralizing regulations were kept. As Andrew Copson writes, "the French state instituted its own control over large parts of church life: selecting bishops, salarying priests, and

57 Jean Bodin, *Les six livres de la republique* (Paris: Chez Jacques du Puys, 1576).
58 Nongbri, *Before Religion*, 100–01.
59 Nongbri, *Before Religion*, 102.
60 Nongbri, *Before Religion*, 103.
61 Guy Haarscher, *Laickość. Kościół, Państwo, Religia*, trans. Ewa Burska (Warszawa: Instytut Wydawniczy Pax, 2004), 19.

regulating the seminaries where they were trained."[62] In Guy Haarscher's view, the Napoleonic rule definitively proved that religion was "in" the state, but the state was no longer "in" religion.[63]

This French model of managing religious diversity and church—state relationships spread throughout Europe during the Napoleonic conquests. The fall of Napoleon and the Bourbon restoration might have started a long period of clashing republican, monarchist, and imperial models. However, the new ideas inspired attempts at conscious "religion-making" in the works of thinkers such as Auguste Comte and Karl Marx. Both were influenced by the Revolution and the post-revolutionary order. Both can serve as examples of an increasing functionalization in thinking about religion during the nineteenth century, while their differences show the emergence of multiple ideas for how such a functionalization should be approached.

Comte was one of the most influential philosophers of the first half of the nineteenth century, most widely known for developing positivism, a philosophical system that rejected metaphysical considerations and aimed to base all knowledge on scientifically verifiable facts and laws.[64] Encapsulated in the idea of a "law of three stages," Comte presented human history as an account of progress, a transition from a theological stage, through a metaphysical one, to what he called a positive stage. This transition was concerned with the interest of the human mind. In the first stage, the human mind was interested in the causes of different phenomena, ascribing supernatural agency whenever a natural explanation was insufficient. In the second, metaphysical stage, supernatural agents were replaced by abstract entities. This stage, in Comte's view, was transitional. It allowed for the transition to the third, positive stage. In this final stage, the human mind was no longer interested in causes, leaving behind the search for absolute notions and instead focusing on studying the laws guiding phenomena.[65]

That epistemic transition required a change in the approach to knowledge and other areas of life, including religion, which had to be reformulated in positivistic terms. Comte founded the so-called Religion of Humanity, a belief system that infused forms taken over from Catholicism with

---

62 Andrew Copson, *Secularism: A Very Short Introduction* (Oxford: Oxford University Press, 2019), 20.

63 Haarscher, *Laickość*, 21.

64 Auguste Comte, *The Positive Philosophy of Auguste Comte*, trans. Harriet Martineau, Volume 1 (London: John Chapman, 1853), 2. For more see, for example, James R. Bailey and Wayne N. Eastman, "Positivism and the Promise of the Social Sciences," *Theory & Psychology* 4, no. 4 (2016): 508–10, https://doi.org/10.1177/0959354394044003.

65 Comte, *The Positive Philosophy*, Volume 1, 2.

a non-supernatural, positive meaning. Although wary of the chaotic aspects of the French Revolution, Comte continued its functional approach. His Religion of Humanity was an attempt to introduce order in place of the disorder of the French Revolution.[66]

Comte laid the foundations for the Religion of Humanity in the concluding chapter of *A General View of Positivism*. He argued that two elementary powers are needed for a well-functioning society: "the moral power of counsel, and the political power of command."[67] Distinguishing morals from politics, Comte believed that Christianity was an imperfect attempt at systematizing the former, a comprehensive ethical system on which the positivist could build.[68] His "Religion of Humanity" was supposed to improve upon Catholicism by stripping it of all the seemingly irrelevant aspects. Thus, Comte advocated a belief in humanity, the main object of worship of the new system, based on three main principles: Love, Order, and Progress. The new religious authority was supposed to support people in overcoming their innate selfishness and promote universal brotherhood. He wanted to institute new rituals, including extensive use of poetry and the arts. He proposed new festivals following an annual cycle no longer based on the life of Christ but on the human life cycle and stages of history. Comte wrote explicitly that "Widely different as are their circumstances and the means they employ, they desire to regard themselves as the successors of the great men who conducted the progressive movement of Catholicism."[69]

While relatively unsuccessful at gathering a broader following, Comte's proposal gave the initial spark for the later emergence of secular humanism, which grew in significance throughout the nineteenth and twentieth centuries. Comte's and his successors' attempts at creating a post-Christian civil religion highlight their pervasive assumption that some kind of cult is necessary to promote social cohesion, morality, and moral action. These attempts also show an understanding of religion as a vital element of communal and individual life. In Martha Nussbaum's words, Comte's approach to ritual provided "a common ground among participants, creating areas of shared expression and memory."[70] At the same time, as Nussbaum notes:

66 Enes Kabakcı, "Trajectoire Du Positivisme Comtien (1820–1857) De La Philosophie Positive A La Religion De L'humanite," *Sosyoloji Dergisi / Journal of Sociology*, no. 23 (2011).

67 Auguste Comte, *A General View of Positivism*, trans. J. H. Bridges (London: Trübner & Co., 1865), 343.

68 Comte, *A General View of Positivism*, 347–48.

69 Comte, *A General View of Positivism*, 371–72.

70 Martha Nussbaum, "Reinventing the Civil Religion: Comte, Mill, Tagore," *Victorian Studies* 54, no. 1 (2011): 11, https://doi.org/10.2979/victorianstudies.54.1.7.

> Comte's religion of humanity responded to a genuine need, but did so in a way that left much to be desired. Although he offered legal protection for the freedom of speech, he still envisaged an all-embracing type of social control, as his philosophical clergy pronounced norms of moral correctness that were to suffuse each person's daily life in just the way that the norms and moral/spiritual authority of the Roman Catholic Church had done during the Middle Ages. He did not want breathing space for dissent or experimentation, nor to entrust ordinary individuals with the job of working out difficult questions on their own.[71]

Both Comte and the two-decades-younger philosopher from Trier, Karl Marx, were products of their time, aiming to understand the direction of history, inspired by the events of the French Revolution. However, while Comte saw a need to introduce order in place of revolutionary disorder, Marx saw the events in France from the turn of the century as paradigmatic, establishing a standard for future proletarian revolutions.[72] Like Comte, Marx viewed history as an account of progress, shared the notion of the human provenience of religion, and viewed religious forms as historically conditioned. However, Marx drew different conclusions from these developments, viewing religion as ultimately obsolete.[73] Marx perceived religion as a manufactured remedy to soothe the daily struggles of the underprivileged. In his view, religion was in a dialectical relationship with the state and society. The state and society created religion as the representation of their consciousness. As soon as a society moved beyond the system of class oppression, the ailment of the underprivileged would disappear, and with it the need for religion.

Viewing religion as obsolete, Marx did not want to reform it. Instead, he became preoccupied with the question of emancipation. At first, Marx wanted to eliminate the category of religion and religious identity altogether. For example, discussing the contemporary proposals to provide Jews with individual liberties while depriving them from communal rights, Marx was interested in neither. He argued that such a resolution would introduce a distinction between the political and the civil, benefitting only the state, but not

71 Nussbaum, "Reinventing the Civil Religion," 29.

72 Gerhard Kluchert, "The Paradigm and the Parody. Karl Marx and the French Revolution in the Class Struggles from 1848–1851," *History of European Ideas* 14, no. 1 (1992): 87, https://doi.org/10.1016/0191-6599(92)90294-M. See also Henry Heller, "Marx, the French Revolution, and the Spectre of the Bourgeoisie," *Science & Society* 74, no. 2 (2010), https://doi.org/10.1521/siso.2010.74.2.184.

73 Joseph Blankholm, "Remembering Marx's Secularism," *Journal of the American Academy of Religion* 88, no. 1 (2020): 43, https://doi.org/10.1093/jaarel/lfz104.

individuals, who would become dependent on the state for their rights. Rejecting such a dichotomous view, Marx argued that true emancipation required for the very category of religion to disappear.[74]

However, at the later stages of his life, Marx moved to a more moderate view. He preferred to leave the ontological questions out of the equation of political identity, keeping them in the sphere of the private and personal. Joseph Blankholm argues that one could differentiate two versions of Marx. Young Marx approached religion in an "eliminativist" way, aiming to remove religion entirely. The mature Marx could be considered more of a "supersessionist," insisting on the separation of religion and politics but allowing for personal differences of opinion and waiting for religion to wane.[75] Marx's contemporary and proponent of secularism, George Holyoake summed up the difference between these two approaches in the following words: "The destruction of religious servitude may be attempted in two ways. It may be denounced, which will irritate it, or it may be superseded by the servitude of humanity."[76]

Similarly to Comte, Marx had a significant influence on his contemporaries and on future approaches to politics and religion. In Blankholm's words, "Marxian secularists have had an enormous influence on the secularization of people and states around the world."[77] However, in the reception of Marx, the pragmatic supersessionist version seems to have prevailed over the eliminativist. For example, Marx himself influenced the working-class movements of the nineteenth century and, in turn, was influenced by them. The events of 1871 testify to the penetration of secularist principles among the socialists. During its short reign, the Parisian Commune instituted, among other things, a strict separation of church and state. The aim of separating religion and politics, rather than eliminating religion, remained stable for decades. Even Vladimir Lenin, who in his later years went in the opposite direction, in 1905 distinguished between the "worldview secularism of atheism and the political secularism of 'disestablishment'," which was needed to uphold the unity of revolutionary struggles.[78]

By the end of the nineteenth century, there was a firm consensus around the idea that an analytically differentiated religion could be approached functionally. Comte and Marx exemplify well how the early ideas of tolerance merged with 'legible' developments to produce different visions for what functions

74 Blankholm, "Remembering Marx's Secularism," 44–45.

75 Blankholm, "Remembering Marx's Secularism," 46–47.

76 George Jacob Holyoake, *The Last Trial for Atheism in England: A Fragment of Autobiography* (London: Trübner & Co., 1871), 34.

77 Blankholm, "Remembering Marx's Secularism," 36.

78 Blankholm, "Remembering Marx's Secularism," 47.

religion could provide. Comte viewed religion as a comprehensive ethical system with ritual elements necessary for social cohesion. The state and those working on reforming it were supposed to improve upon the imperfect forms of the existing religious traditions. Marx viewed religion as a temporary fix, a soothing remedy for poor living conditions. Thus, while the mature Marx wanted to separate religion from politics, he viewed individual religiosity as something to be superseded rather than eliminated (as the young Marx had wanted). Comte started the line of thinking in which some sort of civil religion was viewed as necessary for an orderly society. This line was later continued, among others, by sociologists such as Émile Durkheim or Marcel Mauss.[79] Marx established the line of thinking concerned with emancipation from religion, whether by supersession or elimination. While Comte associated religion with morals, social ethics, and social cohesion and was inspired by Catholicism, Marx took a belief-centered approach more in line with Protestantism that viewed religion as a projection of human self-consciousness.

2.2 *Religion Is Dangerous*

The analytical conceptualization of religion as a distinct category did not only lead to functionalist thinking. It also meant that the notion of religion could be infused with meaning and generalized. It meant that it was possible to speak of what religion is and what its main characteristics are. For example, religion could have been viewed as inherently violent, which is what came out of the modern reformulation of international relations. The so-called Peace of Westphalia is often credited with the emergence of such a view, although it is not necessarily clear whether due to its content or its subsequent mythologization.

Signed in October 1648, the treaties of Osnabrück and Münster, known jointly as the Peace of Westphalia, have been viewed as a breakthrough moment in the history of Europe. Ending the bloodshed of the Thirty Years' War, the treaties have been viewed as the beginning of a new international order, the so-called Westphalian paradigm, Westphalian sovereignty, Westphalian model, or Westphalian system, based on the principles of territorial sovereignty, the gradual replacement of war with diplomatic relations, and the beginning of modern religious tolerance.[80] Emma Ahlm points

79 For more, see Kabakcı, "Trajectoire Du Positivisme Comtien."

80 David Jayne Hill, *A History of Diplomacy in the International Development of Europe* (New York and London: Longmans, Green, and Company, 1906); Leo Gross, "The Peace of Westphalia, 1648–1948," *The American Journal of International Law* 42, no. 1 (1948), https://doi.org/10.2307/2193560; Mark S. Janis, "Sovereignty and International Law: Hobbes and Grotius," in *Essays in Honour of Wang Tieya*, ed. Ronald St. John MacDonald (Leiden: Brill and Nijhoff, 1994); Derek Croxton, "The Peace of Westphalia of 1648 and the Origins of Sovereignty," *The International History Review* 21, no. 3 (1999), https://doi.org/10.1080/070

out that "it is by far the most common understanding of the origins of international law."[81]

The Peace was viewed as the triumph of "particularists," including Denmark, the Dutch Republic, France, Sweden, and some German princes, over "universalists" led by the Habsburgs and their supranational aspirations. Nevertheless, since the beginning of the twenty-first century, a growing number of authors have questioned the underlying presumptions of this understanding. For example, Andreas Osiander argues that this interpretation is dubious, as it implies that Habsburgs posed an existential threat to the involved states. But none of them warred with the others in a defensive capacity.[82] Instead, Osiander argues that this view resulted from the nineteenth and twentieth-century historical accounts of 1648, influenced by the subsequent anti-Habsburg propaganda and the fixation on the concept of sovereignty.[83] Thus, Osiander describes the most common interpretation of the Peace of Westphalia as a "Westphalian myth," a fictional account justifying the contemporary international order.

The mythical character of the Peace of Westphalia as the beginning of state sovereignty has been also underlined by Stéphane Beaulac, who substantiated his point by referring to the situation before and after 1648. On the one hand, the universalizing authority of both the pope and the emperor had been significantly reduced long before the treaties were signed, which allowed for significant territorial autonomy. On the other hand, the situation did not change dramatically after the Treaty. The empire did not disappear for the next century and a half, and its territories did not transform into independent polities. Thus, "1648 constitutes no more than one instance where distinct separate

75332.1999.9640869; James A. Nathan, *Soldiers, Statecraft, and history: Coercive Diplomacy and International Order* (Westport: Praeger Publisher, 2002); José E. Alvarez, "State Sovereignty is Not Withering Away: A Few Lessons for the Future," in *Realizing Utopia: The Future of International Law*, ed. Antonio Cassese (Oxford: Oxford University Press, 2012); Pierre-Marie Dupuy and Vincent Chetail, *The Roots of International Law / Les fondements du droit international* (Leiden: Brill, 2014); Steven Patton, "The Peace of Westphalia and it Affects on International Relations, Diplomacy and Foreign Policy," *The Histories* 10, no. 1 (2019).

81 Emma Ahlm, *EU law and religion: a study of how the Court of Justice has adjudicated on religious matters in Union law* (Uppsala: Juridiska institutionen, Uppsala universitet, 2020), 37.

82 Andreas Osiander, "Sovereignty, International Relations, and the Westphalian Myth," *International Organization* 55, no. 2 (2001): 252, https://doi.org/10.1162/002081801511405 77.

83 Osiander, "Sovereignty, International Relations," 251.

polities pursued their continuing quest for more authority over their territory through greater autonomy."[84]

However, the mythical character of Westphalia does not mean that its ideas can be simply rejected. On the contrary, Beaulac points out that Westphalia is ingrained in our legal order and collective consciousness far beyond the simple assumption. He writes:

> By holding as unquestionably true and valid what is in fact a human-made fabrication, the aetiological myth of *Westphalia* has built a belief-system. This social production has thus provided a shared explanatory structure for the socially constructed international reality and, in doing so, has had an extraordinary impact upon the shared consciousness of humanity. Furthermore, given that this myth managed its way into the very fabric of our international legal order—as the model for the idea, and the ideal, of state sovereignty in international law—the social power that *Westphalia* has continuously demonstrated within human reality increased considerably.[85]

It is not my intention to support any of these views on the role of the Peace of Westphalia here, but rather to underline its paradigmatic character. Regardless of the factual accuracy of the breakthrough account, this account testifies to the importance that sovereignty and territoriality principles began to play in centuries after. Whether factual or mythical, the ideal of Westphalia created a "liberalizing" narrative that fueled the internal power of the states and their drive towards full autonomy, becoming a common point of reference.

This was also important regarding religion. The Peace of Westphalia has often been considered foundational for contemporary religious toleration.[86] However, similarly to the questions of territorial sovereignty, it could be argued

84 Stéphane Beaulac, "The Westphalian Model in Defining International Law: Challenging the Myth," *Australian Journal of Legal History* 8 (2004): 210–11.

85 Beaulac, "The Westphalian Model," 211.

86 This was especially evident during the celebrations of the 350th anniversary of the Treaties, see Veranstaltungsgesellschaft 350 Jahre Westfälischer Friede mbH, *1648: Krieg und Frieden in Europa. Münster/Osnabrück 24.10.1998–17.01.1999* [*Katalog zur 26. Europaratsausstellung*], ed. Klaus Bußmann and Heinz Schilling (Münster: Veranstaltungsgesellschaft 350 Jahre Westfälischer Friede mbH, 1998); Ronald G. Asch, "Religious toleration, the Peace of Westphalia and the German territorial estates," *Parliaments, Estates & Representation* 20, no. 1 (2000). https://doi.org/10.1080/02606755.2000.9522099. Also see, for example, Martin Heckel, *Gesammelte Schriften*, Band V: Staat—Kirche—Recht—Geschichte, (Tübingen: Mohr Siebeck, 2004). https://doi.org/9783161483202.

that it was instead a step in a longer process. On the one hand, the Peace of Westphalia upheld and expanded the territorial aspects of the Peace of Augsburg by including, among others, Reformed Christianity alongside Catholicism and Lutheranism. It also reduced the scope of the *cuius regio, eius religio* principle. Apart from the *ius emigrandi*, the right to migrate to another territory, the Peace of Westphalia introduced the right of assembly (*exercitium publicum*, which was important to Catholics[87]) and private observance (*devotio domestica*, which was more critical to Protestants[88]) to those whose religion was not established. On the other hand, by upholding the right of the ruler to choose the religion of the territory, the increase of toleration mentioned above could not be considered paradigm-changing, but an adaptation of what, in Osiander's words, "proved destabilizing and ultimately unworkable."[89] As Ronald Asch points out, after the Peace of Westphalia, the principle of territoriality was largely upheld. German territories remained largely homogeneous, and the state churches were legally solidified in a way that "was alien to religious freedom."[90]

Again, in this context, the later ideal of Westphalia proved highly potent. In *The Myth of Religious Violence*, William T. Cavanaugh argues that the confessionalism brought by the Reformation introduced the idea of religion as a creed or a set of beliefs to be confessed, distinguishing it from politics as a separate phenomenon.[91] This allowed religion to become a separate cause of disagreement, one that violence could be ascribed to. In turn, it created what Cavanaugh describes as the "myth of religious violence … the idea that religion is a trans-historical and trans-cultural feature of human life, essentially distinct from the 'secular' features such as politics and economics, which has a peculiarly dangerous inclination to promote violence."[92]

Cavanaugh views the narratives surrounding the Thirty Years' War and the so-called Wars of Religion in the sixteenth and seventeenth centuries as foundational for this myth. According to him, religion, as a separate, inherently dangerous phenomenon, was invented at that time. This invention allowed for the creation of a hierarchy of different motives for political action. Subsequent

---

87 Asch, "Religious toleration," 82.

88 Asch, "Religious toleration," 78. Both points in the Treaty of Osnabruck, IPO V, 34.

89 Osiander, "Sovereignty, International Relations," 272.

90 Asch, "Religious toleration," 83. See also Winfried Schulze, "Pluralisierung als Bedrohung: Toleranz als Lösung," in *Der Westfälische Friede*, ed. Duchhardt Heinz (Oldenbourg Wissenschaftsverlag, 1998).

91 William T. Cavanaugh, *The Myth of Religious Violence. Secular Ideology and the Roots of Modern Conflict* (Oxford: Oxford University Press, 2009), 73.

92 Cavanaugh, *The Myth of Religious Violence*, 3.

authors, starting with Baruch Spinoza and followed by Thomas Hobbes, John Locke, and other Enlightenment writers, clearly ascribed the fault for infighting to either religious motives or the lack of tolerance towards differing opinions. This created a narrative of religion as prone to violence and the need for the liberating intervention of the state, which should separate religion from public concerns. Cavanaugh explains:

> The story goes that, after the Protestant Reformation divided Christendom along religious lines, Catholics, and Protestants began killing each other for holding to different doctrines. The wars of religion, which encompassed over a century of chaos and bloodletting, demonstrated to the West the inherent danger of public religion. The solution to the problem lay in the rise of the modern state, in which religious loyalties were marginalized and the state secured a monopoly on the means of violence. Henceforth, religious passions would be tamed, and Protestants and Catholics could unite on the basis of loyalty to the religiously neutral sovereign state.[93]

Cavanaugh points out that the Reformation provided grounds for the growth of the territorial states, both in terms of territorial expansion via the "secularization" of church lands, and in terms of the growth of their autonomy, with the reversal of the medieval order—the emergence of "the thoroughly 'modern' (i.e., new) character of ... state control over the church."[94] It also provided the princes with greater secular authority.

It must be noted that Cavanaugh's argument has been made in a particular context of the justification of the post-2001 War on Terror[95] and as a response to arguments of the so-called New Atheists like Christopher Hitchens or Sam Harris, who argued for precisely the opposite, namely that religion was inherently violent and dangerous.[96] That is why all of his considerations revolve around this particular issue, and why he views the emergence of religion with concerns about tracing all violence to it. Cavanaugh most strongly criticizes

93 Cavanaugh, *The Myth of Religious Violence*, 123.

94 Cavanaugh, *The Myth of Religious Violence*, 169.

95 For more on that see Chapter 7 of Ulrich Schmiedel, *Terror und Theologie: der religionstheoretische Diskurs der 9/11-Dekade* (Tübingen: Mohr Siebeck, 2021).

96 Sam Harris, *The End of Faith: Religion, Terror, and the Future of Reason* (New York and London: W. W. Norton & Company, 2005); Christopher Hitchens, *God is not Great* (New York and Boston: Twelve, 2007).

the essentialism of such an approach—the fact that religion is viewed as a trans-cultural phenomenon with a specific essence.[97]

However, as we saw with Nongbri's analysis, the emergence of religion is a much broader development, not only concerned with religion as violent and not necessarily essentialist. Religion emerges as a separate object of consideration and reform, an object that, in some cases, can be manipulated and adapted to specific needs. For example, in terms of Locke, while Cavanaugh accuses him of treating religion as a source of conflict,[98] Nongbri discusses how Locke aimed to transform religion into a new model.[99]

Cavanaugh and Nongbri do not have to be viewed as disagreeing. While the former focuses on one concrete development, the latter is interested in tracing a broader pattern, each seeing a part of the picture required for their task. However, both notice the emergence of religion as a concept that can be filled with meaning, put under normative measures, and treated as a rhetorical object.

Both scholars also write from the perspective of hindsight. However, these changes were far from clear when the Peace of Westphalia was signed. While the individual state gained more significance through the Peace, the doctrines of the two swords and of the two kingdoms largely held for a long time after the treaties were signed. Similarly, the situation of religious tolerance did not change rapidly. Regardless of the exact significance of the Peace of Westphalia, its subsequent mythological status signifies the subsequent radical reorganizations of international relations, the role of the state, and the functioning of religion, which was conceptualized as a distinct sphere of activity. The discussions concerning the Peace of Westphalia showcase well the essentialist approach to religion—the notion that religion and religious diversity are inherently dangerous—providing an important backdrop for subsequent policy interventions.

3 Legible Religion Begins to Take Shape

Throughout this chapter, I have attempted to sketch the foundational elements and assumptions of what I call legible religion. As I noted following Scott, modern states have a tendency towards a centralized reformulation of the phenomena under their jurisdiction, based solely on the interests of the administrative

97 Cavanaugh, *The Myth of Religious Violence*, 57.
98 Cavanaugh, *The Myth of Religious Violence*, 126.
99 Nongbri, *Before Religion*, 101–04.

beholder. I argued that the same applies to religion, but for that to happen, several historical developments were necessary. As we observed throughout the chapter, religion had to be first separated as a distinct category, and it had to develop also into the notion that allows us to speak of religions in the plural. Then, a model of the relation between state and religion had to evolve in a way that it was acceptable that the former could govern the latter—as well as manipulate it.

Such a distinct notion of religion, as governable and manipulable by the state, could then be turned into a state policy interest. I sketched two main ways of thinking about religion that followed: the functional view of religion as a utility, as described on the example of thinkers such as Comte and Marx; and the essentialist view of religion as dangerous, which emerged out of the narratives concerning the Peace of Westphalia, regardless of whether we consider them factual or mythical. At this stage, however, we only saw the conscious attempts at changing the approach to religion. In the next chapter, we will look at how legible religion became hegemonic.

CHAPTER 2

The Establishment of Legible Religion

The Emergence of a Modern Consensus

The reader might be familiar with a whole range of terms with etymological provenience in the Latin *Saeculum*, from the adverbial "secular" through the verb "to secularize" to nouns such as "secularity," "the secular," "secularism," and "secularization." Each of these terms developed to signify something worldly. Each of them stands for multiple meanings and, thus, requires further clarification.[1]

Secularism needs to be differentiated from its cognates, especially the two most interchangeably used—secularization and secularity. In an encyclopedic definition of these three terms, Hans Raun Iversen distinguished secularism as an *attitude* or *political ideology*, secularity as a *condition of absence* of religion in certain areas of society, and secularization as a *process* of moving away from religion.[2] However, Iversen also underlined the deep interrelation of these three. Secularization is "often leading to (and partly caused by) a politics of secularism."[3] Secularity "may be caused by a specific politics of secularism."[4]

This mutual interrelation of secularism and secularization, as leading to and caused by the other, is at the core of this chapter. This chapter argues that secularization and secularism are closely interrelated in Western Europe. On

1 For example, the "worldly" character of the *saeculum* can be understood as either at odds with God or simply with no explicit reference to religion. Charles Taylor writes about it in the introductory chapter of his monumental work, *A Secular Age*. Taylor employs numbers from one to three to differentiate between different connotations of the term secularity and to qualify which of them he uses when: with number one, he refers to secularized public space and its features; with number two, he points to debates about the decline of belief and/or practice; with number three, he discusses a change in general consciousness, in which religious beliefs becomes a choice among others. Charles Taylor, *A Secular Age* (Boston, MA: Belknap Press, 2018), 1–4. See also Lois Lee, *Recognizing the Non-Religious: Reimagining the Secular* (Oxford: Oxford University Press, 2015), 21–22.

2 Hans Raun Iversen, "Secularization, Secularity, Secularism," in *Encyclopedia of Sciences and Religions*, ed. Oviedo L. Runehov A.L.C. (Dordrecht: Springer, 2013), 2116. Alternatively, Ulrich Schmiedel differentiated between the three as secular—point, secularization—process, and secularism—politics. See Ulrich Schmiedel, *Elasticized Ecclesiology. The Concept of Community after Ernst Troeltsch* (New York: Palgrave Macmillan, 2017).

3 Iversen, "Secularization, Secularity, Secularism," 2116.

4 Iversen, "Secularization, Secularity, Secularism," 2116.

the one hand, secularization could be considered a result of state adaptations of secularism. As we saw previously, already in the nineteenth century, political thinkers such as Comte and Marx had set up secularist agendas that were adopted by their followers. Merged with the legibility concerns that reduced religion to its functional features and presented it as something dangerous, secularism encouraged secularization.

On the other hand, the narratives of secularization provided the initial fuel for secularism. Theories of secularization that followed up on the introduced adaptations sank back into the general consciousness as simplified, reified narratives and as such supported secularism. In this way, the theories-turned-narratives strengthened secularism. Both secularism and secularization imbricated themselves into the ways of thinking about the public square. Even when the return of religion emerged as a counter-narrative to secularization, it continued with assumptions inherited from both, now adapted to changing circumstances. Supported by the centralized administrative attempts at achieving legibility, secularization and secularism exercised a significant consciousness-shaping effect. This process is what I will describe in this chapter as the "secularizing cycle of legible religion."

My considerations might seem rather abstract at this stage. The reader might wonder what significance they have for, for example, the particular furnishing of multi-faith spaces, which will be discussed in part 2. I argue that this interrelation of secularization and secularism turned certain ways of thinking from the conscious to the unconscious. It caused our concepts of religion to become mainly invisible. Such invisibility allowed some behaviors and approaches to seem neutral, even though they are not. Moreover, this turned a broad range of different social actors into agents of legibility attempts: from politicians and government officials at the highest levels, through managers of institutions and, for example, chaplains at the mid-level, to individual representatives of religious communities at the grassroots level.

Thus, for example, the idea that socially acceptable religion no longer requires visible manifestations of religiosity, because it is focused on the *forum internum* instead, made separate rooms for religion a necessity if it was to manifest itself in the public space at all. It also made largely empty and bland spaces seem like a viable choice for rooms inclusive of all forms of religion. The idea that civil values come before any religious adherence resulted in, for example, the refusal of gender separation in such spaces.

The chapter will comprise three parts. First, I will discuss the initial engines of legible religion: secularization and secularism. Second, I will discuss how the secularizing cycle of legible religion and the modern European consensus turned them into a neutral baseline. Finally, I will discuss how such neutrality impacted the formulation of alternatives with the emergence of the notion of the return of religion.

1 Initial Engines: Secularization and Secularism

1.1 *Secularization: the Justifying Narrative*

Secularization as a term has quite a long history and entails a whole range of meanings. Historically, this term referred to, among others, something of this world or life at odds with God.[5] In its earliest canonical understanding, secularization referred to a transfer—of either a person from the ecclesiastical to a lay state or a property from the hands of the church to a civil entity. This meaning is still used within canon law[6] and, as described in the previous chapter, was significant during the French Revolution. In these meanings, one can already see the feature that links all the meanings of secularization—namely, a move towards a "secular" of some kind.

While the term had been in use beforehand, the narrative of secularization has its roots in the Enlightenment,[7] in which the idea of endless progress replaced the medieval notion of providence.[8] Gradually, the idea of progress was associated with a move from the "religious era" to a "secular one", as, for example, in Comte's division of history into three stages or Marx's idea that religion would over time become redundant.[9]

---

5 William H. Swatos Jr. and Kevin J. Christiano, "Secularization Theory: The Course of a Concept," *Sociology of Religion* 60, no. 3 (1999): 211.

6 Solange Lefebvre, "Secularism, Secularization, Public theology, and Practical theology," in *Catholic Approaches to Practical Theology*, ed. C. E. Wolfteich and A. Dillen (Leuven: Peeters Publishers, 2016), 208.

7 One can find traces of this narrative even further in the past, and it could be argued that it was established much earlier. However, the policy approaches that are of interest for my analysis were primarily influenced by the Enlightenment thinkers, which is why the Enlightenment is treated here as the turning point. For more on the earlier expressions see, for example, Jayne Svenungsson, *Divining History: Prophetism, Messianism and the Development of the Spirit* (New York: Berghahn Books, 2016).

8 Angelos Mouzakitis, "Modernity and the Idea of Progress," Hypothesis and Theory, *Frontiers in Sociology* 2, no. 3 (2017), https://doi.org/10.3389/fsoc.2017.00003.

9 Karl Marx, "'A Contribution to the Critique of Hegel's Philosophy of Right: Introduction'," in *Marx: Early Political Writings*, ed. Joseph J. O'Malley and Karl Marx, Cambridge Texts in the History of Political Thought (Cambridge: Cambridge University Press, 1994). See also his views in Karl Marx, "Critique of Hegel's Philosophy of Right," in *Marx on Religion*, ed. J. Raines (Philadelphia: Temple University Press, 2002). A good summary on Marx's views can be found in Mitsutoshi Horii, "Contextualizing "religion" of young Karl Marx: A preliminary analysis," *Critical Research on Religion* 5, no. 2 (2017), https://doi.org/10.1177/2050303217690 8.

The emergence of the sociology of religion in the twentieth century turned these scattered philosophical views into data-driven theories that sank into broader consciousness and, ultimately, into the policy approaches to religion that this study is interested in. Two figures played a key role in this development, Max Weber and Émile Durkheim, laying the foundations for the sociological meaning of secularization by introducing such accompanying notions as "rationalization" or "disenchantment."

Weber proposed that sociology should be interpretive, that is, it should provide an "understanding of social action in order to arrive at a causal explanation of its course and effects,"[10] an approach that has been described by the German term *Verstehen*.[11] This understanding of sociology impacted his understanding of religion (sometimes described as "substantive").[12] Although quite elusive in defining it, Weber approached religion as a cause of social action.[13] This understanding of religion and sociology established the main framework through which Weber interpreted the changes he observed—a transformation of consciousness.

In an entry in the *Stanford Encyclopedia of Philosophy*, Sung Ho Kim argues that the key thematic issue uniting all of Weber's work is that of Western rationalization; the idea that the West is unique in its historical trajectory of civilizational achievements in building a rational, scientific view of the world which puts people in control of their reality.[14] In Weber's approach, such a cumulative rationalization leads to a gradual disenchantment—a process that changes people's perspective on reality. Weber wrote about this extensively in "Science as Vocation." There, as William H. Swatos, Jr. and Kevin J. Christiano argue, the term rationalization is "used as a virtual synonym" of *secularization*.[15] Weber

10 Max Weber, *The Theory of Social and Economic Organization*, trans. A. M. Henderson and Talcott Parsons (New York: Oxford University Press, 1947), 88.

11 For more on what Weber understands under this term see William T. Tucker, "Max Weber's "Verstehen"," *The Sociological Quarterly* 6, no. 2 (1965).

12 See, for example, Peter L. Berger, "Some Second Thoughts on Substantive versus Functional Definitions of Religion," *Journal for the Scientific Study of Religion* 13, no. 2 (1974).

13 For more on that, see Mitsutoshi Horii, "Historicizing the category of "religion" in sociological theories: Max Weber and Emile Durkheim," *Critical Research on Religion* 7, no. 1 (2019), https://doi.org/10.1177/2050303218800369.

14 Sung Ho Kim, "Max Weber," in *The Stanford Encyclopedia of Philosophy*, ed. Edward N. Zalta (Winter 2019), Section 3.2. https://plato.stanford.edu/archives/win2019/entries/weber/. See also the author's introduction in Max Weber, *The Protestant Ethic and the Spirit of Capitalism*, trans. Talcott Parsons and R.H. Tawney (New York: Dover Publications, 2003).

15 Swatos Jr. and Christiano, "Secularization Theory," 211. Also, as they point out on 212: "Weber gave the name secularization to this double-sided rationalization-disenchantment process in religion. Secularization was both the process and the result of the process; however, it is also the case that the term occurs only rarely in Weber's writing." See also

argued that the advances in knowledge do not necessarily mean the increase in general knowledge of individuals, but their awareness that, should they want, they could increase it and find rational explanations for every phenomenon. It means that individuals no longer need to look for magical explanations, and so the world becomes disenchanted.[16]

Such disenchantment, however, is a source of ambivalence. While on an individual level, it might relegate the ultimate values to the personal sphere, on a societal level, it creates a sense of impersonality. Therefore, as Kim points out, Weber anticipated two risks related to disenchantment. On the one hand, there was a risk of the impersonal bureaucratization of reality. On the other, there was a risk of re-enchantment. As Weber argued, at first, disenchantment allowed monotheistic religions to establish themselves as unifying meaning systems. However, disenchantment did not stop there—it went further, ultimately resulting in the rejection of even these forms of unification. As a result, the previously overarching cosmos was fragmented and led, paradoxically, to a certain re-enchantment, as the responsibility for meaning-making returned from the organizational to the individual level; this process being what Weber viewed as a type of renewal of polytheism.[17] However, the new re-enchantment differs from the previous enchantment—it lacks the ultimate values present before. Thus, this process should not be viewed as simply cyclical. Instead, secularization brings permanent consequences on the societal level, even if it may bring re-enchantment on the individual level.

In contrast to Weber, Durkheim assumed cyclicality between secularization and the return of religion. Durkheim is known best for his definition of religion as "a unified system of beliefs and practices relative to sacred things, that is to say, things set apart and forbidden—beliefs and practices which unite its adherents in a single moral community called a church."[18] His approach, often described as functional[19] as it was interested in religion's function in society, was presented in the first chapter of *The Elementary Forms of Religious Life*. He viewed religion as constitutive of society, crucial for the development of its institutions.[20]

Max Weber, "The Protestant Sects and the Spirit of Capitalism," in *From Max Weber: Essays in Sociology*, ed. H. H. Gerth and C. Wright Mills (London: Routledge & Kegan Paul LTD, 1970).

16 Weber, "Science as Vocation," 139, 55.

17 Kim, "Max Weber," Section 4.2. Weber, "Science as Vocation," 148. See also Weber, "Religious Rejections of the World and Their Directions," 357.

18 Émile Durkheim, *The Elementary Forms of the Religious Life*, trans. Carol Cosman (Oxford: Oxford University Press, 2008), 46.

19 Pals, *Nine Theories of Religion*, 105.

20 Durkheim, *The Elementary Forms*, 313–14.

Daniel L. Pals notes that for Durkheim, social facts were more fundamental than individual ones, a notion that was quite revolutionary in his time.[21] In Durkheim's approach, to understand individual behavior, one had to understand society and its constitutive features. Like Weber, Durkheim noted a fundamental change in society. In the wake of both the French Revolution and the Industrial Revolution, fundamental shifts occurred in terms of social systems, morality, politics, and even personal affairs, as their old organizational forms experienced a decline.[22] However, in Durkheim's approach, society required organizational forms for each of these aspects. Therefore, a new form of religion would have to emerge in place of the old, dysfunctional one. The decline of the old forms was a temporary state.[23]

Karel Dobbelaere argues that Durkheim and Weber established the two main ways of thinking about secularization. Those who followed Durkheim opposed secularization and underlined the continuing importance of religion. However, they viewed the situation of religion in the twentieth century as a temporary state of the decline of the "old" before a new alternative would emerge during the "times of creative effervescence."[24] Those following Weber, like Peter Berger or Bryan Wilson, noted a sustained decline in the impact of religion on social life. They referred not to the functionalist but the substantive definition of religion[25] as "based on the sacred cosmos, that is later carried by a special institution."[26] They saw secularization as a struggle on three lines: "community/society, rational/emotional, and private/public."[27] Thus, even in that line of thinking, there was a potential for the return of religion, even if the fragmentation of the religious cosmos would be difficult to overturn.

While the Durkheimian line from the beginning anticipated the return of religion as a logical next step, even in the Weberian line, there was an opening for a partial reversal of secularization because of the re-enchantment induced by the disenchantment.[28] Each of these lines influenced legible religion too. The Weberian line introduced the notion that secularization at a social level in late

21 Pals, *Nine Theories of Religion*, 81.

22 Pals, *Nine Theories of Religion*, 85–86.

23 Durkheim, *The Elementary Forms*, 322–23.

24 Karel Dobbelaere, *Secularization: An Analysis at Three Levels* (Brussels: P.I.E.-Peter Lang, 2002).

25 Developed after Weber, as Weber did not propose any definitions himself.

26 Dobbelaere, *Secularization*, 85.

27 Dobbelaere, *Secularization*, 86.

28 For more on Weber's account, see Robert A. Yelle and Lorenz Trein, *Narratives of Disenchantment and Secularization: Critiquing Max Weber's Idea of Modernity* (London: Bloomsbury Academic, 2021).

modernity is irreversible. Religion becomes individualized and privatized, with each member of society being responsible for their meaning-making system. Only in these forms can it return to the forefront. The Durkheimian line promoted a functional outlook on religion as an aspect of social cohesion, necessary for the functioning of society. Thus, it viewed the return of religion as a necessary follow-up to the temporary secularization. Both lines of thinking were heavily theorized in the 1960s, resulting in the subsequent boom of secularization theories, with detailed theories concerning different types of phenomena and levels of social organization, showcasing the dominance of these narratives.[29] The development of secularization in theory and research was paralleled by an increasing policy interest in secularism, which we will now investigate.

1.2 *Secularism: the Programmatic Formula*

In the last chapter, I have discussed how, in little more than a century, France completely overhauled its approach to religion. Before the French Revolution, France was one of the most significant Catholic bastions. In the nineteenth century, it rapidly became what many view as an extreme example of the separation between state and church. France emerged as a country that completely privatized religious beliefs and practices and put civil values before any religious adherence, at least in principle.[30] The French model of *laïcité* became a standard reference for discussions about the second important notion we need to discuss to understand the establishment of legible religion—secularism.

The precise beginnings of secularism are hard to establish and depend on how one defines it. For example, in *Short History of Secularism*, Graeme Smith begins with an understanding of secularism as "a way of thinking about the world and life which makes no reference to supernatural beliefs."[31] Smith points out that the foundations of secularism can be sought as far back as in the figure of Anaxagoras, born around 500 BCE.[32] Similarly, Copson looks for early secularisms in the arrangements of the Greek *polis*, in which "gods and goddesses were not involved in 'politics'," and "the question of what was 'best and highest' was to be approached entirely in this-worldly terms, not in terms

29 For more, see, Dobbelaere, *Secularization*; Larry Shiner, "The Concept of Secularization in Empirical Research," *Journal for the Scientific Study of Religion* 6, no. 2 (1967), https://doi.org/10.2307/1384047; C. John Sommerville, "Secular Society/Religious Population: Our Tacit Rules for Using the Term 'Secularization'," *Journal for the Scientific Study of Religion* 37, no. 2 (1998), https://doi.org/10.2307/1387524.

30 Whether that happened in practice will be discussed at the beginning of Chapter 3.

31 Graeme Smith, *A Short History of Secularism* (London and New York: I.B. Tauris, 2008), 22.

32 Smith, *A Short History*, 22.

of the divine."[33] More narrowly, in what Smith describes as the traditional account of its rise, secularism started at the end of the Middle Ages, with the advent of humanist thought, which explored an epistemology detached from references to the divine.

However, the definition used by Smith is too broad for our task here, as I am interested in state-sanctioned approaches to religion and religious diversity in what Copson defined as the "full modern sense" rather than approaches to religion and religious diversity *per se*.[34] The English vocabulary lacks a term that denotes precisely the type of secularism that I am interested in here, unlike, for example, French, which has the term *laïcité*.[35] Even the term's original use, when it was coined in the mid-nineteenth century by the British newspaper editor George Holyoake, denoted a "general test of principles of conduct apart from spiritual considerations." Later, it was also associated with a movement that embraced a holistic approach rather than a political one.[36]

Unlike the English term secularism, *laïcité* is more precise in denoting a particular model of the relationship between the state and religions. Haarscher defines *laïcité* by starting from its etymological roots. Based in the Greek *laos*, meaning "the people," *laïcité* refers to political models that refuse to privilege any particular group of people in the state. Instead, the politics of *laïcité* relegate ownership of the state to the people, which also entails a rejection of any discrimination based on an individual's worldview.[37] Michael Kelly points out that while *laïcité* is most often translated as secularism, "the 'lay principle' may be a better equivalent."[38] However, as Haarscher and Kelly underline, *laïcité* is not a contextually neutral term. Haarscher notes that it is used both broadly, in the sense mentioned above, and narrowly to denote a specifically French approach with all of its history and traditions.[39] In Kelly's words, it "has so much history behind it that you need to know something about France to

33 Andrew Copson, *Secularism: A Very Short Introduction* (Oxford: Oxford University Press,2019), 6.

34 Copson, *Secularism*, 6.

35 Some authors refer to "laicism" as an anglicized equivalent. See, for example, Elizabeth Shakman Hurd, *The Politics of Secularism in International Relations* (Princeton and Oxford: Princeton University Press, 2008), 2.

36 George Jacob Holyoake, *English Secularism. A Confession of Belief* (Chicago: The Open Court Publishing Company, 1896), 47.

37 Guy Haarscher, *Laickość. Kościół, Państwo, Religia*, trans. Ewa Burska (Warszawa: Instytut Wydawniczy Pax, 2004), 5.

38 Michael Kelly, "France's laïcité: why the rest of the world struggles to understand it," *The Conversation* (20 November 2020). https://theconversation.com/frances-la-cite-why-the-rest-of-the-world-struggles-to-understand-it-149943.

39 Haarscher, *Laickość*, 5.

understand its nuances."[40] In the broad meaning, one can find this term also in other Romance languages, like Italian *laicità*, developed in constitutional terms such as *principio di laicità*,[41] Spanish *laicidad* or, even in non-Romance languages like Polish *laickość* or Turkish *laiklik*.

The narrower meaning, however, requires further scrutiny. Haarscher notes that the basic assumptions behind the "lay principle," freedom of consciousness and disestablishment of religion, were introduced in the late eighteenth century in the United States, long before the same principles were introduced in Europe.[42] However, that *laïcité* is so firmly ingrained in the public consciousness as a typically French invention signifies its ground-breaking character, at least in the European context in which I am primarily interested. It also points to a specificity of the French approach, which is often misunderstood.[43]

Copson notes that the French Revolution was a "decade-long series of innovations" that established new ways of thinking about the church—state relationship.[44] While, as pointed out by Rémond, the French Revolution did not yet assert secularism in any manifest form, it embodied the core principles of *laïcité* understood as the "lay principle."[45] It asserted power in the people's name, providing, in the Declaration of the Rights of Man and of the Citizen from 1789, liberty of religious opinions, and, by dissociating citizenship from Catholic affiliation, turned to extra-religious sources of national unity. The subsequent secularization (in the original use of the term) of clerical properties, the creation of an ecclesiastical budget, and the transformation of clergy into state officials subjected many aspects of the church to the principles of popular sovereignty. In addition, new public bodies were given the tasks that were previously fulfilled by the church, for example, registration of births, marriages, and deaths, and in 1792 divorce was legalized, further distancing the law from the principles of strictly Catholic religious ethics.

Importantly, freedom of conscience was granted to individuals rather than religious groups. Thus, while this freedom was at first only extended to Roman

40 Kelly, "France's laïcité."

41 For more on that see Luca Pietro Vanoni and Giada Ragone, "From the Secularisation Theory to the Pluralistic Approach: Reconciling Religious Traditions and Modernity in Italian Case-Law," in *Law, Religion, and Tradition*, ed. Jessica Giles, Andrea Pin, and Frank S. Ravitch (New York: Springer, 2018).

42 Haarscher, *Laickość*, 5–6.

43 Anastasia Colosimo, "Laïcité: Why French Secularism is So Hard to Grasp," Institut Montaigne, 2017, accessed 11 December, 2021, https://www.institutmontaigne.org/en/blog/laicite-why-french-secularism-so-hard-grasp; Kelly, "France's laïcité."

44 Copson, *Secularism*, 18.

45 René Rémond, *Religion and Society in Modern Europe*, ed. Jacques Le Goff, The Making of Europe, (Oxford: Blackwell Publishers, 1999), 55.

Catholics and Protestants, it was extended further in 1791 to Jews, who were provided with full civil rights. In the way that Marx would criticize later, individual Jews were free to exercise their religious observance. However, they were not recognized as a collective, a religious group.

The notion of individual freedom encountered some resistance at the collective level. There, the ideas of a centralized overhaul were applied in practice in the search for a replacement for Catholicism. Several short-lived ideas emerged, such as the atheist Cult of Reason inspired by Jean-Jacques Rousseau, later replaced by the deistic reverence to the Supreme Being. Nevertheless, as Copson points out, freedom of conscience, as introduced in 1789, did not survive for long at any level. The new ideas escalated into full-blown anti-Christian persecution with the development of the Revolution and ended abruptly with Napoleon's ascent to power.[46]

The French Revolution provided the first impulse for the emergence of a modern European approach to religious diversity. By establishing freedom of conscience on an individual level, most visible in the principles of Jewish emancipation, the French Revolution strengthened a tendency to treat religiosity as an individual choice. This was broadly summarized at the time by a French politician, Stanislas de Clermont-Tonnerre: "We must deny everything to the Jews as a nation and give everything to the Jews as individuals. They must not form a political body or an order in the state. They must be individual citizens."[47] On a communal level, the French Revolution introduced the principles of functionalization and centralization by remodeling clergy into public officials, overhauling established church structures to fit the revolutionary vision of a lay society, and creating new, centrally designed alternatives for civil religion. In other words, the French Revolution created the foundations for the emergence of legible religion, a version of religion reduced to what was functionally relevant for the state.

The French answer to what makes a state laicized was not the only one. For example, countries such as Britain and Denmark took smaller steps. Haarscher points out that these countries focused on rejecting the ancient rule of *compelle intrare*, the rule that accepted the use of coercion with heretics. This rule had been in place at least since the Theodosian Code, so this rejection constituted a significant change. However, it was not necessarily followed

---

46 Copson, *Secularism*, 20.

47 Own translation of: *Il faut tout refuser aux Juifs comme nation et tout accorder aux Juifs comme individus. Il faut qu'ils ne fassent dans l'État ni un corps politique ni un ordre. Il faut qu'ils soient individuellement citoyens.* After Robert Badinter, *Libres et égaux … L'émancipation des Juifs sous la Révolution française (1789–1791)* (Paris: Fayard, 1989), 149.

by a rejection of the system of privileges and establishment.[48] Others, like Germany, followed more directly in the footsteps of the Napoleonic order, with, in the words of Stefan Korioth and Ino Augsberg, "an intricate balance between a separation as well as a cooperation of state and religious communities."[49]

To delineate and define the divergent tendencies, multiple researchers have tried to propose more nuanced terms than secularism or even *laïcité,* terms that would denote the particular model of the relationship between the state and religions. Thus, for example, as discussed above, Haarscher speaks about broad and narrow approaches to *laïcité,*[50] while French legal scholar, Anastasia Colosimo, speaks about open and strict *laïcité.*[51] The problem is not only limited to the French-speaking context. Scholars such as the former Archbishop of Canterbury, Rowan Williams, or American political scientist Elizabeth Shakman Hurd introduced similar distinctions. Williams distinguished between procedural and programmatic secularisms, aptly summing up the distinction mentioned above:

> Procedural secularism is … a public policy which declines to give advantage or preference to any one religious body over others. It is the principle according to which the state as such defines its role as one of overseeing a variety of communities of religious conviction and, where necessary, assisting them to keep the peace together, without requiring any specific public confessional allegiance from its servants or guaranteeing any single community a legally favoured position against others. Programmatic secularism is something more like what is often seen (not always accurately) as the French paradigm, in which any and every public manifestation of any particular religious allegiance is to be ironed out so that everyone may share a clear public loyalty to the state unclouded by private convictions, and any signs of such private convictions are rigorously banned from public space.[52]

While Williams is more inclined towards procedural secularism, describing it as "posing no real problems to Christians,"[53] Hurd approaches both parts

48 Haarscher, *Laickość,* 19.

49 Stefan Korioth and Ino Augsberg, "Religion and the Secular State in Germany," in *Religion and the Secular State / La religion et l'État laïque,* ed. Javier Martinez-Torrón and W. Cole Durham Jr. (Provo, UT: The International Center for Law and Religious Studies, Brigham Young University, 2010), 322.

50 Haarscher, *Laickość.*

51 Colosimo, "Laïcité."

52 Rowan Williams, *Faith in the Public Square* (London: Bloomsbury, 2012), 2–3.

53 Williams, *Faith in the Public Square,* 3.

of the division more critically. She distinguishes between "Laicism" and "Judeo-Christian Secularism."[54] Laicism, in her approach, "is associated with attempts to force religion out of politics." In contrast, in Judeo-Christian Secularism, "religion is seen as a source of unity and identity that generates conflict in modern international politics." She points out that both forms of secularism are portrayed "as a unique Western achievement that both distills and expresses the essence of Euro-American history, civilization, and culture."[55] Instead of siding with any of them, she sees problematic aspects in each. She argues that, while theoretically distinct, they are relatively close in practice:

> Each of these forms of secularism is a contingent and productive form of power located on a much broader spectrum of theological politics. They are not mutually exclusive. There is no strong or necessary dividing line between them. An individual or an institution may draw upon the substantial discursive resources of both traditions simultaneously to legitimate a particular political position.[56]

The question of to what extent these two tendencies converge or diverge is crucial for the argument of this book. While they might differ in details, I would argue that they were directed at the same questions. What function should religion play in society? Should it be a force for social cohesion, only a personal business, or a combination of both? Thus, I follow Hurd in her assessment that different forms of secularism are not entirely divergent. On the contrary, they share foundational assumptions and can function alongside each other. In other words, they operate in the same overarching paradigm. The overlap in these foundational assumptions was crucial for establishing their hegemonic status, to which we now turn.

2 Neutral Baseline: Secularizing Cycle and a Modern Consensus

How was it possible that secularization and secularism were established as the neutral baseline of public policy and thinking about religion in the public sphere? It is, of course, impossible to give a complete or comprehensive answer to this question. Below, I attempt only to suggest possible reasons for this situation based on the framework described so far. I argue that two factors contributed to this. First, the secularization theories and programs of secularism,

54 Hurd, *The Politics of Secularism*, 2.
55 Hurd, *The Politics of Secularism*, 23.
56 Hurd, *The Politics of Secularism*, 23.

combined with centralized attempts at achieving legibility, exercised a consciousness-shaping effect on individuals and reshaped social reality. Second, the hegemonic status of secularism has been achieved thanks to the loss of its most prominent opponent. The Roman Catholic Church initially opposed legibility attempts and the politics of secularism. However, the Church changed its approach in the twentieth century. The reliance on Concordats, the use of the law, and the emergence of Catholic modernity meant that the main opposition to legibility disappeared, allowing the secularizing cycle of legible religion to merge into the background and become invisible. The following two sections will discuss each of these points.

2.1 *The Secularizing Cycle of Legible Religion*

Previously, I have discussed several changes that occurred in the relation between state and religion before the end of the nineteenth century. I traced the emergence of religion as a separate category that can be governed and manipulated by the state. When combined with the emergence of modern statecraft in the way proposed by Scott, these features allowed for the creation of what I called legible religion, that is, a conceptual framework in which religion is reduced to the features deemed relevant by the administrative beholder, in this case, a utility and a threat. The regulation of religion became an administrative exercise. Moreover, as underlined by Scott, such exercises had a consciousness-shaping aspect. They shaped the way we see reality.

However, to reshape reality significantly, as Scott argues, the regulations need an additional element: ideological support. The mutual interrelation of secularization, as a justifying narrative, and secularism, as a program, provided such a support. One leads to the other. For example, the accounts of both Comte and Marx were based on secularization as a postulate rather than an empirically verifiable process. In Comte's approach, the ideals of the positive stage had to be brought about by the embrace of a new Religion of Humanity. In Marx's view, people had to be emancipated from religion, which would become obsolete after the success of the proletarian revolution. In both, the principles of secularism resulted from the will to bring about secularization. Their ideas of secularization had a normative element. In this respect, their accounts differed significantly from later sociological theories, such as those of Weber and Durkheim, which instead tried to make sense of a changing social reality. A significant alteration of consciousness had occurred in the meantime.

To better understand such change in consciousness, one needs to consider the two types of secularism discussed in the previous section. Secularism transformed into much more than a political program. Hurd points out that both types of secularism, laicism and Judeo-Christian secularism, exercise a consciousness-shaping effect. In her view, both go beyond the simply juridical or administrative terms of relations between the state and religions. Hurd argues that "the forms of secularism described in [her] book are part of the basic values and fundamental beliefs that 'feed into a set of political predispositions'."[57] Secularism in Hurd's approach, then, is not only an array of formal organizing principles but a much broader "set of discursive traditions that seeks to construct both the secular and the religious in particular ways. … These secular visions and the attitudes, sensibilities, and habits that sustain and shape them do not merely reflect social reality; they construct it."[58]

These discursive traditions resulted from several developments: first, the conditions of possibility that were described in Chapter 1; second, the narratives of progress and secularization that provided a part of the ideological justification for their establishment; third, the political programs of secularism that provided their primary content. Different emphases resulted in the particular constructions of the secular and the religious in various European states. They provided the direction that an administrative reduction of religion could follow; most importantly, functionalization and individualization. Finally, when applied politically by the growing European nation-states with their increasing centralizing tendencies, these elements reshaped social reality and general consciousness.

I propose the term "secularizing cycle of legible religion" to capture these interlocking elements. Each of the abovementioned elements is connected to the other in a dialectical relationship. The developments concerning the separation of church and state, the analytical differentiation of religion from other categories, and the functional approach to religion, when merged with the Enlightenment idea of progress, created conditions for the emergence of secularization narratives. Initially more a postulate than a reality, secularization constituted a foundation for the political programs of secularism to bring about that reality. The centralized administrations of modern nation-states provided tools for implementing these political programs, affecting individual and collective behaviors and attitudes. When noticed by the emerging sociology of religion, the change in attitudes provided fuel for theories of secularization, which understood it more as a description of the situation than a postulate. With secularization narratives becoming increasingly taken for granted, the whole cycle began again, impacting policy-making and general consciousness.

The secularizing cycle of legible religion resulted in the normalization of secularism and its postulates to the point that secularism could be perceived as

57 Hurd, *The Politics of Secularism*, 14.

58 Hurd, *The Politics of Secularism*, 44.

a neutral position. As I will discuss based on the example of multi-faith spaces in chapters 4 and 5, the concomitant change in consciousness impacted the place of religion within the public sphere, making its presence seem intrusive and in need of regulation. But before secularism could achieve that neutral character, its leading opponent had to step back, which is the subject of the next section.

2.2 *The Emergence of a Modern Consensus*

All elements of the secularizing cycle of legible religion were initially contested. While secularization and secularism gained prominence throughout the nineteenth century, they were far from the only viable options available. The adoption of secularism by modern statecraft alone cannot account for the practical lack of mainstream alternatives to secularism. The examples of other attempts summed up by Scott as "high modernism"[59] had alternatives, just as a centrally planned economy competed with the free-market ideas. Thus, an additional question requires an answer: Why did secularism ultimately surpass all other options and become a European standard in the 1950s and 60s?[60] Furthermore, why did they become so ingrained that today, as Hurd argues, "Most of us, perhaps unconsciously, perhaps less so, think, work, struggle against, and live in and around variations of the two traditions of secularism"?[61]

Secularism is usually associated with different strands of Protestantism. There is a notion that Protestantism allows for the view of religion as primarily cognitive, individual, private, and even internalized, rather than collective and requiring external manifestations of religiosity. While the first expressions of this idea could be observed in Weber,[62] it seems to be commonplace among contemporary scholars. For example, José Casanova speaks about the

59 James C. Scott, *Seeing like a State: How Certain Schemes to Improve the Human Condition Have Failed* (New Haven: Yale University Press, 1999), 4.

60 I specifically mention Europe here, because the USA have been viewed as the antithesis of secularization theories. As this study is interested in Europe, there is no space to offer a proper analysis for this difference. I can only suggest that this difference might come down to the lack of high modernism in the USA, at least in the approach to religion. It seems that instead of interfering with religion as such, in the USA, another cult of nationalism and civil values was built alongside the religious landscape, rather than in opposition to it. Thus, the religious scene left to its own devices could remain much more dynamic and adaptable to local needs. See also William T. Cavanaugh, *Migrations of the Holy. God, State, and the Political Meaning of the Church* (Grand Rapids, MI and Cambridge, U.K.: William B. Eerdmans Publishing Company, 2011).

61 Hurd, *The Politics of Secularism*, 45.

62 Weber, *The Protestant Ethic.*

Protestant bias of secularism,[63] Rajeev Bhargava argues that Western secularism "can live comfortably with … Protestantized … religions,"[64] while Silvio Ferrari points out that no country with a Protestant majority population was ever convicted for violation of Article 9 of the European Convention of Human Rights by the European Court of Human Rights in Strasbourg, unlike Catholic, Orthodox, Muslim, or religiously diverse countries.[65]

However, this is not the whole picture. The idea of a Protestant bias could be congruent with the types of secularism that follow the supersessionist line of thinking, as exemplified by Marx. However, Catholicism is not inconsequential here. As already visible in the example of Comte, Catholicism contributed, for example, to the line of thinking that could be understood as more focused on social cohesion. Additionally, I argue that Catholicism actively contributed to the development of different understandings of secularism in Europe, at least since the Second World War. By engaging with the work of two American scholars, Giuliana Chamedes and James Chappel, and applying some conclusions made above, I want to outline the significance that the Catholic Church had for the success of secularism.

During the French Revolution, the Catholic Church in France was one of the parties most affected by the Revolution, which led to strong opposition from parts of the local clergy and the Vatican. The Catholic Church became one of the staunchest opponents of secularism in both its liberal and, later, communist forms. Catholic opposition led to many attempts at mending the widening rift between church and state, from the unstable Concordat of 1801 in France, through the attempts at building Christian states all over Europe, to the attempts at what Giuliana Chamedes describes as a "Twentieth-century Crusade," a concerted juridical and diplomatic effort at protecting Europe from liberalism and socialism.[66]

According to Chamedes, the Catholic Church, under the leadership of Pope Benedict XV, attempted to create a viable alternative to both the liberal and the socialist visions of the world. On the one hand, the Catholic Church hoped to counteract secularizing tendencies. On the other, Benedict XV tried to solve

63 José Casanova, *Public Religions in the Modern World* (Chicago and London: The University of Chicago Press, 1994), 216.

64 Rajeev Bhargava, "Rehabilitating Secularism," in *Rethinking Secularism*, ed. Craig Calhoun, Mark Juergensmeyer, and Jonathan VanAntwerpen (Oxford: Oxford University Press, 2011), 101.

65 Silvio Ferrari, "Law and Religion in a Secular World: A European Perspective," *Ecclesiastical Law Journal* 14, no. 3 (2012): 364, https://doi.org/10.1017/S0956618X1200035X.

66 Giuliana Chamedes, *A Twentieth Century Crusade. The Vatican's Battle to Remake Christian Europe* (Cambridge, MA: Harvard University Press, 2019).

the European crisis of the First World War. The Vatican proposed an approach based on the principles of re-Christianization, national self-determination, and greater emphasis on international law. Using its broad diplomatic network and charismatic ambassadors like Eugenio Pacelli, the future Pope Pius XII, the Vatican once again relied on concordats to establish treaties that would suit the ends of both the Catholic Church and the engaged states. Chamedes writes:

> Concordats would provide legitimacy to emerging political leaders and help newly constituted nation-states firm up their claims to territorial sovereignty, by making diocesan lines coincide with desired national boundaries. The legal agreements would also provide new leaders with a way to oppose the influence of liberalism and the rise of left-wing revolution. In exchange, these treaties would greatly expand the Vatican's control over everything from education to family law, from press freedom to the organization of local churches. By making religious instruction in public schools mandatory, giving the church jurisdiction over a range of civil-law matters, and increasing monies funneled from the state to the church, the treaties spelled out relationships of tight church—state collaboration. The papal use of law thus aimed to be, borrowing from Clifford Geertz's phrasing, "constructive of social realities rather than merely reflective of them."[67]

Through concordats, the Vatican wanted to reformulate the relationship between the church and the state, once again placing the former above the latter. The Church wanted to be the source, or at least the solidifying agent, of territorial sovereignty, political legitimacy, and a body with large areas of social life under its jurisdiction. Once again, the law was the tool of choice for the popes. Thus, Benedict XV, and later his successor Pius XI, followed in the footsteps of their eleventh-century predecessor Gregory VII by relying on legal means of exercising influence. Like the eleventh-century revolution, the twentieth-century attempts had the same weaknesses—too much interference in contemporary politics meant that the church was much more susceptible to changes in political currents and attitudes. Thus, the politics of concordats in the inter-war years aligned the church with right-wing parties as "authoritarian and Fascist leaders promised to respect and implement both the papacy's legal revolution and its cultural anticommunist crusade" against the politics

67 Chamedes, *A Twentieth Century Crusade*, 3.

of both Woodrow Wilson and Vladimir Lenin.[68] After the Second World War, these close alliances, based on rigid distinctions between friends and foes, discredited many principles set by papal politics.

Chamedes points out that the concordats were an element of a broader centralizing strategy, which started with the proclamation of papal infallibility in 1871. Several other centralizing measures followed. For example, the pope proclaimed a new Code of Canon Law in 1917, which radically increased papal prerogatives by placing the appointment and removal of bishops in the hands of the pope alone. After the First World War, the Vatican doubled down on expanding Catholic civil society institutions, including new youth organizations and working-class groups for factory and agricultural workers. Lay activism was put under the strictly hierarchical surveillance of the clergy, being reliant on parish priests, bishops, and the pope himself. Increasingly afraid of the development of communism, in the 1930s Pius XI started an anti-communist campaign under the name of the Catholic International. It opposed the Comintern, using new media and communication channels to create and solidify a unified vision of what it meant to be a Catholic in the twentieth century.[69]

Thus, from the end of the nineteenth century, while opposed to the foundational ideas of secularism, the Catholic Church followed in many aspects the centralizing principles described by Scott. Catholic identity and institutions were streamlined and made more legible for the pope. They were subordinated to the ecclesiastical hierarchy at the cost of local and internal diversity, which led to alignment with political currents. Thus, the leading oppositional force to the secularizing tendencies employed the same functional principles as the proponents of secularism. The principles of centralization and legibility, a significant element of the secularizing cycle of legible religion, were broadly accepted within most contemporary political positions, from liberalism, through fascism and communism, to Catholic internationalism.

The other pillar of the cycle followed not much later. While, as James Chappel points out in his study *Catholic Modern*, the Catholic Church was staunchly antimodernist until well into the 1920s, Catholics engaged in pragmatic collaborations with both fascists and communists. Nonetheless, they rejected the core principles of the modern secular nation-state. At that time, such a stance still had a degree of plausibility because of the shaky political situation. However, events such as the Great Depression and the emergence of totalitarian forms of government made any wishes of returning to Catholic empires increasingly implausible. Thus, in the 1930s, "the framing of Catholic debate shifted from

68 Chamedes, *A Twentieth Century Crusade*, 14–15.
69 Chamedes, *A Twentieth Century Crusade*, 4–10.

'how can we overcome the secular state?' to 'how can we shape the secular state?'"[70] In "a desperate bid for relevance in a Europe that was coming apart"[71] the Church accepted secularism's basic principles, such as the uncoupling of religion and politics and the division between public and private spheres. In mere decades, the Catholic Church moved from antimodern positions in the 1920s to the mainstream embrace of modernity in the 1950s.[72] Worrying that liberal democracy would not hold ground against fascism and communism, Catholics developed two parallel approaches to modernity called by Chappel "paternal" and "fraternal" Catholic modernism.[73]

Paternal Catholic modernism was willing to build coalitions with fascists to oppose communists as the worse enemy of the two. It defined the private sphere as the sphere of the reproductive family, which underlined the paternal hierarchy and a gendered division of roles. Paternalist social thinking was primarily concerned with the good of the family, with generous family welfare programs (as opposed to individual welfare programs), conservative reproductive legislation, law and order policies, and easier acquisition of private property.[74]

Less mainstream, fraternal Catholic modernism completely rejected fascism. To fight fascists, fraternal Catholic modernists were willing to collaborate with communists. Modernists conceptualized the private sphere as a collaborative space of brotherly solidarity. They viewed marriage as a union of love. Childrearing was a secondary purpose. They also wanted to build a vibrant civil society with trade unions, youth movements, and a free press.[75]

While Chappel simplifies a highly complex picture, the two broad categories he sketches exemplify the general tendencies in coalition-building and dominant political stances built upon them. Nonetheless, the end of the Second World War brought significant disappointment with both forms of totalitarian politics, and Roman Catholics ultimately rejected both fascism and communism. Instead, a new form of Catholic Modernity emerged: Christian Democracy. A combination of previous tendencies, Christian Democracy embraced religious plurality and conceptualized the private sphere in terms of family. However, Christian Democracy changed how that family was understood. The natalist and nationalist conceptions of a reproductive family known from

70 James Chappel, *Catholic Modern. The Challenge of Totalitarianism and the Remaking of the Church* (Boston, MA: Harvard University Press, 2018), 12.

71 Chappel, *Catholic Modern*, 2.

72 Antimodernism often refers to a theological debate which is just a part of the larger picture discussed here.

73 Chappel, *Catholic Modern*, 12–18.

74 Chappel, *Catholic Modern*, 69–105.

75 Chappel, *Catholic Modern*, 115–39.

paternal Catholic modernity were replaced with the notion of a consuming family. Therefore, the proposed social ethics were primarily concerned with protecting consuming families through family welfare, access to private property, support for free trade unions, worker empowerment, and focus on economic growth.[76]

While short-lived, the consensus of the 1950s Christian Democracy solidified the secularizing cycle. This consensus might be why the interest in theories of secularization peaked around the same time. While the 1960s brought the breakdown of the consensus and paved the way for the emergence of widespread dissent from official Catholic teachings, visible especially in the wake of *Humanae Vitae*, the cycle was in full swing, making it hard to go beyond the foundational principles of secularism. The boundaries between the religious and the secular seemed fixed and self-evident. Secularism became the air that everyone breathed.[77]

Secularism's increasing success thus largely depended on support from the main religious groups in Europe. While Protestantism could be understood as introducing a focus on creedal adherence, freedom of choice, belief-centeredness, and internalization of religious practice, creating a part of the foundations for the emergence of secularism, Catholicism also ultimately contributed to it. The Catholic Church, initially the strongest opponent of modernity and many elements of the legible religion framework, began to contribute to it, first, by employing centralization in its operations, and, later, by accepting the core premises of a secular state. Instead of rejecting the *status quo* and aiming to transform it, the Catholic Church began to think how to influence it. In this way it solidified the hegemonic status of the legible religion. This hegemonic status meant that, even when alternatives to secularism and secularization theories began to emerge, they inherited many of their assumptions. Let us take a closer look at those.

3 Novel Alternative? The Return of Religion

3.1 *The Critique of Secularization*

Although dominant and therefore consciousness-shaping for a long time, the notion of secularization was not universally accepted. On the contrary, from

76 Chappel, *Catholic Modern*, 189–225.

77 The countries with Protestant majorities also started the quest for modernization of, for example, their social issues. For more on this, for example, in Sweden, see Gert Nilsson, *Socialetik i Svenska kyrkan under 1900-talet* (Skellefteå: Artos Norma Bokförlag, 2020).

early on, secularization has been criticized for assuming its own inevitability, its definition of the religious and the secular, including their implied polarity, and for its ideological and ethnocentric character. For example, already in 1965, when interest in secularization peaked, David Martin argued that the term should be eliminated as "the uses to which the term 'secularization' has been put ... (or perhaps, more accurately, misuses) are a barrier to progress in the sociology of religion."[78] He argued that while secularization as a particular process can be observed on a case-by-case basis, it implies a broader narrative that assumes an indefensible definition of religion. Martin pointed out that while one can characterize different institutions as religious, it is difficult to define them as a class sharing "common characteristics apart from the sharing of an adjective."[79] Thus, it is impossible to speak of secularization as a generalized tendency of religious decline because features of what is classified as religious cannot be satisfactorily defined.

Similarly, two years later, in a meta-analysis of the different strands of thinking about secularization, Larry Shiner criticized the term from the perspective of the definition of religion and the polarity implied. He wrote:

> It is evident that the criticism made ... aimed at a view of religious phenomena which narrowly restricts them to certain external elements in the Western tradition, e.g., church attendance and financial support, conventional forms of public and private devotional practice, belief scales based on traditional creeds.[80]

Shiner pointed out that such definitions of religion and religious are restricting and ethnocentric. Moreover, such an approach creates a specific polarity with the secular, which might not be justified. Shiner referred here to Paul Tillich and his suggestion that the existence of a religious, as opposed to a secular, realm expresses "the tragic estrangement of man's spiritual life from its own ground and depth."[81] Shiner also pointed out that this polarity is based on the Western model of church and state relations, which is inapplicable to situations where such a polarity has never been established. Shiner argued also that

78 David Martin, "Towards Eliminating the Concept of Secularization," in *Penguin Survey of the Social Sciences*, ed. Julius Gould (London: Penguin Books, 1965), 169.

79 Martin, "Towards Eliminating," 175.

80 Shiner, "The Concept of Secularization," 217.

81 Paul Tillich, *Theology of Culture* (New York: Oxford University Press, 1959), 8. quoted in Shiner, "The Concept of Secularization," 217.

the two are not necessarily mutually exclusive and that the line between them is not as stable as implied.[82]

These two examples highlight the main lines of the criticism of secularization theories developed from the 1960s onwards. Increasingly, critics began to reject secularization as ideological, incoherent, normatively charged and ethnocentric. Moreover, the critique began to extend even more, with increasing suspicion towards the very possibility of defining religion and a clear-cut religious/secular binary. Interestingly, already at that time, there was a notion that these theories restrict religiosity to specific forms: forms that were discussed as Protestantized, Western, or reduced only to external elements.

The 1990s could be considered the low point for secularization theories. In 1994, José Casanova pointed out that "religion in the 1980s 'went public' in a dual sense. It entered the 'public sphere' and gained, thereby, 'publicity'."[83] In Casanova's view, such events as the Iranian, Nicaraguan, and Romanian revolutions, the impact of the Catholic Church on the fall of Communism concluding with Mikhail Gorbachev's meeting with the pope, the controversy around Salman Rushdie's *Satanic Verses*, or the religiously fuelled conflicts in Northern Ireland and Yugoslavia, showed that religion was far from disappearing. Quite the opposite; religion still had an enormous sway, even, or sometimes especially, in its traditional forms. Casanova continued:

> What was new and unexpected in the 1980s was not the emergence of "new religious movements ... but rather revitalization and the assumption of public roles by precisely those religious traditions which both theories of secularization and cyclical theories of religious revival had assumed were becoming ever more marginal and irrelevant in the modern world.[84]

Casanova argued that, apart from a few "old believers," nearly no one believed in the "myth" of secularization anymore.[85]

And indeed, the disillusionment of many of the "old believers" represents this process well. In his *Sociology of Religion: An Historical Introduction*, Roberto Cipriani describes the path undergone by Sabino Acquaviva, from his first notes on the crisis of the sacred in 1961 to the publication of *Fine di un'ideologia: la secolarizzazione* (*The End of an Ideology: Secularization*) in 1989, which

82 Shiner, "The Concept of Secularization," 218.

83 Casanova, *Public Religions*, 3.

84 Casanova, *Public Religions*, 5.

85 Casanova, *Public Religions*, 11.

forecasted the decade to come.[86] In this book, written together with Renato Stella, Acquaviva argued that the decline of one form of religiosity, namely the magical use of the sacred, created a space for another:

> secularization as a process can by itself give rise to new ways of being religious. It is evident that if religion is robbed of its exterior forms, it allows in the end new ways of living the experience of the sacred precisely because the rules of the game change.[87]

Similarly, Peter Berger moved away from his affirmation of secularization theories in the *Sacred Canopy*. In 1996, Berger wrote "Secularism in retreat," in which he argued that secularization "was essentially mistaken"[88] and, three years later, he edited an influential volume focused on the opposite tendency of "desecularization."[89] There, Berger argued that modernization not only leads to the decline of religion but, quite the opposite, strengthens it. As he summed up in 2008, "modernity is not necessarily *secularizing* but *pluralizing*."[90]

However, the most significant impact was made by Rodney Stark's article "Secularization, R.I.P." from 1999. In this article, Stark traced the narrative of secularization as far back as the British Restoration in 1660. As Stark pointed out, every generation since has presented some belief that humans will surpass faith in the supernatural in a few decades. Stark also described five beliefs on which secularization prophecies were based. First, that secularization was linked with modernization, as its necessary consequence; second, that secularization resulted in a visible decline in individual piety; third, that science was one of the principal reasons for the decline of religion; fourth, that

86 Roberto Cipriani, "Secularization," in *Sociology of Religion. An Historical Introduction* (New York: Aldine De Gruyter, 2000), 167.

87 Sabino S. Acquaviva and Renato Stella, *Fine di un'ideologia: La secolarizzazione* (Rome: Borla, 1989), 9. After Cipriani, "Secularization," 167.

88 Peter L. Berger, "Secularism in retreat," *The National Interest*, December 1, 1996, https://nationalinterest.org/article/secularism-in-retreat-336.

89 Peter L. Berger, *The Desecularization of the World* (Washington, D.C.: William B Eerdmans Publishing Co, 1999). Berger has also been viewed as exemplary for the rise and fall of secularization's influence—see, for example, Dylan Reaves, "Peter Berger and the Rise and Fall of the Theory of Secularization," *Denison Journal of Religion* 11, no. 3 (2012).

90 Peter L. Berger, "Secularisation Falsified," *First Things*, no. February (2008), https://www.firstthings.com/article/2008/02/secularization-falsified. See also Peter L. Berger, *The Many Altars of Modernity* (Boston and Berlin: De Gruyter, 2014).

secularization was irreversible; fifth, that secularization could be applied globally, despite most discussions being focused on Christendom.[91]

However, Stark argued based on historical and contemporary evidence that these beliefs are problematic and should be dismissed. Stark concluded: "Therefore, once and for all, let us declare an end to social scientific faith in the theory of secularization, recognizing that it was the product of wishful thinking."[92] Such criticism of the secularization concept allowed alternative theories to emerge.

By the end of the 1990s, secularization as a theory was in disrepute. Several former proponents offered critical accounts going as far as to state its death. Others pointed towards the empirical inconsistencies, speaking, like Casanova, about the dynamics of desecularization. Some, like Stark, acknowledged that much wishful thinking was involved, highlighting the mythological character of the underlying narratives, which many empirically grounded theories wanted to prove. However, despite these doubts, the emerging alternatives did not necessarily reject all the assumptions of secularization.

3.2 *Individualization, Pluralization, and Others*

Multiple alternatives were proposed in place of secularization. However, as I argue below, most of them shared a common root and several assumptions with secularization. Gert Pickel argues in his introductory volume to the sociology of religion that two main alternatives to secularization emerged: *individualization* and *pluralization*.[93]

According to Pickel, theories of *individualization* are based on the idea that the decline in church affiliation in the West is not equivalent to the decline of religion. Instead, the modern loss of the importance of institutionalized religion involves the subjectivization of religion, which shifts it from the collective to the individual level.[94] As he defines it, "Individualization is the process of increasing self-determination by the individual with a simultaneous decrease in external control through external social instances and factors (social

---

91 Rodney Stark, "Secularization, R.I.P.," *Sociology of Religion* 60, no. 3 (1999): 251–53, https://doi.org/10.2307/3711936.

92 Stark, "Secularization, R.I.P.," 269.

93 Gert Pickel, *Religionssoziologie. Eine Einführung in zentrale Themenbereiche* (Wiesbaden: VS Verlag, 2011), 218. The German terms used in the book were translated by their author in Detlef Pollack, Olaf Müller, and Gert Pickel, *The Social Significance of Religion in the Enlarged Europe: Secularization, Individualization and Pluralization* (Aldershot: Ashgate, 2012). *Marktmodell des Religiösen* was translated into pluralization and *Individualisierungsthese* into individualization.

94 Pickel, *Religionssoziologie*, 179.

structure)."[95] Thus, as Pickel concludes, there is no conflict between modernity and religion in these theories—religion is simply adapting to societal changes and deregulation.

The *pluralization* theory, by contrast, is based on rational choice theory. It assumes that the decline in some of the religious indicators results from the available supply on the "religious market." Individuals are by nature religious, but they make cost/benefit calculations in their choice of religious "providers." The vitality of the religious market, and the activity of individual actors, is reliant on the providers. If they fail to adapt to the needs of their "consumers," these consumers will seek other options or refrain from choosing any providers at all. Thus, what Peter Berger described as the breaking down of the cosmos into individual sub-worlds, with a resulting pluralization, is not harmful to religion but brings some fresh air instead, which might revitalize it in the future.[96]

Both approaches rely heavily on the functional approach to religion, as presented by Durkheim. In both, religion cannot simply disappear because of the innate religious needs of individuals, even if they differ in how they interpret its influence on the transformation of religious beliefs. Pickel points out that the individualization theory was developed by Thomas Luckmann. The pluralization theory is based on the theory of religion developed by Stark and William Sims Bainbridge. Again, both heavily rely on Durkheim in their approach.[97]

In their approaches, the proponents of both individualization and pluralization are building upon the secularization narratives and reformulated the secularization theories instead of offering entirely new ways of thinking. As a result, they accepted many assumptions inherent in secularization. For example, Stark explicitly wrote in "Secularization, R.I.P." that there is "nothing to argue about" in terms of secularization understood as the weakening of religious institutions. It is evident in many parts of the world that religious institutions hold less power than they used to.[98] Some, like Oliver Tschannen, went as far as to group these approaches as secularization theories.[99]

Even the theories that do not neatly fit into any of the three categories (secularization, individualization, or pluralization), for example, Casanova's account, follow similar footsteps. Casanova explicitly disputes the claims made by all three currents and criticizes Weber and Durkheim for separating

95 Pickel, *Religionssoziologie*, 180.
96 Pickel, *Religionssoziologie*, 198–200.
97 Pickel, *Religionssoziologie*, 200ff.
98 Stark, "Secularization, R.I.P.," 252.
99 Oliver Tschannen, *Les theories de la secularisation.* (Geneva: Droz, 1992). For further discussion see Ulrich Schmiedel, *Elasticized Ecclesiology. The Concept of Community after Ernst Troeltsch* (New York: Palgrave Macmillan, 2017), 147.

the question of the truth of religion from that of its symbolic structure and social function.[100] Nevertheless, he accepts several assumptions from secularization theories. He writes:

> the theory of secularization is so intrinsically interwoven with all the theories of the modern world and with the self-understanding of modernity that one cannot simply discard the theory of secularization without putting into question the entire web, including much of the self-understanding of the social sciences.[101]

Out of the three propositions hidden behind the secularization label that Casanova identifies—differentiation, decline, and privatization—he rejects only the latter two.[102] He writes:

> It is simply fallacious to argue, for instance, that the permanence or increase in religious beliefs and practices, and the continuous emergence of new religions and the revival of old ones in the United States or anywhere else, serves as empirical confirmation that the theory of secularization is a myth. It only confirms the need to refine the theory ... Similarly, it is incorrect to claim that the role religion has recently played in political conflicts throughout the world serves to invalidate empirically the theory of secularization. But no less incongruous is the position of those defenders of the theory of secularization who use the thesis of privatization to accuse religion of trespassing illegitimately on the public sphere or of crossing systemic boundaries by assuming nonreligious roles.[103]

Instead, Casanova offers an account of deprivatization's dynamics (rather than the process). He acknowledges differentiation as a general trend and pointed out that under certain conditions in limited geographical areas, even the decline thesis can be applicable (for example, if religion resists modernization from the established position). However, he points out that under other conditions, religion, even in its traditional forms, can be subjected to "publicization," provided that its institutions transform from the state- to the society-oriented.[104]

---

100 Casanova, *Public Religions*, 17–18.

101 Casanova, *Public Religions*, 18.

102 Casanova, *Public Religions*, 211.

103 Casanova, *Public Religions*, 212.

104 Casanova, *Public Religions*, 220.

Thus, theorists such as Stark or Casanova primarily criticized the "myth" of secularization—the term used by both in their respective critiques.[105] Their main problem was with the normative implications drawn from the secularization narratives, while the theoretical discussions came second. Casanova explicitly writes that:

> Some of the related propositions presented in the study are that the thesis of religious decline has its origins in the Enlightenment critique of religion; that this critique was not so much a theoretical statement or an empirical proposition as a practical political program; that this practical political program was most effective wherever churches had attained caesaropapist establishment and were resisting the process of differentiation ... that in such cases the Enlightenment critique of religion was usually adopted by social movements and political parties, becoming in the process a self-fulfilling prophecy; that once in power those movements and parties tended to translate the theory into applied state policies.[106]

This statement is important because it highlights the impact that secularization has made on public policies concerned with religion. It also emphasizes that the prophetic character of the notion of secularization was to a great extent self-fulfilling. The belief that modernity would bring secularization led to the development of policies that, in turn, encouraged secularization.

By entering a dispute with the secularization theories but not rejecting them altogether, the new narratives retained many of the former theoretical foundations instead of starting anew. They were acknowledging secularization as a step in the process of modernization. That is why several key ideas circulated by those who were disillusioned with secularization bore specific prefixes that implied that secularization was nevertheless real: "*re*-turn of religion or God,"[107]

105 Casanova, *Public Religions*, 11; Stark, "Secularization, R.I.P.," 253 and 55.

106 Casanova, *Public Religions*, 214.

107 See, for example, Jayne Svenungsson, *Guds återkomst: En Studie av gudsbegreppet inom postmodern filosofi* (Gothenburg: Glänta, 2004); Linda Martin Alcoff and John D. Caputo, *Feminism, sexuality, and the return of religion* (Bloomington: Indiana University Press, 2011); Inger Furseth, "The return of religion in the Public Sphere? The Public Role of Nordic Faith Communities," in *Institutional Change in the Public Sphere. Views on the Nordic Model*, ed. Fredrik Engelstad et al. (Warsaw and Berlin: De Gruyter, 2017), https://doi.org/10.1515/9783110546330-012; Joel Halldorf, *Gud: Återkomsten* (Stockholm: Libris förlag, 2018).

"spiritual *re*-volution,"[108] "*re*-making of world order,"[109] "*de*-secularization,"[110] "*de*-privatization,"[111] or "*post*-secularism."[112] This short review of terminology used to denote what was happening in place of secularization signifies that it was all about a follow-up process, striking back, or an increase in tension between the secular and the religious.

In this context, it might be more helpful to speak of three currents: Weberian, represented by a majority of the proponents of secularization; Durkheimian, represented by the proponents of individualization and pluralization; and the mixed current, represented by, among others, Martin or Casanova, who built upon both accounts.[113] Such differentiation allows us to see more clearly the common root of the narratives of secularization and the return of religion, which might be ostensibly opposite, but in pragmatic terms often merge into one.

4 Legible Religion Firmly Established

This chapter started with Hans Raun Iversen's proposal to consider secularization and secularism as mutually interdependent. Much of the chapter attempted to complexify the understanding of this interdependence. The two are so interrelated that it might be better to think about them in a circular fashion, in what I have called the secularizing cycle of legible religion. Secularization strengthens secularism, which, in turn, provides more arguments in favor of secularization. In both the accounts of secularization and the programs of secularism, we could see the shaping lines of legible religion: the individualization of religious identity, the privatization of religious observance, belief-centeredness, functionalization, and an engineer-like approach to religion, including the control of cult, structures, and a focus on social ethics. The idea of the lay principle also increased the agency of individuals, at least

108 See Paul Heelas and Linda Woodhead, *The Spiritual Revolution. Why Religion is Giving Way to Spirituality* (Oxford: Oxford University Press, 2005).

109 See Samuel Phillips Huntington, *The Clash of Civilizations and the Remaking of World Order* (London: Simon & Schuster, 1996).

110 See Berger, *The Desecularization of the World.*

111 See Casanova, *Public Religions.*

112 See, for example, Jürgen Habermas, "Notes on Post-Secular Society," *New Perspectives Quarterly* 25, no. 4 (2008), https://doi.org/10.1111/j.1540-5842.2008.01017.x; Jürgen Habermas, *An Awareness of What is Missing: Faith and Reason in a Post-secular Age* (Cambridge: Polity Press, 2010); Elaine Graham, *Between a Rock and a Hard Place: Public Theology in a Post-Secular Age* (London: SCM Press, 2013).

113 For Casanova, *Public Religions*, 17–19.

in terms of their personal choice. Together with the broader transformation of statecraft, which employed centralization and social engineering to achieve a greater legibility of religion, secularism became a potent force that imbricated itself not only structurally but also mentally in the consciousness of individual members of society, creating a sense of fixation of the boundary between the religious and the secular.

The increasing prominence of the secularizing cycle was so strong that even the most significant force of opposition against secularism, the Catholic Church, employed secularizing principles. Thus, while the Catholic Church first fought secularism, the turn towards trying to influence it was not as great as some may have thought. Ernst-Wolfgang Böckenförde critically summarized it:

> Against the emancipation of the state from religion implicit in the grant of freedom of religion, the post-1815 Restoration asserted the idea of the 'Christian state'. The 'Christian state' was supposed to halt and even reverse the growing and universally visible trend towards a fundamental secularization. But what did it actually achieve? No more than the imposition of a non-secular veneer over reality, without being in any way able to affect the survival and diffusion of the idea of the state and with it the political principle of secularization. What resulted were makeshifts: monarchy by the grace of God, the alliance of throne and altar, the Holy Alliance, and so on. Christianity became a prop for highly secular transactions, deployed to stabilize power constellations and to sanction specific politico-social circumstances dictated by the times, in an effort to preserve them against efforts to change them.[114]

The Catholic turn toward a general acceptance of modernity, including the separation of religion and politics and the differentiation between public and private spheres, solidified the picture for decades to come, making secularization and secularism seem, in many ways, self-evident. As a result, a functional approach to religion became the norm. For the state, the question was not whether, but how far, it should interfere with and control religion. For the churches, the question was no longer whether to fight the secular state but how to influence it.

However, secularization was still primarily a Western Christian project, not ready for rapid pluralization, the first signs of which would be visible in the

114 Ernst-Wolfgang Böckenförde, "The Rise of The State as a Process of Secularization," in *Religion, Law, and Democracy*, ed. Ernst-Wolfgang Böckenförde, M. Künkler, and T. Stein (Oxford: Oxford University Press, 2020 [1967]), 164.

1960s but would enter full swing around the turn of the century. In light of pluralization and the increasing criticism towards secularization, an alternative in the form of the "return of religion" began to emerge. However, as its name suggests, it was a reaction to secularization that in many ways followed into its footsteps, rather than overthrowing the modern consensus, which might help us explain the challenges that it encountered in the context of pluralization. For example, the lack of agreement to it by some branches of Islam might be one reason why the inherent problems of secularism and its non-neutral character became so evident with the increase of Muslim presence in Europe in the twenty-first century. Moreover, the fixation on what the secular means also led to some problems with the gradual emergence of the so-called "nones." The next chapter will take a closer look at these and other consequences of the "return of religion."

CHAPTER 3

The Adaptation of Legible Religion

Adapting to Pluralist Societies

The previous two chapters discussed the foundations of an overarching tendency in approaching religion in Europe. As I argued, a series of developments, including the conceptualization of religion as a distinct, governable, and manipulable category and the development of two ways of approaching it—namely, as utility and danger—allowed for the development of a reductive framework, gathered under the umbrella term legible religion. These developments reshaped social reality through what I called the secularizing cycle of legible religion. Religion has been adapted to high-level generalizations and reductions to make the identified phenomenon legible. Based on political developments and philosophical and theoretical proposals of thinkers such as Comte, Marx, Weber, and Durkheim, these reductions were focused on specific characteristics: the individualization of religion, the privatization of religion (through the rejection of collective rights to specific groups), creedal adherence, belief-centeredness, as well as an understanding of religion as something primarily cognitive (the expression of a Protestant bias noted in the last chapter). Religion was also placed under the category of civil values, with an expectation that all religious traditions would accommodate them.

The last chapter noted that, around the 1990s, secularization was replaced by the return of religion, a narrative that had equally important consequences for the approach to religious diversity. This chapter will investigate what happened when the return of religion replaced secularization and when the requirements of modern statecraft had to go beyond just internal Christian diversity, with an occasional "Jewish exception."

I will argue that secularism stood at the foundation of the contemporary European policies of managing religious diversity. The novel approaches changed focus without significantly changing the overarching framework. The hegemonic status of legible religion remained largely untouched. The first part of the chapter will discuss a move from "good secular, bad religion" to "good religion, bad religion." While upholding the distinction between the religious and the secular, European states drew a new line of division between different religions: those that fitted into the format of legible religion, however it was shaped in individual states, and those that did not. The second part of the chapter will discuss the emergence of different sub-frameworks due to an interplay of three modalities which influence the rhetoric and the actions of different stakeholders: Christianity, secularism, and religious pluralism. In comparing two thinkers, Samuel Huntington and Jürgen Habermas, I will aim to show how the overarching framework of legible religion contributes to the construction of such sub-frameworks that, while distinct and operating on different sides of the political spectrum, maintain the *status quo*.

1 Good Religion, Bad Religion

As noted in Chapter 2, between the 1990s and the 2010s the narratives of secularization experienced a gradual decrease in popularity. The changing religious landscape created fertile ground for the emergence of the return of religion narratives. Like secularization, the return of religion affected the policies directed towards the now fully distinct area of religion. But how should one understand the notion of "return" in this context?

This part of the chapter will argue that the notion of return resulted from the growing mismatch between legibility requirements and rapidly changing social reality. The pluralizing religious landscape observed an increase in religious beliefs and behaviors that did not conform to legibility standards. The states adapted by differentiating between good and bad religions. The first section will discuss the division into "marked" and "unmarked" religions. The second section will discuss three distinct approaches that gained importance based on this division. (1) Religions that fit into the format of legible religion were, when relevant, treated functionally as tools for achieving specific outcomes. Under this condition, they could operate in the public space. (2) Otherwise, they were dismissed as irrelevant and relegated into the private sphere. Fitting into legible standards allowed them to remain unmarked or "banal." (3) Religions that did not fit into the legible format were not only dismissed but also marked as a potential threat in need of tight control.

1.1 *Marked and Unmarked*

In the article "Secularism, Secularization, Public Theology, and Practical Theology," Solange Lefebvre discusses the gradual disappearance of Christianity into the background of Western countries. She argues that secularization must be understood in light of related concepts, such as confessionalization and cultural Christianity.[1] The post-Reformation confessionalization and the

1 Solange Lefebvre, "Secularism, Secularization, Public theology, and Practical theology," in *Catholic Approaches to Practical Theology*, ed. C. E. Wolfteich and A. Dillen (Leuven: Peeters Publishers, 2016), 209.

development of the principles summed up under the phrase *cuius regio, eius religio* had a decisive influence on the shaping of institutions concerned with healthcare, education, and, in many cases, even charity. Because of that, even after the state took over most of the responsibilities from the church, the way these institutions functioned remained deeply influenced by the respective ecclesial structures and denominational flavoring. Christian roots, however, were obscured in the process of secularization and were no longer recognized as such, at least at first sight.

In its historically established forms, Christianity, like the Catholic Church in France or the national Lutheran Churches in Scandinavia, also retained a privileged position in European societies. It retained a tacit presence in multiple areas of social life, from upbringing, ethical instruction, and rites of passage, through public institutions like hospitals, schools or even geographical demarcations, collective symbols, the calendar, the names of people and places, and even notions of "public morals" or "family values."[2] Hidden in plain sight, it remained to a large extent unnoticed. Multiple sacred buildings in prominent places, the loud sounds of church bells, or nun habits were near invisible while a mosque, a muezzin's call to prayer, or Islam-related head-coverings were viewed as incompatible with a secular state.[3]

Elayne Oliphant describes this dynamic as "the privilege of being banal" in a book under the same title.[4] In a study of Catholicism and its relation to secularism in Paris, Oliphant notes that Catholicism retained a particular

2 Lefebvre, "Secularism, Secularization, Public theology," 210. C.f. Jayne Svenungsson, "Public Faith and the Common Good A Radical Messianic Proposal," *Political Theology* 14, no. 6 (2015), https://doi.org/10.1179/1462317x13z.00000000047; David Thurfjell and Erika Willander, "Muslims by Ascription: On Post-Lutheran Secularity and Muslim Immigrants," *Numen* 68, no. 4 (2021), https://doi.org/10.1163/15685276-12341626.

3 See for example Chouki El Hamel, "Muslim Diaspora in Western Europe: The Islamic Headscarf (Hijab), the Media and Muslims' Integration in France," *Citizenship Studies* 6, no. 3 (2002), https://doi.org/10.1080/1362102022000011621; W. Shadid, "Muslim Dress in Europe: Debates on the Headscarf," *Journal of Islamic Studies* 16, no. 1 (2005), https://doi.org/10.1093/jis/16.1.35; Sarah Carol and Ruud Koopmans, "Dynamics of contestation over Islamic religious rights in Western Europe," *Ethnicities* 13, no. 2 (2013), https://doi.org/10.1177/1468796812470893; David Thurfjell, *Det gudlösa folket. De postkristna svenskarna och religionen* (Stockholm: Molin & Sorgenfrei Förlag, 2016), 202–19; Eva Brems et al., "Head-Covering Bans in Belgian Courtrooms and beyond: Headscarf Persecution and the Complicity of Supranational Courts," *Human Rights Quarterly* 39, no. 4 (2017), https://doi.org/10.1353/hrq.2017.0053. Of course, there are significant differences between different countries and different phenomena, see, for example, Serdar Kaya, "State Policies toward Islam in Twenty Countries in Western Europe: The Accommodation of Islam Index," *Muslim World Journal of Human Rights* 14, no. 1 (2017), https://doi.org/10.1515/mwjhr-2016–0003.

4 Elayne Oliphant, *The Privilege of Being Banal: Art, Secularism, and Catholicism in Paris* (Chicago: University of Chicago Press, 2021), 3.

advantage. She writes that "In a country widely admired for its *laïcité* (secularism), numerous Catholic objects, images, and spaces occupy the Parisian landscape."[5] However, they do so in banal ways. They remain unnoticed, as if their presence does not violate a public space that is supposed to remain free from religious presence. They remain unmarked.

Oliphant's idea refers to the remarks made by *Charlie Hebdo*'s late editor Stéphane Charbonnier known under the pseudonym "Charb." Charb pointed out that the caricatures of the prophet Mohammed had to be produced until "Islam is made as banal as Catholicism."[6] In other words, until the seriousness towards the religious materiality of Islam becomes like that of Catholicism. As Oliphant points out, this came out of a presumption that is foundational for secularism—that to become fitting for modernity, religions have to transform their imagery from sacral objects of devotion into simple objects that can be mocked without offense. Charb's description of Catholicism as banal, in Oliphant's view, means that "Catholics had developed a more appropriately modern relationship with materiality than Muslims."[7] However, while Oliphant agrees with Charb that Catholicism became banal in France, she disagrees that it is a sign of weakness. Referring to Hannah Arendt's notion of banality,[8] she points out that despite France's emphasis on *laïcité*, many Catholic symbols function in self-evidently unproblematic ways. Oliphant argues:

> Banality—far from a sign of weakness—proffers a series of privileges. Such privilege can most readily be seen in how Catholic materiality moves freely between the unmarked background and marked foreground of public life.[9]

Banality in this sense means not only that churches or the sound of church bells can operate unnoticed. Christian art, the symbols of the cross on Scandinavian flags, or end-of-year school ceremonies located in the church[10] can also be perceived as something neutral. They can be framed as a part of

---

5 Oliphant, *The Privilege of Being Banal*, 3.
6 Oliphant, *The Privilege of Being Banal*, 3.
7 Oliphant, *The Privilege of Being Banal*, 3.
8 See Hannah Arendt, *Eichmann in Jerusalem: A Report on the Banality of Evil* (New York: Penguin, 1963). As Olliphant writes: "For Arendt, banality was a means of addressing how actions and practices typically deemed reprehensible or unacceptable come to appear as self-evidently unproblematic, both to individuals and collectively." Oliphant, *The Privilege of Being Banal*, 3.
9 Oliphant, *The Privilege of Being Banal*, 3.
10 For more see, for example, Viktor Aldrin, *Skolavslutningar i kyrkan och spelet om religion i svensk skola* (Skellefteå: Artos & Norma Bokförlag, 2018).

cultural heritage, sinking into the background of everyday life. While Oliphant speaks only about the example of France, the same dynamics could be observed in Europe more broadly. Christianity operates with the privilege of moving between unmarked and marked, a privilege that is the most spectacularly lacking in the case of Islam, as exemplified by Charb's comments. Neither French secularism, as consciously imposing specific rules on the public sphere and individual citizens, nor Islam have the same ability to move between the marked and unmarked. Oliphant explains:

> When it comes to religion, Islam stands in relief as the marked against the marked secular French. Catholicism, by contrast, is equated with the secular in France through practices that make it isomorphic with the history and culture of France and Europe. Catholic material forms, figures, and practices occupy monumental spaces in Paris. They rise above the skyline, and they provide the names of many of the streets, passageways, and metro stations. Quite often, however, this Catholic materiality goes overlooked.

Therefore, the burqa or the niqab stir up heated debates while nuns' habits remain undisputed.[11]

Building on Oliphant's account, I would like to suggest that banality is not only valid for historically established Christian denominations. Instead, I would propose that banality is conferred to those religious traditions that fit into the legible religion framework. This criterion is not only fulfilled by formerly or currently established religious traditions. The same dynamic can be found, for example, concerning Buddhism. At least in its Westernized form, Buddhism fulfills some requirements presented in the previous chapters. It can easily adapt to factors such as the individualization and the privatization of religious

11 Of course, as court cases, such as the famous European Court of Human Rights *Lautsi and Others v Italy* case show, this banality is sometimes uncovered, especially by those coming from a place where such banality is differently configured. In that case, the Finnish-born Soile Lautsi viewed the display of crucifixes as a violation of her negative freedom of religion or belief as indicated in Article 9 of the European Convention of Human Rights. Interestingly, the Italian government argued that the crucifix was, in a sense, "banal" in the aforementioned sense, as it symbolized a cultural symbol of values important in Italy, and thereby was not used in a religious sense. For more, see Paolo Ronchi, "Crucifixes, Margin of Appreciation and Consensus: The Grand Chamber Ruling in Lautsi v Italy," *Ecclesiastical Law Journal* 13, no. 3 (2011), https://doi.org/10.1017/s0956618x11000421; Grégor Puppinck, "The Case of Lautsi v. Italy: A synthesis," *BYU Law Review*, no. 873 (2012); G. Itzcovich, "One, None and One Hundred Thousand Margins of Appreciations: The Lautsi Case," *Human Rights Law Review* 13, no. 2 (2013), https://doi.org/10.1093/hrlr/ngs038.

practice or the cognitive characterization of religion. That might be one reason why a figure of Buddha can be spotted in many public places without raising much attention, and Buddhist-inspired meditation and mindfulness can be publicly advertised.[12] Thus, fitting into the legible framework confers the possibility of remaining unmarked, at least regarding those features deemed irrelevant to the state. As exemplified most significantly by Islam, the lack of that privilege marks everything as potentially dangerous and requiring control.

The distinction between marked and unmarked (and the freedom to move between them) proposed by Oliphant is vital for the question I raised at the beginning of this section: What does the return of religion mean? In the framework of legible religion presented in this book, one can understand the notion of return in a new way. It does not mean that religion gradually disappeared or declined with secularization, only to return at the turn of the century. Instead, it means that the secularizing cycle of legible religion changed the majority traditions (and translated some foreign traditions, such as Buddhism) in each country. The rapid changes and pluralization created novel groups that did not fit or were not perceived as fitting into the legibility requirements. As a result, new challenges for policy and decision-makers emerged. Their response has been directed at amending this situation, making all new traditions legible, as only then would they be neutralized and could be conferred the privilege of banality.

1.2 *Policy and Practice*

We can inspect a particular example to understand the dynamic between different approaches to banal and unbanal religions more concretely. In the introduction, I already mentioned the term multi-faith paradigm, proposed by Adam Dinham. Dinham uses that term regarding a policy change in the United Kingdom during the New Labour government between 1997 and 2010. In an article entitled "The Multi-Faith Paradigm in Policy and Practice: Problems, Challenges, Directions" Dinham analyzes the government's changing approach to religion, highlighting aspects that can serve as an example of the emerging dynamics more broadly.

Dinham writes that during these years, "there was a concerted, growing and active engagement of policy makers with faith communities."[13] This

---

12 The uncontroversial status of Buddhism in Sweden is discussed in David Thurfjell, *Det gudlösa folket. De postkristna svenskarna och religionen* (Stockholm: Molin & Sorgenfrei Förlag, 2016), 157–82.

13 Adam Dinham, "The Multi-Faith Paradigm in Policy and Practice: Problems, Challenges, Directions," *Social Policy and Society* 11 (2012):," 577, https://doi.org/10.1017/S1474746412000255.

engagement, according to Dinham, resulted from an increased focus on "'community cohesion' as a basis for managing ethnic and religious plurality."[14] On the one hand, religious communities were increasingly viewed as potentially valuable repositories of resources that could support the growth of cohesion. On the other hand, in light of terrorist attacks and social unrest, they were viewed as a potential danger to that cohesion. Dinham sums up this ambivalence and problematization with the following words:

> The muddle which results both valorises faiths and at the same time imagines them as something to be feared. It also sets faith groups up as public realm actors with the appearance, but not a method, for enacting the role envisaged for them.[15]

Dinham points out that three concrete lines of engagement with religion emerged based on these two lines of thinking. First, faiths played the role of "heroes" of cohesion by providing a platform to increase civic engagement and active citizenship. Second, engagement with faith communities was supposed to have a preventive aspect, lowering the risk of radicalization and violent extremism. This measure was primarily directed towards Islam, although it included far-right extremism later on. Third, religious communities were viewed as a foundation for faith-based social action, contributing to and supplementing civil society.[16]

As a result, faith communities in Britain engaged more with the government, local authorities, and third sector organizations. They supported them in the struggle for greater community cohesion, becoming the intermediaries in multi-faith environments and increasing their social engagement. However, the three envisioned functions of faith communities (cohesion, prevention, and service provision) proved problematic.

Cohesion-oriented activities raised several issues. It was difficult to account for the effects of engagement. It was impossible to measure whether cohesion was created or consolidated clearly. It was challenging to decide who should represent different parts of the community. Such engagement also raised the visibility of faith communities, revising the question of the role of religion in the public sphere that was considered settled.

---

14 Dinham, "The Multi-Faith Paradigm," 577.

15 Dinham, "The Multi-Faith Paradigm," 584.

16 Dinham, "The Multi-Faith Paradigm," 579.

Similarly, the Prevent strategy, the UK government's approach to counterterrorism focused on tackling radicalization as early as possible,[17] proved alienating and often deepened the existing problems instead of solving them. Especially Muslim communities saw themselves as singled out and blamed for terrorism. The increase in focus on Muslim communities proved quite problematic also for other faith communities. Many non-Muslims did not understand why the resources were disproportionately directed towards Muslims.

Service provision was also far from unproblematic. Low levels of religious literacy required much rudimentary preparation. The differentiation between multi-faith, inter-faith, and faith-based services proved confusing, as did an understanding of the differences between dialogue and social action. All of this resulted in misunderstandings and provided infrastructural challenges. Dinham writes:

> Thus, it is possible to have the dialogue but not really to know who is in it and what it is for. It is possible to have multi-faith services available to anyone, but far harder to provide services as a multi-faith body. It also obscures the occasional need for single-faith services in order to reach out to those who want them.[18]

The service-oriented aspect of the multi-faith paradigm proved problematic because it forced a specific vision of multi-faith coexistence. It necessitated engagement that had to be open-ended and multi-faith from the get-go. There was no space for single-faith actions and provisions even if they increased cohesion and could have resulted in multi-faith effects. Parts of society that would not engage in consciously open and multi-faith projects were excluded from the beginning.

All three aspects of the multi-faith paradigm had an overarching visibility problem. On the one hand, cohesion and service provision raised the presence of religion in the public sphere. Thus, the share of marked activities of the legible faith communities increased, while their ability to move between marked and unmarked was curtailed. On the other hand, the activities of specific groups, such as Muslims, were marked in public eyes.

---

17 See, for example, Fahid Qurashi, "The Prevent strategy and the UK 'war on terror': embedding infrastructures of surveillance in Muslim communities," *Palgrave Communications* 4, no. 1 (2018), https://doi.org/10.1057/s41599-017-0061-9.

18 Dinham, "The Multi-Faith Paradigm," 584.

Dinham defines these developments as a multi-faith paradigm,[19] mainly to highlight a specific change of status of multi-faith and inter-faith activities.[20] Activities based on the collaboration of different faith communities were turned from the interest of a small group of enthusiasts to an object of public policy. The government's goal was to create a "multi faith society," as expressed in governmental policy documents such as "Face to Face and Side by Side: A Framework for Partnership in Our Multi-Faith Society."[21]

Dinham points out that the governmental embrace of a multi-faith paradigm took multi-faith into the mainstream but deprived it of nuance and confused it. He concludes:

> In the end, the multi-faith paradigm proves a conundrum. It has no religious creed, buildings, explicit practices, or formal leaders. It struggles to deliver complex partnership and the broadest of participation. It finds it especially hard to engage with the marginalised, radicalised and extreme whom policy-makers most want to address. In these ways, multi-faith practices risk constituting a parallel world running alongside 'real' faith communities, seeming to respond to policy hopes but unable to bring constituencies of faith with them. To this extent the multi-faith paradigm remains a construct of policy hopefulness.[22]

Dinham's account captures several developments described in the previous chapters. The distinction between heroes and villains of public cohesion combines, on the one hand, the functional conceptions of religion and, on

---

19 A note must be made on the use of the term multi-faith paradigm. The British example has its specificity and is not applicable one-to-one to other European countries. As mentioned before, each country has its own special take on the management of diversity.

20 While Dinham points out that the terms multi-faith and inter-faith are mostly used interchangeably, he briefly mentions the differentiation made by a British scholar of religion, Paul Weller in Paul Weller, *Time for a Change: Reconfiguring Religion, State and Society* (London: T&T Clark International, 2005). As Weller points out, multi-faith usually underlines variety, while inter-faith refers to relationships between different religions. While Dinham does not draw too many conclusions from it, the use of multi-faith can, arguably, constitute an interpretative guide for the differentiation between different types of religious communities, for example, if one returns to Oliphant, between the banal and unbanal, or between those fitting into the framework of legible religion and those that do not.

21 Department for Communities and Local Government, *Face to Face and Side by Side: A Framework for Partnership in Our Multi Faith Society* (London: Department for Communities and Local Government, 2008). See in Dinham, "The Multi-Faith Paradigm," 579.

22 Dinham, "The Multi-Faith Paradigm," 586.

the other, those that view religion as an inherent danger. The reductive treatment of religion and the reformulation of multi-faith show the ways in which administrative strategies make complex phenomena legible. Centralized, overarching definitions of religious communities miss the differences between communities and individuals. Such broad generalizations run the risk of failing to achieve their goal. For example, preventive strategies unfairly single out some groups, like Muslims, and may miss potential threats from others simply because they do not belong to the singled-out group. The administrative simplifications of multi-faith miss crucial elements of reality, such as lack of knowledge concerning specific religious traditions or differences in willingness to engage with others in different communities. They also introduce confusing artificial distinctions between different religions or between dialogue and social action. In the end, the top-down approach misses the complexity of reality. It proves to be more about hopefulness than a sensible policy, with its ideas running alongside reality rather than addressing it.

Despite the particularity of the British context, it exemplifies well how different conceptual elements come together in a concrete policy proposal. The British example presents a transformation resulting from the increasing prevalence of the return of religion narrative. It shows the emergence of three distinct ways in which religion becomes important: two concerning its functional value, treating faith communities as a potential source of social cohesion or a service provider, and one viewing religion as a potential threat, that is, the prevent agenda.

Summing up the whole section, I distinguish three different approaches to religion that emerged with the return of religion. From the state's perspective, religion was of interest either because of its utility or the danger it posed, in line with the tendencies described in previous chapters. It had a possible third option if it conformed to the legibility standards. In that case, it was conferred the privilege of banality and the potential to operate in an unmarked way in the public sphere.

But the increase in the overall visibility of religion threatened this careful *status quo*. As Dinham notes, the return of religion narrative produced a new modality: religious pluralism. A potential disruptor, religious pluralism reinvigorated two other modalities: secularism and Christianity.[23] The interplay of these three modalities will be discussed in the second part of this chapter.

23 Dinham, "The Multi-Faith Paradigm," 579. Based on Weller, *Time for a Change*, 73.

2 The Interplay of Christianity, Secularism, and Religious Pluralism

The interplay of three modalities—Christianity, secularism, and religious pluralism—impacted the programs of both the political right and the political left. As a result, various stances emerged, briefly analyzed here through the examples of Huntington and Habermas. I have chosen these two thinkers because they represent opposite sides of the political debate and are some of the most influential thinkers in their respective camps. Both thinkers are known for their impact on understanding religion in the twenty-first century. Huntington was a crucial influence on the conservative right. Habermas was a leading intellectual figure of the New Left. I argue that, while proposing different responses to religious pluralism, these two thinkers operate within the same overarching, hegemonic framework and, in the end, maintain the existing *status quo*.

2.1 *The Importance of Coalitions*

The importance of Christianity in the shaping of social institutions, including its impact on the creation of the Western legal tradition and its further reconfiguration during the Reformation and the French Revolution, provided historically established forms of Christianity with a unique position. These denominations were reshaped by the secularizing cycle of legible religion. Such reshaping allowed them to operate unnoticed in highly secularized public spheres under the guise of cultural heritage. They constituted a banal presence.

After the Catholic turn to modernity, secularism and Christianity in Europe co-existed in a fragile equilibrium. However, the rapid pluralization of the religious landscape introduced a religious presence that did not fit into this framework. The emergence of religious pluralism as a third modality threatened the equilibrium, reinvigorating the other two modalities and encouraging different ways of engagement.

Among others, combative forms of secularism and Christianity emerged, most commonly associated with the political right. Elaine Graham describes this dynamic in the USA and the United Kingdom based on two movements that she described as "Evangelicals" and "New Atheists." Graham argues that Evangelicals could be identified as a movement that juxtaposes Christian theology against two enemies: multiculturalism and secularism. Suspicious of non-theological arguments and cultural pluralism, this discourse operates with a polarization of the world.[24] It is informed by a vision of the Christian

24 See Paul Tillich, *Theology of Culture* (New York: Oxford University Press, 1959). For more on the subject see William Schweiker, "Theology of culture and its future," in *The Cambridge Companion to Paul Tillich*, ed. Russell Re Manning (Cambridge: Cambridge University Press, 2009).

public vocation "as entailing a personal witness to objective moral truths.[25]" On the other hand, the New Atheists see religion as the epitome of evil, not secularism. Their equivalent of religious belief is total devotion to science, which they view as bearing the marks of humanity's savior. Like Evangelicals, New Atheists see multiculturalism—the religiously plural—as a danger. Both perceive fundamentalist Islam as the most dangerous threat. Both also share a fuzzy notion of the West, claiming that it is under threat.[26]

Thus, both Evangelicals and New Atheists, defined this way, oppose each other and multiculturalism. However, it must be noted that, at least in Europe, neither of these two groups has entered the political sphere as a significant force. Instead, from the 1990s, forms of coalitional thinking defending the equilibrium emerged as politically significant. Over time, the modalities of Christianity and secularism created a consensus against religious pluralism. Especially on the political right, numerous overlapping movements, captured under the terms such as *populist (radical) right*,[27] *far right*,[28] *right-wing*, *national populism*,[29] *national conservatism*,[30] *paleoconservatism*,[31] and many others,[32] explicitly embraced the equilibrium of secularism and Christianity

25 Elaine Graham, *Between a Rock and a Hard Place: Public Theology in a Post-Secular Age*, (London: SCM Press, 2013), 141.

26 Russell Foster, Nick Megoran, and Michael Dunn, "Towards a geopolitics of atheism: Critical geopolitics post the 'War on Terror,'" *Political Geography* 60 (2017), https://doi.org/10.1016/j.polgeo.2017.07.011. See also Tina Beattie, *The New Atheists: The Twilight of Reason and the War on Religion* (London: Darton, Longman and Todd Ltd, 2007).

27 Cas Mudde, *Populist Radical Right Parties in Europe* (Cambridge: Cambridge University Press, 2007).

28 See, for example, Cas Mudde, *The Far Right Today* (Cambridge: Polity, 2019); Spyros Sofos, "Securitizing the "Other" in the European Far-Right Imaginary," *Political Trends & Dynamics in Southeast Europe* 2019, no. 2 (2019).

29 See, for example, Rogers Brubaker, "Between nationalism and civilizationism: the European populist moment in comparative perspective," *Ethnic & Racial Studies* 40, no. 8 (2017), https://doi.org/10.1080/01419870.2017.1294700; Roger Eatwell and Matthew Goodwin, *National Populism: The Revolt Against Liberal Democracy* (London: Pelican Books, 2018).

30 See, for example, Thomas Borén, Patrycja Grzyś, and Craig Young, "Intra-urban connectedness, policy mobilities and creative city-making: national conservatism vs. urban (neo)liberalism," *European Urban and Regional Studies* 27, no. 3 (2020), https://doi.org/10.1177/0969776420913096.

31 See, for example, Chilton Jr. Williamson, "'What Is Paleoconservatism? Man, Know Thyself!," *Chronicles—a Magazine of American Culture* (January 2001), https://doi.org/https://www.chroniclesmagazine.org/what-is-paleoconservatism-2/; Ryszard Bobrowicz and Mattias Nowak, "Divided by the Rainbow: Culture War and Diffusion of Paleoconservative Values in Contemporary Poland," *Religions* 12, no. 3 (2021), https://www.mdpi.com/2077-1444/12/3/170.

32 See also notes on the terminology in Mudde, *Populist Radical Right*; Cas Mudde and Cristobal Rovira Kaltwasser, *Populism: A Very Short Introduction* (Oxford: Oxford University Press, 2017). It must be noted that all of these terms do not capture exactly the same

(although, as I will argue, based on Habermas, the coalitional thinking of this kind was not inconsequential for the left either). Many of these movements were connected to political parties, such as the French *Front National*, recently renamed *Rassemblement National*, the German *Alternative für Deutschland*, the Swedish *Sverigedemokraterna, the* Danish *Dansk Folkeparti*, or the Italian *Lega Nord*,[33] which combined in their rhetoric an embrace of Christian heritage with a defense of secularism, often alternating between seemingly contradictory stances, heavily relying on the privileged banal Christian presence defined as cultural.[34]

The notion of the "clash of civilizations" proposed by the American political scientist Samuel P. Huntington was an important point of reference to these. This notion had a significant impact on understanding the relationship between religion and politics and on approaches to religious diversity. It has remained a potent political force until today. The following section will inspect this idea more closely.

2.2 *Samuel Huntington*

Published first in *Foreign Affairs* in 1993, "Clash of Civilizations" proved extremely popular, making Huntington famous beyond the field of political sciences and international relations.[35] In the text, Huntington argued that the world moved through different phases after the Peace of Westphalia. The conflicts were fought, consecutively, between princes, nations, or peoples, and, during the Cold War, two superpowers. All were mainly limited to what Huntington calls "Western civilization."[36] While the Cold War involved the

phenomena and have different points of emphasis. However, they all embrace a form of coalitional thinking concerning secularism and Christianity.

33 One could also point to the examples from Central-Eastern Europe, but, as discussed in Bobrowicz and Nowak, "Divided by the Rainbow", Central-Eastern Europe is in some respects different.

34 For more on the emergence of the far right and their uses of Christianity, see Hannah Strømmen and Ulrich Schmiedel, *The Claim to Christianity: Responding to the Far Right* (London: SCM Press, 2020).

35 Samuel Phillips Huntington, "The Clash of Civilizations?," *Foreign Affairs* 72, no. 3 (1993). Later, Huntington developed his ideas in the book Samuel Phillips Huntington, *The Clash of Civilizations and the Remaking of World Order* (London: Simon & Schuster, 1996). While the book presents a more complex and nuanced position than the article, its reach has been significantly smaller to that of the article's. If one looks at the citations record, according to Google Scholar his article has been cited 42,934 at the moment of writing (https://bit.ly/3NSr9lx). His book is, unfortunately, missing from the citation records in Google Scholar, as it is from Clarivate's Web of Science. Both the article and the book figure in the database of Microsoft Academic. According to that database, the article has been cited 5,982 times while the book only 1,212 (see https://bit.ly/3qZnSqX) which might be an indicator of the difference in reach of the two.

36 Huntington, "The Clash of Civilizations?," 23.

confrontation of global communism and global capitalism, it resulted in the return of religion as a volatile factor in international relations. As Huntington argued, the end of the Iron Curtain did not mean an end to divisions. Instead, the Iron Curtain was replaced with a Velvet one.[37] The conflict lines were redrawn between civilizations, understood by Huntington as the broadest levels of cultural identity rooted in religion.[38] He differentiated eight such civilizations: Western, Confucian, Japanese, Islamic, Hindu, Slavic-Orthodox, Latin-American, and, with a qualifying "possibly," African. According to Huntington, the primary conflict lines would be drawn between these different civilizations in the twenty-first century.

Concerning religion, Huntington was visibly inspired by the theories and narratives of the return of religion. He wrote:

> The processes of economic modernization and social change throughout the world are separating people from longstanding local identities. They also weaken the nation state as a source of identity. In much of the world religion has moved in to fill this gap, often in the form of movements that are labeled "fundamentalists." … The "unsecularization of the world," George Weigel has remarked, "is one of the dominant social facts of life in the late twentieth century." The revival of religion … provides a basis for identity and commitment that transcends national boundaries and unites civilizations.[39]

In Huntington's view, the cultural and religious differences were much less flexible than, for example, political and economic ones. Thus, they were leaving much less space for change and negotiation. The cultural and religious focus created an "us" versus "them" dynamic, both at the micro-level of communities competing on the same territory and a macro-level, where states from different civilizations competed.

Huntington singled out two civilizations in a specific way. The West was singled out directly, as being at the peak of its power in relation to the others. This is what Huntington described in combative terms by using the phrase "the West versus the Rest."[40] On that basis, he put forward a set of policy proposals. These included increased West-centrism that promotes cooperation and unity among "its own," incorporation of those cultures that seem possible to incorporate, the increase of the military capabilities of the West while limiting

37 Huntington, "The Clash of Civilizations?," 31.
38 Huntington, "The Clash of Civilizations?," 26.
39 Huntington, "The Clash of Civilizations?," 26.
40 Huntington, "The Clash of Civilizations?," 39.

such capabilities among Confucian and Islamic states, as well as exploiting differences and conflicts between them. Beyond the West, a significant portion of Huntington's original essay deals with Islam and its conflicts with neighboring Western, Orthodox, Hindu, and other civilizations. Huntington's approach marks Islam as a major source of the existing and forthcoming conflicts, indirectly suggesting future policy directions.

This singling out is vital in the context of Huntington's influence. As Jeffrey Haynes pointed out in an article written on the twentieth anniversary of the original article, Huntington's essay became the "touchstone for nearly all contemporary debates about the capacity of different groups to live together in relative amity not enmity."[41] Half a decade later, Haynes described the impact of the "Clash of Civilizations" and its focus on Islam on the electoral gains of right-wing parties and their internal organization during the mid-2010s. Haynes wrote that Huntington's paradigm singled out Muslims as the problematic group. It encouraged "some Western politicians and policy makers to view all Muslims in a malign way, without making a distinction between … the mass of 'moderate' … Muslims and … the small minority of Islamist extremists and even smaller number of Islamist terrorists."[42] Adopted to varying degrees, Huntington's views inspired the policies of mainline political parties and found more radical expression in far-right movements.

Huntington is an American scholar, yet his views proved extremely potent in Europe too. An American scholar of nationalism, Rogers Brubaker, points out that the account presented by Huntington proved especially attractive for the emerging populist movements, playing into the need of differentiating people from non-people.[43] Brubaker goes as far as to call the impact of Huntington's ideas "civilizationism."[44] The notion of civilization rooted in Christianity serves as a tool of both identity-building and differentiation from others. Brubaker even traces a particular source of the popularity of civilizationism in Europe to a Dutch politician, Pim Fortuyn, whose reliance on Huntington was

41 Jeffrey Haynes, "Twenty Years after Huntington's 'Clash of Civilzations'," in *The Clash of Civilizations. Twenty Years On*, ed. J. Paul Barker (Bristol: E-International Relations, 2013), 11.

42 Jeffrey Haynes, "From Huntington to Trump: Twenty-Five Years of the "Clash of Civilizations"," *The Review of Faith & International Affairs* 17, no. 1 (2019), https://doi.org/10.1080/15570274.2019.1570755.

43 Rogers Brubaker, "Why populism?," *Theory & Society* 46 (2017): 362–63, https://doi.org/10.1007/s11186-017-9301-7.

44 Brubaker, "Between nationalism and civilizationism," 1193.

so great that he called himself the "Samuel Huntington of Dutch politics."[45] In critical conversation with Brubaker, Ulrich Schmiedel writes, "Huntington's clash of civilizations has had a huge impact on populist politics. In the current migration crisis, the construct has been activated and amplified. Populists cash in on the clash."[46]

Huntington's account and its influence exemplify that the three emerging modalities of religious pluralism, secularism, and Christianity, can enter coalitions, resulting in particular political constellations that may be stronger than on their own. Neither Evangelicals nor New Atheists, as described by Graham, were able to achieve their goals by themselves. In contrast, a coalition of the modalities of secularism and Christianity was able to make much larger political gains, supported by a legitimating narrative of the "clash of civilizations" and building on the broader account of the return of religion. In this coalitional model, neither secularism nor Christianity took precedence. Instead, they formed a joint enterprise of cultural heritage, allowing agents employing this sub-framework to claim arguments from both sides.[47]

Operating within the broader framework of legible religion, these coalitions employed a reduced version of religion as a functional category. On the one hand, a generalized label of Christianity was used as an identity-building tool. On the other, a generic idea of Islam was employed as a differentiating category, naming the other. The former was defended based on cultural heritage. The latter was marked and rejected based on significant civilizational differences—a lack of fit and a danger to the framework of legible religion—while the values of secularism provided a direction in approaching both.

As will become visible in Chapter 5, the civilizationist sub-framework had a significant impact on the perception of the public sphere, impacting the view of the presence of phenomena such as, for example, multi-faith spaces. This was, however, not the only framework at work, which, as I will postulate, is the reason for often-contradictory stances in approaching such spaces. More sub-frameworks were offered, coming from different political standpoints. Yet,

45 Merijn Oudenampsen, *De Conservatieve Revolte—Een Ideeëngeschiedenis van de Fortuyn-opstand* (Nijmegen: Uitgeverij Vantilt, 2018), 219; Matthew Kaminski, "Another Face of Europe's Far Right," *Wall Street Journal*, 3rd of May 2002, https://www.wsj.com/articles/SB1020370399854613 20.

46 Ulrich Schmiedel, "The cracks in the category of Christianism: A call for ambiguity in the conceptualization of Christianity," in *Contemporary Christian-Cultural Values: Migration Encounters in the Nordic Region*, ed. Cecilia Nahnfeldt and Kaia S. Rønsdal (London: Routledge, 2021), 166.

47 See also Mattias Martinson, *Sekularism, populism, xenofobi: En essä om religionsdebatten* (Malmö: Eskaton, 2017).

as argued here, they remained within the broader paradigm of legible religion. To pursue this argument further, I will now move to the other side of the political spectrum and turn to the debates on the place of religious reasons in the public debate and Habermas's proposal on the subject.

2.3 *Jürgen Habermas*

Huntington had a significant impact on concrete policies of the political right. It would be difficult to find a contemporary scholar whose proposals would have the same concrete effect on the policies of the left. Nevertheless, when it comes to the ways of thinking about religion, one could point to the German philosopher Jürgen Habermas. Habermas had a massive impact on the social sciences and humanities at the turn of the millennium. The *Stanford Encyclopedia of Philosophy* describes him as "one of the most influential philosophers in the world."[48] Habermas's reach goes way beyond the scholarly world. He is often viewed as "one of the leading philosophical exponents of the European Union"[49] while *Der Spiegel* named him "the Last European" who views the EU as his and his generation's project.[50] As a system-building philosopher, however, Habermas requires greater introduction than policy-oriented Huntington.

In the context of the place of religion in the public square, Habermas is one of the thinkers whose position on religion changed together with the dominant narratives. He moved from viewing religion as an archaic method of socialization, for example, in *Theory of Communicative Action* in the 1980s,[51] to engaging more with religion post 9/11, with the notion of the post-secular society first introduced in his 2001 *Friedenspreisrede,* a speech on the occasion of the Peace Prize given by the German Association of Booksellers.[52] The visibility of this change was raised even further as a result of the debate with Cardinal

48 James Bohman and William Rehg, "Jürgen Habermas," in *The Stanford Encyclopedia of Philosophy*, ed. Edward N. Zalta (Fall 2017). https://plato.stanford.edu/entries/habermas/#DiaBetNatRel.

49 Tom Whyman, "Happy birthday Habermas, your philosophy has failed us," *The Outline*, July 30th, 2019, https://theoutline.com/post/7734/habermas-failure-political-philosophy.

50 Georg Diez, "Habermas, the Last European. A Philosopher's Mission to Save the EU," *Der Spiegel International*, November 25th 2011, https://www.spiegel.de/international/europe/habermas-the-last-european-a-philosopher-s-mission-to-save-the-eu-a-799237.html.

51 Jürgen Habermas, *Theory of Communicative Action. Volume One: Reason and the Rationalization of Society* (Boston, MA: Beacon Press, 1984).

52 Jürgen Habermas "Glauben und Wissen. Dankesrede," Friedenspreis des Deutschen Buchhandels,2001,https://www.friedenspreis-des-deutschen-buchhandels.de/alle-preistraeger-seit-1950/2000-2009/juergen-habermas.

Joseph Ratzinger.[53] Because of that, just as Huntington's ideas provided an important inspiration for the political right's approaches to the return of religion, Habermas's views could represent the broader mindset behind European policy-making, at least in its left-liberal guises as embodied, for example, in the policies of New Labour described above.

Here, again, Europe followed the American debates. Habermas's engagement with religion builds on an American discussion on the acceptability of religious reasons in the public debates. Thus, this discussion requires a short introduction before I can delve into his own thought on the subject. In the same year as *Clash of Civilizations*, John Rawls published *Political Liberalism*. There, Rawls developed his earlier notion of the overlapping consensus by discussing how to envision a political ideal of public reasoning in a situation of competing comprehensive conceptions of the good. Rawls proposed "a neutral approach"—a "freestanding" solution independent of such comprehensive conceptions, which could operate as a module in each of them. Public debates should be based on public reasoning, limited to "political values alone."[54] In this way, as Hugh Baxter points out, Rawls shaped one side of the forthcoming controversy over the role of religion in public political discussions, "the side arguing that citizens in liberal democracies should exercise restraint on public employment of religious reasons."[55]

However, some of the follow-up to Rawls's idea led to less neutral results. For example, Robert Audi supplemented Rawls's framework with two restrictive secular principles. Audi argued that no one should postulate a restriction of human behavior by law or public policy if one could not provide an "adequate secular reason for this" nor is "sufficiently motivated by ... adequate secular reason."[56] Thus, Audi visibly associated this side of controversy with secularism.

Baxter points out that the other side of the controversy, represented by Paul Weithman and Nicholas Wolterstorff among others, rejected the basic claim of Rawls and Audi's position. They allowed for religious reasons in public debates. They argued that religious reasons can be viewed as adequately substantiating claims by other citizens. Even if others do not share the comprehensive

---

53 Jürgen Habermas and Joseph Ratzinger, *The Dialectics of Secularization: On Reason and Religion* (San Francisco: Ignatius Press, 2007).

54 John Rawls, *Political Liberalism* (New York: Columbia University Press, 2005), 138; 214; 474; 92.

55 Hugh Baxter, *Habermas: The Discourse Theory of Law and Democracy* (Stanford: Stanford Law Books, 2011), 193.

56 Robert Audi, "Liberal Democracy and the Place of Religion in Politics," in *Religion in the Public Square: The Place of Religious Conviction in Public Debate*, ed. Robert Audi and Nicholas Wolterstorff (London: Rowman & Littlefield Publishers, Inc., 1997), 25.

conceptions of the good behind the argumentation, that does not immediately make them incomprehensible. For example, religious individuals can understand a utilitarian argumentation that they do not share. This understanding should work in both directions. Additionally, Weithman and Wolterstorff pointed to the pragmatic role of religious communities in promoting democracy. They argued that in many cases, religious communities encourage and create possibilities for civic engagement, inspiring political action, and providing a "moral vocabulary and set of concerns for democratic political discourse."[57]

To understand Habermas's interest in these debates, one also needs to understand the theoretical basis of his thought. Many have pointed out that Habermas's work is notoriously complex because all of his works are interconnected in a system based on a multi-level research program.[58] Habermas's theory is founded on several fundamental ideas. The notion of the public sphere is among them. While Habermas first discussed this notion in the context of concrete historical developments, he ultimately developed it into a never-realized ideal that would impact his later thought. The public sphere entailed a discursive community that "disregarded status completely," problematized "areas that until then had not been questioned," taking away the subject prerogatives of the church and the court, and became inclusive and general "not merely in … significance, but also … accessibility."[59] Based on such an ideal, Habermas built interconnected ideas of, among others, the pragmatic theory of meaning, communicative action, discourse, and deliberative democracy.

Habermas took a pragmatic stance on speech. In his view, understanding the conditions of acceptability was crucial for understanding a speech act. He wrote:

> we understand a speech act when we know the kinds of reasons that a speaker could provide in order to convince a hearer that he is entitled in the given circumstances to claim validity for his utterance—in short, when we know what makes it acceptable.[60]

---

57 Baxter, *Habermas*, 197.

58 James Gordon Finlayson, *Habermas: A Very Short Introduction* (Oxford: Oxford University Press, 2005), XVIII.

59 Jürgen Habermas, *The Structural Transformation of the Public Sphere: An Inquiry Into a Category of Bourgeois Society* (Cambridge, Massachusetts: MIT Press, 1998), 36–37.

60 Jürgen Habermas, *On the Pragmatics of Communication*, ed. Maeve Cooke (Cambridge, MA: MIT Press, 1998), 232.

Thus, Bohman and Rehg point out that Habermas saw a necessary tie between speech acts and reason-giving. They write:

> speech acts inherently involve claims that are in need of reasons—claims that are open to both criticism and justification. … A speech act succeeds in reaching understanding when the hearer takes up "an affirmative position" toward the claim made by the speaker … When the offer made by the speaker fails to receive uptake, speaker, and hearer may shift reflexive levels, from ordinary speech to "discourse"—processes of argumentation and dialogue in which the claims implicit in the speech act are tested for their rational justifiability as true, correct or authentic. Thus the rationality of communicative action is tied to the rationality of discourse.[61]

Transferring these abstracts into the concrete language of politics, Habermas proposed the notion of "deliberative democracy." This notion entails that all decision-making requires engagement in discursive practices to legitimize decisions. Bohman and Rehg sum up this approach by noting that:

> citizens may regard their laws as legitimate insofar as the democratic process, as it is institutionally organized and conducted, warrants the presumption that outcomes are reasonable products of a sufficiently inclusive deliberative process of opinion- and will-formation.[62]

The questions raised by Rawls, Audi, Weithman, and Wolterstorff are then of fundamental importance to Habermas's core ideas. Thus, Habermas engaged with them directly in his 2005 volume *Zwischen Naturalismus und Religion* in a chapter on religion in the public sphere.[63] Translated into English in 2006, both as a part of the book[64] and as a separate paper in the *European Journal of*

61 Bohman and Rehg, "Jürgen Habermas."

62 Bohman and Rehg, "Jürgen Habermas."

63 Jürgen Habermas, "Religion in der Öffentlichkeit. Kognitive Voraussetzungen für den »öffentlichen Vernunftgebrauch« religiöser und säkularer Bürger," in *Zwischen Naturalismus und Religion. Philosophische Aufsätze*, ed. Jürgen Habermas (Frankfurt am Main, Hessen: Suhrkamp Verlag, 2005).

64 Jürgen Habermas, "Religion in the Public Sphere: Cognitive Presuppositions for the "Public Use of Reason" by Religious and Secular Citizens," in *Between Naturalism and Religion* (Cambridge: Polity Press, 2006).

Philosophy,[65] this paper could be considered equal in stature to Huntington's *Clash of Civilizations*.[66]

Habermas even started the whole paper from similar considerations as Huntington. He pointed out that since 1989/90, religious traditions and faith communities have regained importance in an unexpected turn of events. Habermas explicitly referred to the increased fears of the clash of civilizations and an increase in different types of religious engagement such as fundamentalism or religious aspects of ethnic and national conflicts. While Habermas viewed this religious increase as a part of the dynamics of decolonization, he also mentioned the surprising religious renaissance in the United States. Habermas acknowledged the problematic nature of the narratives of secularization, pointing instead to the differences within the West. Habermas acknowledged that these differences might result from the lack of an organized approach to religion in the United States, similar to French *laicism*. In light of the considerations from a previous chapter, one could understand it as the lack of a secularizing cycle of legible religion. Habermas wrote:

> Unlike in France, the introduction of the freedom of religion in the United States of America did not signify the victory of laicism over an authority that had at best shown religious minorities tolerance in line with imposed standards of its own. Here, the secularization of state powers did not serve primarily the negative purpose of protecting citizens against the compulsion to adopt a faith against their own will. It was instead designed to guarantee the settlers who had turned their backs on Old Europe the positive liberty to continue to exercise their respective religion without hindrance. For this reason, in the present American debate on the political role of religion all sides have been able to claim their loyalty to the constitution.[67]

65 Jürgen Habermas, "Religion in the Public Sphere," *European Journal of Philosophy* 14, no. 1 (2006): 3, https://doi.org/10.1111/j.1468-0378.2006.00241.x.

66 According to Google Scholar the English citation of the text in the *European Journal of Philosophy* has 2246 citations: (https://bit.ly/3LJncxS). It is harder to judge what has been cited in the book versions, but the German original has 1,237 citations (https://bit.ly/3x1ULal) while the English translation has 1,336 citations (https://bit.ly/3u8zF87), which is relatively high and the highest among his publications on religion, but well shy of Huntington's 42,934 citations (https://bit.ly/3NSr9lx). However, it should be noted that Huntington's ideas created a whole paradigm for international relations, while Habermas spoke to a much more constrained audience.

67 Habermas, "Religion in the Public Sphere," 3.

The specific example of the United States prompted Habermas to consider the American debate on the use of religious argumentation in public reasoning.

Habermas pointed out that the constitutional freedom of religion is the appropriate political answer to religious pluralism. He argued that only the state's secular character can secure it. The secular character, however, is not enough. Beyond the state, different parties within society must reach a certain level of agreement on the balance between positive and negative religious liberty. Thus, they need to learn to adopt the perspective of others. The best form of political participation for that purpose is deliberative democracy. As the secular government must base its legitimacy on another source than religious belief, implementation of deliberative democracy should fulfill two fundamental conditions: equal participation of all citizens and "the epistemic dimension of a deliberation that grounds the presumption of rationally acceptable outcomes."[68]

These two conditions, according to Habermas, explain why the types of reasons available within the public sphere are of such great importance. All decisions must be justified in a way accessible to others, regardless of their faith or lack thereof. Habermas took what could be considered a middle position between Audi, on the one hand, and Weithman/Wolterstorff, on the other. He agreed with Audi that the principles of secular reasoning should constrain all public officials. However, he viewed this principle as too excessive if applied to other organizations and individual citizens. Simultaneously, he was afraid of basing any decisions on purely religious reasons as "it is unclear why under this premise the political community should not at any time be in danger simply of disintegrating into religious struggle."[69] He wrote:

> The liberal state must not transform the requisite institutional separation of religion and politics into an undue mental and psychological burden for those of its citizens who follow a faith. It must of course expect of them that they recognize the principle that political authority is exercised with neutrality towards competing world views. Every citizen must know and accept that only secular reasons count beyond the institutional threshold that divides the informal public sphere from parliaments, courts, ministries, and administrations. But all that is required here is the epistemic ability to consider one's own faith reflexively from the outside and to relate it to secular views. Religious citizens can well recognize this 'institutional translation proviso' without having to split their identity

68 Habermas, "Religion in the Public Sphere," 5.

69 Habermas, "Religion in the Public Sphere," 12.

> into a public and a private part the moment they participate in public discourses. They should therefore be allowed to express and justify their convictions in a religious language if they cannot find secular 'translations' for them.[70]

Habermas viewed the "institutional translation proviso" as a cooperative task where cognitive burdens have to be shared equally. Habermas pointed out that "monoglot" citizens who cannot find secular ways of expressing their political aspirations should still engage in the civic process with the understanding that other citizens, fulfilling their civic duty, will help them accomplish the translation. Religious contributions can also help those of other convictions find hidden meanings and possible truth contents that could otherwise be missed or not voiced.

At the same time, Habermas pointed out those religious traditions must work internally in a task of hermeneutic self-reflection. They must account for the cognitive dissonances arising in encountering other religions and worldviews, the independence of the secular from the sacred, and the priority of secular reasons in the political arena. In other terms, they need to undergo a "modernization of religious consciousness."[71] In a revised model of citizenship, however, Habermas burdened secular citizens with a similar task:

> secular citizens are likewise not spared a cognitive burden, because a secularist attitude does not suffice for the expected cooperation with fellow citizens who are religious. This cognitive act of adaptation needs to be distinguished from the political virtue of mere tolerance. What is at stake is not some respectful feel for the possible existential significance of religion for some other person. What we must also expect of the secular citizens is moreover a self-reflective transcending of a secularist self-understanding of Modernity.[72]

Habermas then rejected the "narrow secularist consciousness" in favor of a post-secular mindset, a philosophical position that does not judge religious truths but clearly divides between faith and knowledge and is "open to learn from religion but remains agnostic in the process."[73]

---

70 Habermas, "Religion in the Public Sphere," 9–10.
71 Habermas, "Religion in the Public Sphere," 13.
72 Habermas, "Religion in the Public Sphere," 14.
73 Habermas, "Religion in the Public Sphere," 17.

2.4 *Habermas and Huntington Compared*

On the surface, then, Habermas's position completely differs from the one taken by Huntington. In place of creating a stronghold for one's own identity, Habermas postulated opening to others in the process of mutual understanding. However, at a closer look, one may spot that Habermas shares Huntington's attachment to the established overarching framework of what I describe as legible religion, although he emphasizes its different aspects and reaches different conclusions. This difference partially results from a different approach to the three modalities. Huntington largely rejects religious pluralism and puts Christianity and secularism at the same level under the guise of Western culture.

In contrast, Habermas acknowledges all three modalities, although he views secularism as fundamental for the operation of the other two. He also privileges contemporary, mainstream Christianity in the model of religious pluralism. Although he rejects narrow secularism, he still sides with its broader version, which privileges the secular over the religious. The public sphere is primarily secular. Religion is provided a specific space under specific conditions. Although religious concerns may be voiced in an unabridged version at the beginning, they require subsequent translation to constitute justification for decision-making. While Habermas acknowledges the importance of religion for individuals, he views religion primarily in functional terms as something that might provide meaning that could be otherwise lost. Moreover, Habermas sees religion as inherently volatile and potentially dangerous if given unrestricted access to the public sphere. Without specific provisions, religious presence may easily disintegrate into religious struggle. Thus, Habermas introduced the ideal of religious presence in the public sphere, privileging religions that underwent a modernization of their consciousness. He even gave an example of Catholic Christianity and its apologetical efforts as an example.

This privileged positioning is better visible in other texts by Habermas, where some agreement with Huntington's proposals is more visible. On numerous occasions, Habermas underlined the importance of Christian heritage. He viewed it as important in the formation of Europe and foundational for secular ideas like a pan-European consciousness, described in his 2001 considerations of the need for a European constitution.[74] He also saw the fundamental role of Christianity in the development of human rights, as discussed in his dialogue with Joseph Ratzinger.[75]

---

74 Jürgen Habermas, "Why Europe Needs a Constitution," *New Left Review*, no. 11 (2001): 10; 19; 20.

75 Habermas and Ratzinger, *The Dialectics of Secularization: On Reason and Religion*, 24.

However, Christianity is privileged only regarding those denominations that underwent a transformation of consciousness, that is, those that were historically established. Such an approach is especially visible in his 2008 book *Ach, Europa*, translated as *Europe: The Faltering Project,* in a chapter on "What is Meant by a 'Post-Secular Society'? A Discussion on Islam in Europe." There, Habermas reiterated his call for complimentary learning between religious and secular ways of thinking. However, to make it possible, Habermas required religious consciousness to undergo a specific transition, the one that was achieved by the Protestant churches in Germany or the Catholic Church during the Second Vatican Council. The changes symbolically initiated by Martin Luther in 1517 are positioned as a model of such transition:

> When we think of such a shift from a traditional to a more reflexive form of religious consciousness, the model of the change in epistemic attitudes within the Christian churches of the West following the Reformation springs to mind.[76]

This overlooks many Christian communities, for example, some Pentecostal churches.[77] Islam is treated similarly: "Muslim communities still have to undergo this painful learning process."[78]

Thus, in the context of this book, one could say that Habermas differentiates between legible and non-legible religions. While in his thought, the difference between the marked and unmarked described by Oliphant is much less visible than in Huntington's, he nonetheless allows access to the public sphere only to those who adapt to the legible framework. Furthermore, even in terms of legible religions like Lutheran or Catholic Christianity, access is provided under strict conditions of a "translation proviso."

Altogether, then, Huntington and Habermas are theoreticians whose thoughts deeply impacted the political movements on, respectively, the political right and left. They are often portrayed as entirely opposed. In many respects, they are. They differ in their approach to the three modalities noted by Dinham and Weller: religious pluralism, secularism, and Christianity. While Huntington rejects the first in a coalition of the latter two, Habermas privileges secularism, and raises Lutheran and postconciliar Catholicism as models for the other religions. However, within the framework of this book, I believe one

76 Jürgen Habermas, "What is Meant by a 'Post-Secular Society'? A Discussion on Islam in Europe," in *Europe: The Faltering Project* (Cambridge: Polity Press, 2009), 75.

77 Habermas, "What is Meant," 61.

78 Habermas, "What is Meant," 75.

can find some similarities between them regarding the described framework of legible religion. They both build on the narrative of the return of religion. Both take a functional approach to religion, even if they differ in what function they select for it, such as identity-building, differentiation from "others," meaning-making, or loyalty-establishing tools. Both operate on the assumption that some religions are legible and thereby allowed to function in the public sphere, while others are not. Both retain the division between marked and unmarked. Both see religion as a volatile factor and thereby a potential threat, at least in some forms. Both, finally, see religion as primarily cognitive.

Through the example of both Huntington and Habermas, one can observe how the overarching framework of legible religion is adapted to competing sub-frameworks with the turn of narratives from secularization to the return of religion. While the acceptance of modernity by the Catholic Church, as described in the previous chapter, allowed for the legible religion framework to become hegemonic and provided a temporary consensus in which the relationship of Christianity and secularism was locally negotiated, the emergence of religious pluralism disrupted that consensus and necessitated new constellations. As pointed out by Oliphant, it emphasized the privilege of banality provided to the historically dominant denominations, as they contrasted with the traditions and communities that did not undergo legible transformation. The boundaries between the marked and unmarked were reopened to negotiation, in which the privileges of the previously unmarked established actors clashed with the demands for access to the public space of the marked ones. Such a reinvigorated competition might be behind numerous controversies regarding issues such as crosses, handshakes, head-coverings or, as discussed in the following two chapters, prayer rooms. However, the hegemonic status of the overarching framework of legible religion has been maintained, and the adaptations operated as sub-frameworks, with no visible paradigm change.

3 The Defense of Legible Religion

Since the 1990s, the return of religion has not only been discussed among descriptive sociologists but also picked up by normatively inclined thinkers and politicians. This chapter aimed to address the sudden need for the adaptation of political frameworks to a changing situation and a new understanding of religion. At first, building upon Elayne Oliphant's notion of banal religion, I have discussed the difference between marked and unmarked. As I argued, with the changing situation, religions that adapted to the framework of legibility were allowed the privilege of moving between marked and unmarked, and with it, the ability to operate in the public sphere unnoticed. Conversely, religions that did not fit into legible standards did not possess that privilege, being constantly marked as potentially threatening. The "return" in the return of religion, then, means the appearance of a novel presence that did not fit into the legibility framework.

I have discussed this through the example of the British "multi-faith paradigm" as discussed by Adam Dinham based on the policies of New Labour in the years from 1997 to 2010. Following Dinham, I have discussed the re-engagement with religious communities, which followed two main lines: functional (community cohesion and service provision) and preventive (mainly towards the marked Islam). As Dinham noted, this approach ultimately proved quite problematic, running alongside reality rather than addressing it. The central-level administrative simplifications trying to make multi-faith legible proved too reductive to achieve the established aims. Functionalization, ignoring, and prevention were three ways the state approached religion.

Following Dinham and Weller, I have described three modalities that emerged with the introduction of the return of religion: religious pluralism, secularism, and Christianity. The sudden marked presence of other religions, especially Islam, posed a sudden threat to secularists, the banal presence of historically established versions of Christianity, and, most importantly, the established consensus between the two. The seeming consensus of the latter two had been disrupted, and there was a need to readapt to the new, third modality that resulted in the emergence of competing sub-frameworks.

Such sub-frameworks were presented on an example of two distinguished and distinct thinkers: Samuel P. Huntington and Jürgen Habermas. Huntington and Habermas offer two different takes on the kinds of constellations that can be built regarding these three modalities. Huntington wanted to conserve the Western, Christian-secular *status quo* by doubling down on Western identity and resolving the presence of the "other" by entirely rejecting it. Habermas wanted to respond to plurality by engaging with it. However, he wanted to do it on the terms set by secularism, with Christianity, more precisely Lutheranism and Roman Catholicism, as a model for other religions. He proposed an opening for otherness via "institutional translation." As such, Habermas and Huntington could be viewed as opposites.

However, in terms of the overarching framework discussed in this book, they are not as far apart from each other as it might seem. They built their sub-frameworks within the broader paradigm of legible religion. Both wanted to return to the consensus by turning the "other" presence legible. Those following Huntington want to secure the Christian-secular consensus by suppressing the presence of others, vehemently opposing anything that endangers their identity, although they allow for conversions into the West. Those more proximate to Habermas want to "translate" others into the terms that fit neatly into the existing consensus, providing them with space only to the extent that follows the established rules of acceptability and understanding. In both cases, the allowed religion has to mimic the well-known, established forms of religiosity. Both sides view religion as a potential threat—a rogue civilization in our midst in Huntington's approach and a volatile factor in Habermas's point of view. They also see its utility—a robust identity-building factor for Huntington and a space for learning for Habermas. Both require adaptations that follow the principles of the secularizing cycle of legible religion, which prove impossible to many believers. In the end, both reframe older secular solutions to the new situations, leading to the problems described by Dinham.

Thus, the hegemonic status of the legible religion framework remains firmly in place. Despite the addition of religious pluralism to Christianity and secularism, central-level reductions, simplifications, and generalizations are the standard administrative approach that seeps into the general consciousness due to its consciousness-shaping effect. The mismatch between the legible and that which does not comply with the requirements of legibility results in subsequent clashes of highly publicized symbolic cases, including handshakes, crosses, head-coverings, or prayer in public spaces. This approach also translates into concrete adaptations within public institutions, such as the multi-faith spaces discussed in this book. They highlight some of the fallacies of the legible approach.

The analysis presented in this book has until now been made at a largely abstract level of ideas, theories, and principles. However, these ideas, theories, and principles had, and still have, a very direct impact on the concrete arrangements in which European countries operate, both on the community level, as visible in the fundamental legal principle of the so-called freedom of religion or belief, and in the very concrete arrangements of physical space in public institutions. These concrete arrangements will be discussed in the following chapters.

PART 2

Legibility Embodied and Contested

∴

CHAPTER 4

Designing Religion in Public

Multi-faith Spaces as the Embodiment of Legible Religion

Equipped with a better understanding of layers upon layers of meaning accrued over centuries with regard to notions such as religion and religious diversity, we can return to the empty bland room with white walls, gray carpeting, and fluorescent tube lighting described at the beginning of this book. It is this web of significance through which the simple sign "MULTI-FAITH AND CONTEMPLATION ROOM" turns the room into a source of tensions that exemplify larger rifts in the European religious landscape: between majority and minority traditions; between those focused on the individual, internal religious experience, and those with a strong collective, external element; between those who treat their beliefs as a private matter, and those whose religious observance requires visible expressions of faith. Multi-faith spaces, then, offer concrete examples of the problems with contemporary approaches to religious pluralism that have been discussed in the abstract so far.

However, not all spaces gathered under the umbrella term multi-faith spaces look like the one described earlier. Some operate in different ways in the institutional context, outside of it, or as an example of local initiative. The design of some spaces differs to the extent that it could be challenging to find many similarities between them, and the spaces mentioned above. Yet, as I argue, even among those spaces, one can see traces of the legible tendency to approach religion from a functional angle, including a focus on social cohesion or service provisions described earlier.

In the following two chapters, I argue that most multi-faith spaces constitute an embodiment of the legible religion. They are one of the most concrete examples of the influence this paradigm exercises in practice. First, their materiality is often shaped by the legible preference. Most typical multi-faith spaces provide more suitable conditions for people whose religiosity is individual, private, internalized, iconoclastic, cognitive, and silent. Second, even spaces that do not follow the most typical design tend to represent the approach that focuses on treating religion as either a potential threat or a functional tool. Third, the context, discussions, and conflicts around these spaces constitute an arena where it is possible to study the consciousness-shaping effect that the broader framework of legible religion exercises, how the difference between marked and unmarked operates, and how the three modalities of religiously plural, secular, and Christian, as discussed in Chapter 3, influence the perception of the space.

This chapter will focus on the normative assumptions inherent in the design of multi-faith spaces, which will be considered in two sections. The first will look at the history and early examples of multi-faith spaces that proved formative for the general trends in designing such places. The second will consider questions of definition and typology to identify these general trends and discuss their implications. Thus, this chapter will discuss the first and, partially, the second of the abovementioned points. This chapter will argue that the early examples of multi-faith spaces, although unique at first, later started to function as models for an increasing number of both intra- and extra-institutional multi-faith spaces. Those within public institutions were subsumed under the institutional logic expressing a preference for individual, private, internalized, iconoclastic, cognitive, and prayer-oriented religiosity. Those outside of institutions had to adapt to the requirements of the public space. Both needed to find their place within the legible religion paradigm. The proposed typology will highlight how they did so in practice, differentiating between spaces that imposed control over religion, and those that employed it as a functional tool for achieving specific goals, most importantly, social cohesion; those that subtracted from the possible ways of being religious, and those that added an alternative to the existing ones. Chapter 5 will continue the discussion. In this way, the framework of legible religion will be translated from abstract theoretical considerations into the concrete practice of physical institutions, the environments of public institutions, and contemporary debates.

1 The Emergence of Multi-faith Spaces

Shared religious spaces have been a constant feature of religious coexistence throughout history.[1] One of the most famous landmarks in Rome, the Pantheon, a temple of all the gods, is a visible manifestation of a long pedigree of multi-faith spaces (even if it was later turned into a Christian basilica). The attempts at mixed religious settings have been repeated in Europe over the centuries, both in inter-denominational contexts, like the *Simultankirche* introduced in Bautzen in 1524, and in inter-faith ones, like the Long Stables converted into

1 Terry Biddington, *Multi-faith Space: History, Development, Design and Practice* (London: Jessica Kingsley Publishers, 2020), 36.

the Prayer Room in Friedrich Wilhelm I's Potsdam Sanssouci Palace.[2] These spaces were often an attempt at creating a more cohesive community based, among others, on the shared use of such spaces or their symbolic value.

However, in their contemporary version, multi-faith spaces have been a recent invention. An early example of a standalone multi-faith space could be observed during the New York World's Fair in 1939: the so-called Temple of Religion. A joint effort of Jewish, Catholic, and Protestant leaders, this circular building had a modernist outlook with a large courtyard surrounded by arcades. The inscription at the entrance welcomed "all who worship God and prize religious freedom."[3] The arcades were decorated with murals presenting the History of Religious Architecture from different parts of the world. The building itself was an auditorium that seated up to 1,200 people and was meant for presentations expressing the value of spiritual issues. The building remained unconsecrated and was demolished a year after it was raised, never holding any explicitly religious services.[4]

Some of the earliest traces of a modern multi-faith space within an institutional context can be observed a few years after the inception of the United Nations, with a leading role played by its second Secretary-General, Dag Hammarskjöld. The original architectural plans of the UN Headquarters in New York reserved a small space for an inclusive place of withdrawal, stillness, and silence. Raising aspirations, Hammarskjöld, in collaboration with a group composed of different members of Judaism, Christianity, and Islam, developed plans for space with grandeur, raised funds for it, and spearheaded its development in 1957 with great attention to detail.[5] A Room of Quiet featured only benches, an altar-like slab of iron ore in the middle of the room, and geometric

2 Terry Biddington, "Towards a Theological Reading of Multi-faith Spaces," *International Journal of Public Theology* 7, no. 3 (2013), 316, https://doi.org/10.1163/15697320-12341293.

3 International Hildreth Meière Association, "New York 1939 World's Fair: Temple of Religion, Flushing, NY," 2021, accessed 17th of September, 2021, https://www.hildrethmeiere.org/commissions/new-york-1939-worlds-fair-temple-of-religion-arcade-facing-courtyard.

4 Paul M. Van Dort, "Temple of Religion," 1939 New York World's Fair, 2021, accessed 17th of November, 2021, https://www.1939nyworldsfair.com/worlds_fair/wf_tour/zone-2/temple_of_religion.htm. For more see J. Terry Todd, "The Temple of Religion and the Politics of Religious Pluralism: Judeo-Christian America at the 1939–1940 New York World's Fair," in *After Pluralism: Reimagining Models of Religious Engagement*, ed. Courtney Bender and Pamela Klassen (New York: Columbia University Press, 2010); Courtney Bender, "Temple of Religion, New York World's Fair (1939–1940)," SSRC Forums, 2014, accessed 17th of November, 2021, http://forums.ssrc.org/ndsp/2014/08/04/temple-of-religion-new-york-worlds-fair-1939-1940/.

5 United Nations, "'A Room of Quiet' The Meditation Room, United Nations Headquarters," United Nations, 2018, accessed 18th of September, 2021, https://www.un.org/depts/dhl/dag/meditationroom.htm.

art on the central wall. It had meticulously selected lighting, carpeting, and wall paint. This space was a result of a coherent vision expressed by Hammarskjöld in an introductory text distributed to the visitors:

> People of many faiths will meet here, and for that reason none of the symbols to which we are accustomed in our meditation could be used. …
>
> But the stone in the middle of the room has more to tell us. We may see it as an altar, empty not because there is no God, not because it is an altar to an unknown god, but because it is dedicated to the God whom man worships under many names and in many forms. …
>
> It is [also] a reminder of that cornerstone of endurance and faith on which all human endeavour must be based.
>
> The material of the stone leads our thoughts to the necessity for choice between destruction and construction, between war and peace. Of iron man has forged his swords, of iron he has also made his ploughshares. Of iron he has constructed tanks, but of iron he has likewise built homes for man. The block of iron ore is part of the wealth we have inherited on this earth of ours. How are we to use it? …
>
> There is an ancient saying that the sense of a vessel is not in its shell but in the void. So it is with this room. It is for those who come here to fill the void with what they find in their center of stillness.[6]

In these passages, one may see the main principles guiding Hammarskjöld: stillness and individual internal reflection, apophatic symbolism, an inclusivist approach to religious pluralism, or even a degree of syncretism. One may notice an understanding of faith as a basis for social action, although Hammarskjöld also sees a place for a measure of spirituality in all human endeavors.[7] Interpreting iron as a symbol of choice between peace and war, while not stated anywhere, could be arguably understood in this context as highlighting the utility-based approach to religion, viewed as a double-edged sword.

---

6 United Nations, "'A Room of Quiet.'"

7 Hammarskjöld, in many ways, represented a classical liberal vision of religion. For more on Hammarskjöld's religion see, for example, James Wm. McClendon Jr., "Dag Hammarskjöld—Twice Born Servant," in *Biography as Theology: How Life Stories Can Remake Today's Theology*, ed. James Wm. McClendon Jr. (Eugene, OR: Wipf and Stock Publishers, 2002); Alynna J. Lyon, "Moral motives and policy actions: The case of Dag Hammarskjöld at the United Nations," *Public Intergrity* 9, no. 1 (2007), https://doi.org/10.2753/PIN1099-9922090105; Morariu Iuliu Marius, "Aspects of political theology in the spiritual autobiography of Dag Hammarskjöld," *HTS: Theological Studies* 74, no. 4 (2018), http://dx.doi.org/10.4102/hts.v74i4.4857.

The UN Meditation Room was a forward-looking invitation to rethink shared spaces. It constituted a new approach to the coexistence of people representing different beliefs and worldviews in public institutions. Installed in the newly constructed headquarters of an organization meant to learn from the insufficiencies of the League of Nations and establish world peace, it proposed a novel model of coexistence in conditions of increasing plurality. However, this proposal came from a very specific context—it expressed specific liberal sensitivities and the Scandinavian background of its main contributors (the king of Sweden and the Swedish government donated the block of iron ore, while a Swedish artist, Bo Beskow, painted the mural). Thus, it might have been more sensitive to specific types of religiosity or spirituality, while underappreciating others. It underlined the universalizing approaches to faith, as expressed by popular theologians such as Paul Tillich.[8] Remembering this background is important when looking at its successors. While a valuable symbol as a unique installation, if used as a model for creating similar spaces worldwide, it could have proved potentially problematic.

Thus, while multi-faith spaces have many historical predecessors, I argue that in these two examples one may see the emergence of new directions in how they began to function in the twentieth century and onwards. First, one can see extra- and intra-institutional spaces. Second, one can see the implementation of "unity by exclusion," that is, the idea that the space will become neutral and inclusive by excluding any visible symbolism. Third, in Hammarskjöld's vision for the UN Meditation Room, one can also see traces of liberal religiosity, or more narrowly, spirituality, that was destined to be more and more dominant in the public spaces in the decades to come.

1.1 *The Importance of Chaplaincy*

While ground-breaking, the UN Meditation Room remained unique for several decades. To gain a broader following, it required another development. Chaplaincy and the view of faith provisions as an intra-institutional service had to emerge first. In his history of workplace chaplaincy, a British priest and scholar, Malcolm Torry, sees chaplaincy primarily as a response of the Christian churches to subjectively understood secularization. Chaplains were supposed to carve a space for faith within secular contexts. Torry points out that, at first, chaplaincy emerged in the early modern navy and army. Its development followed a dual strategy: it aimed at the evangelization of individuals, on the one hand, and the broadening of parochial ministry into new contexts,

8 See, for example, Paul Tillich, *Systematic Theology (in 3 volumes)* (Chicago, Illinois: University of Chicago Press, 1951–1963).

on the other. With the end of the Second World War, the high number of former military priests paved the way for a fast-paced development of chaplaincy in new, institutional, and industrial contexts. Thus, the so-called workplace chaplaincy emerged and the accompanying workplace chapels with it. The new developments led to the increase in the significance of chaplains to the point at which, during the 1980s, chaplains became agents of social change, attempting to tackle such social issues as unemployment, racial inequality, or even questions of corporate responsibility.[9] The fast-paced development of chaplaincy coincided with the period in which secularization as a narrative was most potent, which is why its development responded, at least partly, to its proposals.

Between the end of the Second World War and the 1990s, workplace chaplains turned from a disparate phenomenon into a modern profession providing services in growing numbers of airports, hospitals, schools, universities, prisons, and other modern institutions.[10] These institutions played a growing role in how people perceived religion. By joining the developing institutions of a modern state, chaplains became important representatives of religion. As Lena Kühle and Henrik Reintoft Christensen underline, the approach to religion in public institutions can help us better understand the state's approach to religion. Through these institutions, most individuals experience the 'state.'[11] Chaplains play a significant, intermediary role in that.[12]

When secularization began to be replaced by the return of religion, chaplaincy also changed. Kühle and Reintoft Christensen identify three primary roles in which chaplains operate today. First, they negotiate space with secular institutions, becoming the middleman, the "third person," positioned somewhere between the institution, the chaplain's religious community, and their respective institution's clients. Second, they are often directly responsible for the management of religious diversity. Such responsibility is especially significant in the European model, where chaplaincy is based on specific denominations. The majority confession chaplains often have to facilitate access to various resources and cater to the needs of those without their own chaplain. Finally, their work depends on the institutional logic, context, the arrangement

9 Malcolm Torry, *Bridgebuilders: Workplace Chaplaincy—A History* (London: Canterbury Press, 2010).

10 See Biddington, *Multi-faith Space*, 37–60.

11 For more on the subject see also Michael Lipsky, *Street Level Bureaucracy Dilemmas of the Individual in Public Services* (New York: Russell Sage Foundation, 1980). http://www.jstor.org/stable/10.7758/9781610447713.

12 Lena Kühle and Heinrik Reintoft Christensen, "One to serve them all. The growth of chaplaincy in public institutions in Denmark," *Social Compass* 66, no. 2 (2019): 183–84, https://doi.org/10.1177/0037768619833331.

of private/public distinction, and the increasingly secular predispositions of the populations they serve. Thus, chaplains' work functions to a large extent like a litmus test for the current state of approaches to the management of religious pluralism. Kühle and Reintoft Christensen conclude, similarly to Torry:

> Chaplaincies are changing as a result of secularization and pluralization, as well as being under pressure from policies and reductions of welfare services associated with new public management. These changes may result in the growth of chaplaincy, the introduction of chaplaincy to new domains, or the development of multi-faith chaplaincies. However, none of these changes can happen without the work of the chaplains themselves.[13]

Thus, chaplaincy entered a new phase at the end of the twentieth century. Chaplains increasingly developed concrete solutions to cater to a broader audience than their own confession, and the UN Meditation Room served as an ample example. Terry Biddington, the author of the first systematic handbook to multi-faith spaces, points out that the first "*explicitly multi-faith* space in Europe" was opened in 1988 as a part of the Pastoral Centre at the Vienna Schwechat International Airport.[14] It resulted from the longstanding development of chaplaincy as a service. *Andachtsraum* was built on the initiative of Joseph Farrugia, the Catholic airport chaplain hired by the Diocese of Vienna. Farrugia wanted to introduce a better prayer room that people of all faiths could use.[15] Since then, the airport's Pastoral Center has expanded to three different spaces, each following many of the characteristics known from A Room of Quiet—ambient colors and lights, modest furnishing with an altar-like table, and lack of religious symbols beyond geometric representations. This time, however, the spaces were more pragmatically equipped, with access provided to different religious texts, including the Bible, the Quran, Buddhist prayer books, and prayer mats.

In 1989, a year after the creation of a multi-faith space at Vienna Airport, the University Medical Center in Utrecht opened its own Room of Silence. Similarly, the room was designed by the local Catholic chaplain, Jack de Valk. Again, the room expressed the need to cater to members of different faiths. It followed the precedence set by the previously described spaces. However,

13 Kühle and Christensen, "One to serve them all," 186.

14 Biddington, *Multi-faith Space*, 39.

15 APA-OTS, "Seit 20 Jahren gibt es in Wien-Schwechat die 'Flughafenkapelle'," *APA-OTS*, 3rd of July 2008, http://www.ots.at/presseaussendung/OTS_20080703_OTS0034.

this room proposed an innovation: confessionally marked spaces. Biddington described the space in the following words:

> A raised central area with a granite block is surrounded by faith areas or "identity zones" (de Valk's phrase) on the lower ground space. The block, painted with red concentric circles, can serve as a Christian altar, or as a non-Christian table for offering flowers and fruit, for lighting candles or for creating impromptu shrines with memorials, photographs, and other symbolic items. Around the edges and in the corners of the room are areas for ecumenical Christian worship ... an open area for Islamic worship ... and a quiet area for Humanists/Atheists.[16]

The original room kept its shape until today, and a stillness center, *Stiltecentrum*, was subsequently built around it. The number of such spaces at the whole university also increased.[17]

The changes in chaplaincy expressed the increasing significance of considerations for, and the need to cater to, various religious beliefs. Such significance was most pronounced in highly globalized spaces such as airports, universities, or hospitals. Within those institutions, multi-faith spaces appeared in increasing numbers. While today it is hard to estimate their exact number, one can point to some counts to give a sense of how widespread they are. For example, the 2011 estimate counted at least 1,500 multi-faith spaces in Britain alone.[18] Most of the 81 hospital chaplaincies in Sweden have some kind of alternative prayer space.[19] The 2017 investigation of the Danish Ministry of Science and Higher Education found that three quarters of universities, and half of vocational colleges reported offering a prayer room.[20] Institutionalizing the innovation of chaplains, some European government agencies recommended these spaces.[21] Thus, these spaces were, as the title of the most extensive study

16 Biddington, *Multi-faith Space*, 45.

17 Utrecht University, "Meditation, lactation and first-aid rooms," 2021, accessed 25th of September, 2021, https://students.uu.nl/en/meditation-lactation-and-first-aid-rooms.

18 Andrew Crompton, "The Architecture of Multi-faith Spaces: God Leaves the Building," *The Journal of Architecture* 18 (2013), 475, https://doi.org/10.1080/13602365.2013.821149.

19 Biddington, *Multi-faith Space*, 46.

20 Uddanelses- og Forskningministeriet, Opgørelse over antallet af bederum eller lignende faciliteter på de videregående uddannelsesinstitutioner, (Copenhagen: Uddanelses- og Forskningministeriet, 2017).

21 For example, Spain, see Francisco Diez de Velasco, *Guía Técnica Para La Implementación Y Gestión De Espacios Multiconfesionales*, Observatorio del Pluralismo Religioso en España (Madrid, 2011). or UK, see Peter Collins et al., *NHS Hospital 'Chaplaincies' in a Multi-Faith Society. The Spatial Dimension of Religion and Spirituality in Hospital*, Durham University and NHS (Durham, 2007).

of multi-faith spaces up to date suggests, "Symptoms and Agents of Religious and Social Change."[22] They were symptoms because they signified the changing approach and adaptations of the European public space. They were agents because their context, presence, and use had a significant influence on, among others, how religious presence was treated within institutional contexts, what kinds of practices were sanctioned, and how inter-faith relations were structured.

To sum up, the development of chaplaincy in the twentieth century, especially after the Second World War, was, at least to a certain extent, a response to encroaching secularization. Chaplains approached it by carving out physical spaces within the broader institutional context, introducing chapels in such disparate places as schools, hospitals, airports, or shopping malls. Increasingly professionalized and constrained by institutional logic, chaplains became the intermediaries between the institutions, their clients, and their own religious communities. Within state-led institutions, chaplains became liaisons of the state. Their approach to religion, thus, reflected on the state's approach to religion (and vice versa).

With the change of the narratives from secularization to the return of religion, chaplains' approaches changed. Nevertheless, like the broader patterns discussed in Part 1 of this book, the former methods were adapted to the new contexts rather than overhauled. As chaplains continued to carve out the space for faith, chapels were turned into multi-faith spaces. In addition, the intermediary role of the chaplains from majority confessions was expanded with added tasks of catering to people from other religious communities.

While, at first, chaplains were the primary agents of finding space for religion in public institutions, over time, their inventions were institutionalized and, in many cases, separated from the chaplains themselves. As a result, multi-faith spaces took on a life of their own, sometimes even gaining governmental recommendation. Because of that, the spaces themselves became symptoms and agents of religious and social change. However, to better understand these two roles, one needs to understand better what hides behind the term multi-faith space.

---

22 *Multi-Faith Spaces: Symptoms and Agents of Religious and Social Change* was a three-year collaboration between the Universities of Manchester and Liverpool funded by the AHRC and ESRC. The study has documented 36 UK spaces and 12 spaces from other countries existing in a variety of institutional contexts, with a detailed study of the 14 of them. The results of the research project are encapsulated in a traveling exhibition entitled *multi-faith [spaces]* that can be viewed online at https://cargocollective.com /wwwmulti-faith-spacesorg.

2 A Typology of Multi-faith Spaces

After inspecting the early developments of multi-faith spaces, I can now focus on their analysis. As I will argue at the beginning of this part, the term multi-faith spaces is extremely broad and challenging to define satisfactorily. Thus, instead of overtly focusing on definition, I will propose a typology of these spaces. Considering the goal of this book, the most typical multi-faith spaces will tell us more about the dominant tendencies in thinking about religion. Thus, in developing typology first, I will argue that three elements are especially important in analyzing the spaces themselves: how they are designed, where they are placed, and what effect the combination of design and placement has. Second, based on that, I will propose two primary ideal types, spaces that subtract and spaces that add, and analyze examples of both. In the final section, I will argue that despite their differences, both types fit well into the framework of legible religion; one focused more on the control of religion and the other on its function.

2.1 *Defining a Multi-faith Space*

The four examples of early multi-faith spaces previously mentioned, the Temple of Religion in New York, A Room of Quiet at the UN Headquarters, the *Andachtsraum* at Vienna Airport, and the Room of Silence at the UMC in Utrecht, offer a good cross-section of what the umbrella term of multi-faith space signifies. They show that multi-faith spaces can operate as standalone spaces, like the Temple of Religion, or as intra-institutional spaces, like all the others. They can play a symbolic role, as the Temple of Religion or A Room of Quiet or make up a pragmatic solution for catering to people of different faiths, as *Andachtsraum* and the Room of Silence. They can be devoid of any visible, confessional manifestations or divide the room into a shared space and "identity-based" zones. They can result from the grassroots involvement of local communities, an effort of the institutional leadership, or a chaplain carving out a space for religion within a particular institution.

These differences show that the notion of multi-faith space is a catch-all term. This conclusion is one of the results of the Symptoms and Agents of Religious and Social Change project mentioned earlier. The project team points out in the *multi-faith [spaces]* exhibition, which described the project's results, that "Multi-faith Spaces … have no precise definition; existing only in the eye of the beholder. They are places where a range of faith-based or spiritual activities can be undertaken, wherein each user should find something of appeal."[23]

23 Ralf Gregor Brand, Andrew Crompton, and Chris Hewson, "Multi-faith Spaces—Symptoms and Agents of Religious and Social Change," *University of Manchester and*

However, I would argue that there is a need to make further definitional efforts. If one would stay at this stage of the definition, each space might count as a multi-faith space—the entire world could be considered as such. The *multi-faith [spaces]* exhibition describes specific features to delineate the term further. According to its authors, multi-faith spaces are not fixed. Their character may change with use. They are usually not consecrated and should not be treated as holy sites. They operate within a larger context, even if that context is not institutional. They are further defined by use, which is sanctioned both by the design of the space and further written instructions.

However, that still leaves much space to include broadly diverging phenomena under this term, which might be why their naming is so disparate. Multi-faith spaces are usually named using a combination of a broad range of adjectives, such as reflection, quiet, silent, multi-faith, inter-faith, rest, contemplation, prayer, reconciliation, worship, wellbeing, living, serenity; and nouns such as lounge, space, chapel, chaplaincy, room, center.[24]

But the *multi-faith [spaces]* exhibition also points to a normative assumption behind these spaces. As it reads:

> MFS contain a strong human component. This can be characterized as the shared manifestation of a methodical, yet creative desire to 'get along'. MFS are thus markers of pluralism and tolerance, indicators of the ever-shifting role of religion within the public realm, and a sign of a continued need to research the physical and material aspects of religious practice.[25]

That is why the character of multi-faith spaces is a result of their materiality and placement, as will be discussed below, and the meaning that lies in the eye of the beholder—the users, and the observers, define what these spaces signify. The intentions in approaching the space also impact what role they play and how they are perceived. As already mentioned above, some of these spaces proved to be causing significant tensions instead of expressing the desire to "get along."

Summing up these considerations, the term multi-faith space could be defined as any place consciously devoted to a broad range of beliefs and practices. They are further defined by their context, use, and perception. This definition may still prove unsatisfactory for many, as it gathers a vast number of different phenomena. That is why I argue that differentiating the most

---

University of Liverpool, 2012, accessed 17 September 2021, http://cargocollective.com/www multi-faith-spacesorg, Models section.

24 Brand, Crompton, and Hewson, "Multi-faith Spaces," Naming section.

25 Brand, Crompton, and Hewson, "Multi-faith Spaces," Models section.

common types of spaces may be more helpful in analyzing these spaces and the approaches to religion behind them. In the next section, I will propose a typology for precisely that purpose.

2.2 *The Design, the Placement, and the Effect*

In the following three sections, I will develop a typology of multi-faith spaces to understand the approaches to religion behind them better. Following Weber's notion of "ideal types,"[26] I will accentuate certain predominant features and tendencies among the existing spaces. Like all typologies, it draws in broad strokes. However, I will try to highlight the divergences from the ideal types whenever possible to provide the reader with a fuller picture of the situation at hand.

In the section on chaplaincy, I have noted the importance of the institutional context for the emergence of multi-faith spaces. Three out of four examples discussed by far operate in secular institutions. That is because most multi-faith spaces exist in such a context. Courtney Bender points out that while one can point to multiple shared sacred spaces, the great majority of modern multi-faith prayer rooms, chapels, and buildings are built and designed within secular institutions.[27]

And yet, even Bender, in her portal on the Architecture of Multi-Faith Spaces, shows examples of spaces that do not operate in this institutional context, such as the already mentioned Temple of Religion[28] or the House of One in Berlin.[29] With the distinction between institutional and extra-institutional spaces, contextual placement could posit the first element of differentiation in our typology.

However, in this book, I am interested in the tendencies in approaching religion that stand behind multi-faith spaces. Contextual placement on its own does not offer us enough information to understand that. Multi-faith spaces can differ broadly within and outside of the institutional context. Andrew Crompton differentiates between two types of spaces based on their design. In

26 Max Weber, "Objectivity in Social Science and Social Policy," in *The Methodology of the Social Sciences*, ed. E. A. Shils and H. A. Finch (New York: Free Press, 1949). See also Susan Hekman, *Weber, the Ideal Type, and Contemporary Social Theory* (Notre Dame, IN: University of Notre Dame Press, 1983).

27 Courtney Bender, "The Architecture of Multi-faith Prayer: An Introduction," SSRC Forums, 2014, accessed 17th of November, 2021, http://forums.ssrc.org/ndsp/2014/08/04/the-architecture-of-multi-faith-prayer-an-introduction/.

28 Bender, "Temple of Religion."

29 Courtney Bender, "Bet- und Lehrhaus (The House of Prayer and Learning)," SSRC Forums, 2014, accessed 17th of November, 2021, http://forums.ssrc.org/ndsp/2014/08/04/bet-und-lehrhaus-the-house-of-prayer-and-learning/.

an article with the suggestive title, "The architecture of multi-faith spaces: God leaves the building," Crompton criticizes most existing spaces for being rather mundane and bland, attempting to create an inclusive space by excluding any traces of identity. Crompton writes:

> The most common and characteristic type [of multi-faith spaces] is a windowless white room with a few religious texts on a shelf and the paraphernalia of religion, when not actually in use, kept out of sight in boxes.
>
> These universal interfaces with God are not, as one might have thought, a sublime expression of a deep unity of which individual religions are merely a particular expression.
>
> Empty white rooms have become the default solution because there is an assumption that we should not be exposed to symbols of other people's faith if that can be avoided. Whether shielding people from other religions is reasonable or legal seems not to matter. In practice the most important issue in multi-faith design has become how to prevent a space becoming meaningful in an inappropriate way.[30]

Crompton differentiates two ideal types of shared space: negative and positive.[31] The negative spaces follow the "unity by exclusion" principle and rely on as minimal design as possible. In contrast, positive spaces follow the "unity by inclusion" principle, which allows for multiple symbols, artifacts, styles, and layers of meaning within one space.[32] While negative spaces are usually built from scratch, positive spaces can exist in formerly mono-confessional spaces. For example, a former Christian chapel might be converted into a multi-faith space by allowing other confessional groups to inhabit the space and bring their symbols into it.

Crompton points out potential problems with both approaches. According to him, the positive type privileges the denomination that created the chapel[33] and thus requires careful balancing by a dedicated inter-faith minister to ensure

30 Crompton, "The Architecture of Multi-faith," 475.

31 Crompton, "The Architecture of Multi-faith," 479.

32 Crompton, "The Architecture of Multi-faith," 479.

33 Or, potentially, the majority confession. In this context one may find interesting the example of the Abraham Ecumenical Centre built for the 1992 Summer Olympics in Barcelona. There, the space that was originally meant to serve different Christian denominations, Islam, Buddhism, and Judaism was converted at the end of the event into the Catholic Church of the Patriarch Abraham through the addition of the crosses to the building's façade. See Courtney Bender, "Abraham Centre/Parroquia Patriarcha Abraham," SSRC

universal access and does not acknowledge the power of symbols. Its attempts at creating a mechanical solution for transforming the space, like turntable altars or washing facilities that can be hidden, often risks being "theatrical, expensive and potentially comic."[34] In contrast, if executed poorly, the negative design risks becoming meaningless and appealing "only to those who follow the *via negativa*."[35] As stated in the above-mentioned quote, that is the fallacy to which most existing spaces adhere.

The distinction between positive and negative spaces is significant for this book because, as Crompton notes, these design approaches come from two different understandings of religion. He writes:

> Whether one takes the positive or negative approach depends upon what one supposes the gods to be. If they are taken to be a surface upon which we project our social needs and interests, then mixing religions is analogous to mixing cultures and the positive approach is appropriate. In that case multi-faith spaces should be … rooted in one tradition but open to all in a spirit of hospitality. How affairs are arranged between rival users is a matter for casuistry.
>
> Alternatively, those who believe that their God is real, but, in a spirit of tolerance, recognize that others may hold the same opinion of theirs, will treat multi-faith spaces as places where a free choice is made among real alternatives. Time-sharing an empty room is then the equitable solution. Here sacred symbols are taken seriously. Paradoxically the refusal to display them in a public space acknowledges their power.[36]

While I concur with Crompton that both designs have implicit understandings of religion, I do not entirely agree with his assessment. Instead, I suggest that there is a need to dig deeper in the search for what hides behind them. As an architect, Crompton focuses on the design of these spaces. However, as with the institutional context, the design of the space alone will not present a complete picture of the vision of religion behind it.

The distinction between the positive and negative could be conceptualized regarding the design and the effect. A multi-faith space with a negative design within the institutional context will have a different effect than one outside of

Forums, 2014, accessed 17th of November, 2021, http://forums.ssrc.org/ndsp/2014/08/04/abraham-centreparroquia-patriarcha-abraham/.

34 Crompton, "The Architecture of Multi-faith," 484.

35 Crompton, "The Architecture of Multi-faith," 484.

36 Crompton, "The Architecture of Multi-faith," 480.

it. As I will show in the analysis of concrete multi-faith spaces in the following two sections, inside an institution, if multi-faith spaces constitute the only place for religious observance, the negative design will subtract, limiting the possibilities for kinds of religiosity allowable. Outside institutional context, multi-faith spaces add a new possibility on top of the existing ones, regardless of their design. Thus, I differentiate between the spaces that subtract and those that add.

2.3 *Spaces That Subtract*

In those places, where multi-faith spaces make up the only place where religiosity can take place, multi-faith spaces subtract. When one is waiting on a plane, has a short break between university classes, or is awaiting treatment in a hospital room, multi-faith spaces often constitute the only place where religion is allowed. Their design will instruct and limit the religiosity that can take place within its constraints. Thus, what they subtract is of crucial importance to our analysis. By analyzing what is subtracted in those spaces, one can see the tendencies in approaching religion that hide behind them. We can better understand what kind of religiosity is preferred and what is discouraged. As I will argue, by dedicating a separate room for religion, multi-faith spaces often subtract religion from other places within the institution. By focusing on minimal, neutral design, they subtract visible manifestations of religiosity. They also limit the possible exercise of belief to individual, internal practices such as contemplation or meditation, and pose silent prayer as the "proper" activity for believers.

As mentioned earlier, in Europe, multi-faith spaces within public institutions underwent a certain degree of institutionalization. They are no longer tied only to chaplains but can be introduced by various agents for various reasons. Regardless of those reasons, however, they must adapt to those institutions' logic and, sometimes, also direct government recommendations. This leads to a certain level of standardization. As already mentioned in the introduction to this book, motivations and intentions are of lesser importance than the established models. In most cases, these spaces follow the same negative design and are remarkably similar between different European countries. Analyzing four concrete cases may help us better understand how they are organized and furnished in different institutions in countries with different historical, cultural, and religious backgrounds.

In Poland, a country with a still-fresh communist past and relatively high (if waning)[37] levels of religious observance and affiliation to the Catholic Church,

37 Marcin Przeciszewski and Rafał Łączny, *Kościół w Polsce*, Katolicka Agencja Informacyjna (Warszawa, 2021), https://ekai.pl/wp-content/uploads/2021/03/Raport-Kosciol-w-Polsce-2021.pdf.

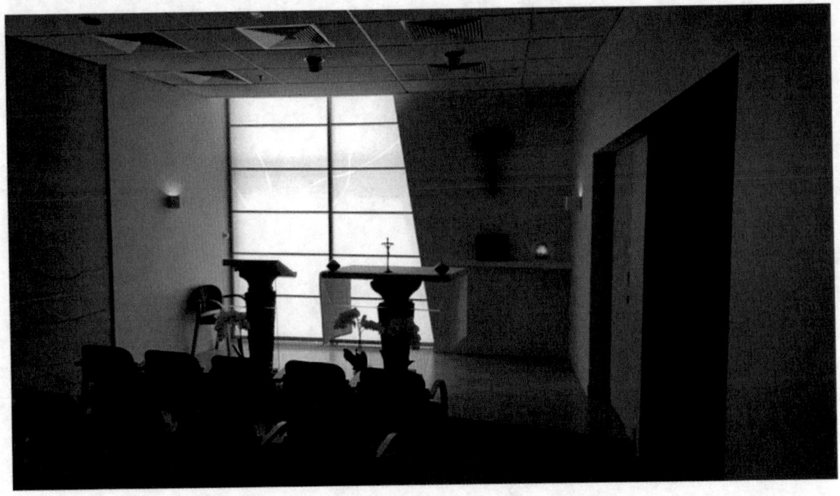

FIGURE 1 Warsaw Chopin Airport chapel (Altar)
SOURCE: USED WITH KIND PERMISSION BY AUTHOR

FIGURE 2 Warsaw Chopin Airport chapel (Wall)
SOURCE: USED WITH KIND PERMISSION BY AUTHOR

a country which is viewed by many as the anti-thesis to the secularization thesis,[38] the Warsaw Chopin Airport, one of the country's most important transportation hubs, has two chapels, one of which (in Terminal A) is described as ecumenical. The chapel itself has a typical Christian setting: Christian

38 See, for example, José Casanova, *Public Religions in the Modern World* (Chicago and London: The University of Chicago Press, 1994).

FIGURE 3 Warsaw Chopin Airport room for all denominations
SOURCE: USED WITH KIND PERMISSION BY AUTHOR

newspapers and brochures by the entrance and a mass schedule; one wall covered by a giant image of Christ; a few rows of chairs directed towards the altar; a small shrine devoted to Mary, Patron of Airmen, with an image of the pope sitting in the aircraft, and a book for prayer intentions; half of the wall behind the altar has a visible cross and a tabernacle with the Eucharist (see Figures 1 and 2).

However, the wall with the face of Christ separates the chapel from another room—a separate space next door "for passengers of all religions and denominations" (see Figure 3).[39] It is a rectangular room with white walls, neutral wooden elements, bland lights, and a light carpet. One wall is made of opaque glass panels with light behind them. The floor has two levels to provide space for, for example, guided meditations. There are three chairs next to the wall—the only element of the room that is not fixed.[40]

Let us move about 650 kilometers north-west to Lund and its university. We find a remarkably similar space in the Centre for Languages and Literature building close to the university library. Although this space is situated in Sweden, a country that could be considered significantly different from Poland

39 Lotnisko Chopina, "Chaplaincy," 2021, accessed 8th of October, 2021, https://www.lotnisko-chopina.pl/en/chaplaincy.html.

40 Interestingly, the two rooms are connected in multiple ways. They can be joined by folding the wall with Christ's face. They are also linked by the opaque glass wall, as it continues from the prayer room to half of the altar wall in the chapel. Both rooms also have similar sliding, tinted glass doors opened with a click of a button. In a way, this could be considered symbolic for the relations between the majority and minority traditions.

FIGURE 4 Stilla rum at SOL building, Lund University
SOURCE: USED WITH KIND PERMISSION BY AUTHOR

in terms of religious heritage, with a strong Lutheran background, and which is seen as one of the most secularized in the world, it is hard to find many differences between it and the two room in Warsaw. This space in Sweden is called *Stilla Rum*, a Quiet Room. It is harder to find than the one at the Polish airport. One needs to follow the inconspicuous signs through several corridors to locate the space in the remote part of the building's basement. The room is rectangular, with white walls, gray carpet, fluorescent lighting, and some sitting space close to one wall. Instead of a wall of opaque glass, it has abstract art on three glass panels with lighting above them (see Figure 4).

In the United Kingdom, a country whose colonial notion of Commonwealth required significant efforts in managing religious pluralism, close to the motorway in Lancashire, two rooms on the opposite sites of the Rivington Services duplicate the same design—empty, rectangular space with white walls and fluorescent lighting (but a darker carpet for a change).

In one of the recently built hospitals in Barcelona, instead of introducing a chapel as in the old building, a new *sala multiconfesional*, a multi-faith space, has been introduced. As Anna Clot-Garrell and Mar Griera described it, the room is as empty as possible to be, in the eyes of the administration, as neutral as possible and suitable for all users. Again, it is a narrow rectangular room with white walls and no apparent design or architectural inclination.[41]

41 Anna Clot-Garrell and Mar Griera, "Las salas multiconfesionales en el contexto hospitalario catalán: negociaciones y tensiones en la gestión de la diversidad," *Salud Colectiva* 14, no. 2 (2018): 295, https://doi.org/10.18294/sc.2018.1534.

Four countries in four different corners of Europe and four different institutional contexts (airport, university, motorway, and hospital) share a remarkably similar approach to multi-faith—unity by exclusion. That, however, does not mean that these spaces are neutral. What they subtract is significant.

To make this consideration more concrete, one may go back to the exercise from the beginning of this book. Imagine one of these spaces. How do they make you feel? Do they fit your expectations of such a space? How about your needs? If the task is to stand or sit and silently contemplate/meditate/pray, these spaces are well equipped for the purpose. But now imagine the situation of those who do not fit into this pattern. Imagine that you need a prayer mat and a specific direction to pray. Will it not make you feel awkward if others are also in the space? What if you need to pray aloud—will you not disturb others in the space? How about if you want to use the space with others—will it not be seen as "taking over" of the space by others? What if candles are essential in your ritual? Or if you need washing facilities for ritual ablution? What if you need any physical objects—would you be comfortable taking them out (if you brought them yourself) and putting them out in the open in that space?[42]

As I argued before, these spaces have an implicit understanding of religion inscribed into them, and the spaces described above help us define what that understanding is. First, by having a dedicated room for all religions, religion can be implicitly or explicitly subtracted from all other places in the building. The dedication of one room to religion implicitly suggests that the rest of the space is meant for other activities. It also makes it easier for the institutional management to actively relegate all religious behavior to this one space. Of course, the design and placement cannot on their own warrant this conclusion. Thus, further investigation into the policy and perception of multi-faith spaces is needed, which will follow in the next chapter.

Second, by removing religious symbols and artifacts, these spaces subtract visible, external manifestations of religiosity. Thus, they show a certain preference for an internalized religiosity and one that is, at least locally, iconoclastic. We will not even find religious texts in the abovementioned spaces, which is not true for all multi-faith spaces. For example, in the Retreat Room at the Southern Campus of the University of Copenhagen or in the multi-faith spaces at the Gatwick London Airport, one can find religious texts placed on a shelf or in a cupboard. The texts, however, unlike symbols, turn us towards a cognitive, rather than ritualistic, character of beliefs. The lack of external differentiation

42 Biddington, *Multi-faith Space*, 106–07. offers a helpful general overview of different needs.

combined with inviting people of different beliefs may also suggest hope for syncretism, possibly a catch-all spirituality,[43] although it does not warrant it.

Third, because the spaces are small, the size of a room, with seating for up to three people, they encourage individual and private prayer, meditation, or contemplation.

Fourth, they encourage a certain type of religious observance—silent prayer—as a proper activity for all religious people. Bender puts it, questioning the inherent assumptions:

> not only [multi-faith spaces] seek to put people from different religions under the same roof, but … they expect them all to do something that can be called prayer. Why and when did we decide that "prayer" (or its cognate "prayer and reflection") signals something that all religious people might wish to do, that requires special space, and that is benign enough to take place across a wide range of secular settings?[44]

Thus, these rooms encourage, and sometimes even impose, a specific type of religiosity—individual, private, internalized, iconoclastic, cognitive, and prayer-oriented. Rather than offering a neutral, all-inclusive space, they express a legible preference—the institutional logic of catering to all thus risks losing all that do not fit into the room's features.

Many of these features follow the same lines discussed in previous chapters. The similarity of different multi-faith spaces points to an implementation of a top-down model rather than an organic development. At the same time, their character represents a reductive vision of religion stripped to what is viewed as essential. In line with the notion of individual emancipation discussed based on Marx in Chapter 1, these spaces primarily focus on individuals, limiting the interest in their collective identity. Focused on the cognitive aspects of religion, internal and private practice, and positing silent prayer as the proper form of religious observance, they could be considered an expression of Protestant bias. By limiting religion to a secluded room and limiting individuals' exposure to the religiosity of others, these rooms also seem to embrace the view of religion as something potentially dangerous, imposing a degree of control over it.

---

43 See Sophie Gilliat-Ray, "'Sacralising' Sacred Space in Public Institutions: A Case Study of the Prayer Space at the Millennium Dome," *Journal of Contemporary Religions*, no. 20 (2005): 367, https://doi.org/10.1080/13537900500249921.

44 Bender, "The Architecture of Multi-faith Prayer: An Introduction."

The imbalance between different religions becomes even more pronounced in cases like Warsaw Chopin Airport. There, a space for the majority confession is set next to the multi-faith space. A similar case in a different setting can be found, for example, at the Istanbul Airport, where a mosque and 44 Islamic prayer rooms are accompanied by just three all-inclusive multi-faith spaces.[45] In both cases, a majority confession is entirely catered to, while everyone else stands before a test of adherence to legible standards. If they fulfill them, they may practice their religion. Otherwise, there is no place for them. In this, one can see in a concrete example the same dynamic of marked and unmarked as described in Chapter 3. The legible majority confessions are given a significant degree of leeway. All other religious presence is marked and strictly controlled within the confines of a limited amount of space to lower the exposure. It can function within the public space only in narrowly defined ways.

Such an understanding of religion has been raised to the level of art in a master thesis project in architecture at the University of Udine, highlighting central planning in the negative design. *Nova project—multi faith space* by Davide Bottos and Elena Calabrò created three rectangular units out of stark white honeycomb cardboard placed in the Scientific Center of Rizzi court. Completely empty inside, the rooms received external light via the openings in one wall. The authors write in the description:

> For each studied religious beliefs we were able to synthesize the major movements of the body, obtaining the minimum spatial units. The numbers of units of this project are the result of a careful analysis and synthesizing of the main elements that are common to all worship places analysed.
>
> The analysis led us to the functional identification, with breakdown thereafter, of individual volumes that characterize all the places of worship. From this breakdown we were able to identify three recurrent volumes: a classroom that connects and hosts collective religious practices; a smaller and intimate volume, like a crypt, where to settle the icon, holy books, or religious symbols, and finally a vertical element, that connects the faithful and the divinity, as well as an eye-catcher to the true duties of the faithful.[46]

---

45 Istanbul Airport, "Prayer Rooms," 2021, accessed 17th of November, 2021, https://www.istairport.com/en/passenger/services/airport-services/prayer-rooms.

46 Davide Bottos and Elena Calabrò, "Nova project - Multi faith space," Divisare, 2016, accessed 8th of October, 2021, https://divisare.com/projects/325458-davide-bottos-elena-calabro-nova-project-multi-faith-space.

Although highly sophisticated, the project by Bottos and Calabrò offers a full explication of the legible religion approach discussed in part 1. Bottos and Calabrò reduced religiosity to what seemed essential from their point of view. They created an engineered multi-faith space based on a detailed study of the model versions of different religions, with spaces measured to allow the standard religious practices, leaving no place for innovation. They comprehended religion as something static and stable, the operations of which can be planned entirely from the outset.

While seemingly bland, minimalistic, and neutral, the institutional multi-faith spaces following the negative design are not inconsequential. Quite the opposite; they introduce a clear preference for a specific type of religiosity—individual, private, internalized, iconoclastic, cognitive, and prayer-oriented. These features are imposed on everyone, or at least on those who do not belong to majority confessions, underlining the difference between banal and unbanal, marked and unmarked. While the majority confession is sometimes allowed more leeway by virtue of being banal, all other religions are controlled and prevented from being practiced if not fitting into the set standards. The spaces also express a level of central planning in their design, as most visible in the architectural project by Bottos and Calabrò. They follow the principles of legible religion.

2.4 *Spaces That Add*

While multi-faith spaces have been institutionalized and, at least to a certain extent, standardized within public institutions, they do not face the same constraints outside of the institutional context. Multi-faith spaces outside of institutions do not subtract as much as intra-institutional spaces do. If introduced outside of secular institutions, both negative and positive designs can make up novel, creative solutions for coexistence in the conditions of religious pluralism. What becomes more important in a non-institutional context for the understandings of religion behind multi-faith spaces is what these spaces add to the pool of existing solutions and what logic these additions follow. To answer these questions, I have selected four examples of extra-institutional spaces: *Ceremonirummet* in Copenhagen, Denmark, a section of the *Stora Tuna Kyrkogård* in Borlänge, Sweden, *House of One* in Berlin, Germany, and *Guds Hus* in Fisksättra, Sweden. These spaces have been chosen to represent different aspects of standalone spaces: negative and positive design; spaces in development and those already finished and functioning; spaces initiated by secular individuals, and spaces led by religious leaders; spaces sponsored by the state, and those with no state involvement.

Ceremonirummet refers to conceptual plans rather than a finished space. Unfortunately, the municipality of Copenhagen rejected the proposal to build it despite strong, grassroots backing[47] sustained even years later.[48] Nonetheless, it has been fully conceptualized and designed, showcasing a potential type of standalone multi-faith space in the urban context.

The space has been designed by a Danish architectural company, *Svendborg Architects*. As a result of the bottom-up initiative, this space responded to the perceived need for a space for non-religious and those not belonging to major traditions; an alternative place to the church or the town hall in which to celebrate rites of passage.[49] Placed in a part of the existing columbarium and water tower at Bispebjerg Cemetery, close to plots dedicated to people of faiths other than Christianity, the circular building of glass and bare concrete would offer a spectacle of light and surrounding nature. The architects write in their description of the proposal:

> The Ceremony Room takes its setting within the rising diversity of Danish society. As our modern society grows, more and more people wish to hold life ceremonies outside the traditional framing of the state church and adjust the experience to their individual ideology. The Ceremony Room is about creating a neutral architecture in a context with a dignified, solemn setting that can include all people regardless of their faith, belief, or spirituality.[50]

Ceremonirummet is an interesting example of a negative design operating outside secular public institutions. Relying on its context and the surrounding nature, it followed many of the same minimalist design principles, involving raw architectural materials, such as concrete and glass. The architects understand this design approach as inclusive and neutral, while the space creators

47 Mette Skov Hansen, "København siger nej til neutralt ceremonirum," *Kristeligt Dagblad*, 14th of September 2016, https://www.kristeligt-dagblad.dk/kirke-tro/koebenhavn-siger-nej-til-neutralt-ceremonirum.

48 Anna Balk Møller, "Der er behov for alternative ceremonirum i Danmark," *Politiken*, 18th of December 2018, https://politiken.dk/debat/kroniken/art6874853/Der-er-behov-for-alternative-ceremonirum-i-Danmark; Anna Balk Møller, "Ti år med frivilligt arbejde. Giver det mening?," *Ceremonirum*, 26th of September, 2019, http://www.ceremonirum.dk/ti-aar-med-frivilligt-arbejde-giver-det-mening/. The CeremoniRum group constantly advocates for its creation since 2009 when it was formed. See http://www.ceremonirum.dk/

49 Louise Voller, "Ceremonier uden religion til folk, der lever uden Gud," *Information* 2008, https://www.information.dk/kultur/2008/08/ceremonier-uden-religion-folk-lever-uden-gud.

50 Svendborg Architects, "Ceremony Room in Existing Buildings," 2021, accessed 15th of September, 2021, http://www.svendborgarchitects.dk/Ceremony-Room-Existing-Buildings.

view *Ceremonirummet* as a response to the pluralization of society. Despite these similarities to the intra-institutional spaces, the effect of this space would be different. Unlike intra-institutional spaces, it would not replace the church or other temples but supplement them, offering an alternative to those who want to use it at their discretion.

While *Ceremonirummet* has remained in the conceptual phase, the other spaces described below are either works in progress or have already been finished. *Stora Tuna Kyrkogård* is a graveyard located next to the historically significant *Stora Tuna* church in the Borlänge municipality in Central Sweden. Both the church and the cemetery were established as early as the thirteenth century and continue to play a vital role in the life of the local parish. In 2016, Borlänge received increased media coverage by opening the country's first religiously neutral cemetery in an empty part of the church's area. Although run by the Church of Sweden, which retained the responsibility for burial places in Sweden after the formal split of the state and church in 2000, it is supposed to be open to people regardless of their convictions and beliefs. The only requirement to get a plot is to refrain from using any religious or ideological symbols on gravestones.[51] The new space was an initiative of a local teacher and councilor, Josef Erdem. He saw the need for such a space both among the native Swedes and those who, like Erdem, migrated to the country and do not identify with the major traditions. These are the people who do not have dedicated burial places.[52]

Similar to *Ceremonirummet*, the religiously neutral section of *Stora Tuna Kyrkogård* could be considered an example of a negative design, as it subtracts something visually. However, it differs significantly from the spaces discussed so far. It has no inherent design itself. It relies on the design choices proposed by individuals responsible for burials. It operates only on the rule that it rejects any religiously- or ideologically-infused symbols. This changes the character of the space, providing a sense of grassroots development rather than a top-down pronouncement. Again, the negative design does not have the same implications as it would in an intra-institutional context. It does not replace the space of the majority confession, nor the minority ones. It functions as an optional

51 An interesting and in some ways similar case in the North American context, and connected to the problems of religious freedom, is discussed in Winnifred Fallers Sullivan, *The Impossibility of Religious Freedom*. (New Jersey: Princeton University Press, 2018).

52 Linda Mankefors, "Här får de neutrala den sista vilan," *dt.se*, 23rd of September 2016, https://www.dt.se/artikel/har-far-de-neutrala-den-sista-vilan.

alternative to these. It responds to a particular need voiced by a specific part of society.[53]

While the former two spaces operate on negative design, the next two focus on the positive one. After ten years of envisioning, visualizing, designing, and a global fundraising campaign, the cornerstone of the House of One was laid on the 27th of May 2021. An initiative of three religious leaders working in Berlin, minister Gregor Hohberg, imam Kadir Sanci, and rabbi Tovia BenChorin, the building in construction is supposed to house three temples under one roof: a church, a mosque, and a synagogue joined by a shared hallway.

The building is multi-faith in two principal ways. First, the whole building can be considered multi-faith, as it houses temples of three religions. Second, the actual multi-faith space is in the middle of the building, in the structure's hallway, where believers of the three religions are supposed to meet and mingle.

The multi-faith space follows a positive design with a visible representation of faiths included in the project. Interestingly, as other positive spaces described by Crompton, it could be considered placed within a former building of the majority confession. While constructed from the ground, the building is raised on the foundations of the thirteenth-century *Petrikirche* destroyed during the Second World War and removed during the GDR era.

The project also has specific goals in mind. The project initiators write on their website:

> In Berlin, where once religious emancipation and enlightenment became a European project through the friendship of Lessing and Moses Mendelssohn, where in 1989 the "iron curtain" fell by the power of words and the power of non-violent resistance, the House of One will be a place where the coexistence of religions is lived peacefully, in great openness and appreciation of diversity.[54]

The project then is viewed as both symbolic and exemplary. It symbolizes the rich history and hope for an equally prosperous future of peaceful religious coexistence. It aims to serve as an example of diversity that functions well.

53 The claim to neutrality of both examples, however, and their proposed all-inclusiveness posed some challenges in their reception. For more, see Ryszard Bobrowicz and Jakob Wirén, "Cemeteries as Spaces of Interreligious Encounter? The Use of Different Types of Neutrality in the Context of Graveyards in Scandinavia," *International Journal of Public Theology* 17, no. 4 (2023), https://doi.org/10.1163/15697320-20230106.

54 House of One, "The Concept" 2019, accessed 18th of November, 2021, https://house-of-one.org/en/concept.

In these goals, the project allied with the German state, especially the federal government, whose different branches are among the top sponsors of the project. The cornerstone has been laid by the President of the Bundestag, Wolfgang Schäuble, who, as *The Guardian* reported, "called it a 'location of tolerance and openness,' which he said had the 'theological aspiration to be open to other spiritual perspectives with equal respect.' He stressed the importance of the project to promote dialogue between the religions and to fight fanaticism and violence."[55] In Schäuble's comments, one may see traces of the functionalized approach. He views the project as playing a specific role—promoting interreligious dialogue and the fight with fanaticism and violence. In other words, it is an example of thinking about religion as a force for social cohesion.

Like the other standalone spaces, the House of One is not obligatory or replacing any existing possibilities. Instead, it is a novel alternative to more traditional, mono-confessional temples and thus supplements the urban religious environment of Berlin.

The last example I want to consider here is *Guds Hus* in Fisksätra near Stockholm. *Guds Hus* has functioned successfully since 2003, joining three religious communities, the Parish of Nacka, part of the majority Church of Sweden, the Roman Catholic Church Diocese of Stockholm, and the Association of Muslims in Nacka. The website of the project states that in the *Guds Hus* building, one may "meet people from different ethnic, linguistic, cultural, religious, and social realities."[56] Thus, *Guds Hus* provides a space for "cross-border cooperation" and it functions as a learning center for how to live with diversity.[57]

Like the House of One, *Guds Hus* is a formerly mono-confessional space that opened to others.[58] While the building remains a Christian Church, the plot next to the church has been allocated for a new mosque. Again, the place in between the two temples, envisioned as a glass atrium, is supposed to serve as the proper multi-faith space, hosting the joint events of all three communities involved.

Despite the similarities of background and design, *Guds Hus* differs in some regard from the House of One. First, the Swedish project does not receive the

---

55 Kate Connolly, "'House of One': Berlin lays first stone for multi-faith worship centre," *The Guardian*, 27th of May 2021, https://www.theguardian.com/world/2021/may/27/berlin-lays-first-stone-for-multi-faith-house-of-one-worship-centre.

56 Guds Hus, "God's House. Where people meet," 2020, accessed 12th of March, 2020, http://gudshus.se/en/.

57 Guds Hus, "God's House. Where people meet."

58 The two project are even partners: House of One, "Guds Hus—Our Partner Project in Sweden," 2019, accessed 18th of November, 2021, https://house-of-one.org/en/news/guds-hus-%E2%80%93-our-partner-project-sweden.

same degree of state support. The state is not mentioned among the major donors, and no active government representatives are visible among supporting voices. Second, it has more of an organic character, starting from the joint celebrations of two local communities joined by the third, rather than an initiative of religious leaders. As the website reads:

> Christians and Muslims have collaborated for many years in Fisksätra. The organized cooperation began at Pentecost 2003 when about 60 people from the Lutheran Nacka Parish and the Muslims Association in Nacka met for common prayers on the local soccer field. This event became the kickoff for the interfaith dialogue with regular conversations and gatherings both in the church and the basement mosque.
>
> St. Konrad's Catholic Parish has celebrated Sunday Mass in Fisksätra Church for several years and joined the cooperation, together with Stockholm City Mission, when the advice and support center Källan was opened in 2008.[59]

Thus, the building is a further step in the collaboration of three local communities rather than the core of the project.

Despite these differences, there are traces of functional thinking present in the project's self-understanding. *Guds Hus's* website describes the project as "one of integration and inclusion and builds on religion as a resource in the community that can help heal the divisions in Swedish society."[60] *Guds Hus* is meant to "enrich ... cultural community life and help [people] unite to face challenges and offer moments of tranquility, reflection, and recovery from the strain of every-day life."[61] Finally, it works "for xenophilia and to strengthen religious freedom."[62] Again, the notion of social cohesion and the functional relevance of religious collaboration is critical in the project's vision, even if its roots are focused on local collaborations and encounters.

All these spaces pick something up from the four historical examples mentioned earlier. They all have a symbolic value, highlighting the change in society, yet all aim to address a pragmatic need. The symbol-neutral cemetery and *Ceremonirummet* symbolize unity by subtracting visible manifestations of religious affiliation, while the House of One and *Guds Hus* take precedence from

59 Guds Hus, "Om Guds Hus," 2020, accessed 12th of March, 2020, https://gudshus.se/en/om-guds-hus/.

60 Guds Hus, "Om Guds Hus."

61 Guds Hus, "Om Guds Hus."

62 Guds Hus, "Om Guds Hus."

the multi-faith space in Utrecht and provide "identity spaces" for each of the involved groups. Each of these spaces adds something new to the existing picture. *Ceremonirummet* was meant as an alternative to celebrate rites of passage in the conditions of increasing diversity to all those who did not belong to the majority confession. Whether its negative design is neutral remains a question. However, it was not meant to include everyone *per se* but to address the increasing need for individualization of rituals beyond the existing tradition. The religiously neutral, or, maybe more adequately, religiously agnostic cemetery next to *Stora Tuna* church also used a negative design to offer an alternative to all those who do not identify themselves with any of the majority traditions that already had their areas in the existing cemeteries. Thus, while the negative design of these spaces limited their potential "clientele," they did not subtract any of the options but added new alternatives on top of the existing ones.

The positive spaces have a different focus. Each of them aims to represent peaceful coexistence, appreciation of diversity, and openness to others. They are supposed to represent positive examples of how to approach ethnic, linguistic, cultural, religious, and social diversity. In this context, it is interesting that each of them operates only on religious majorities and either contemporarily or historically most significant minorities: Christianity, Judaism, and Islam in the House of One and Lutheranism, Catholicism, and Islam in *Guds Hus*. Part of the justification behind that might be the notion of Abrahamic religions, the notion that these religious communities spring from a common root.[63] Another interpretation, however, could be that the majority confession plays a similar role to that of majority confession chaplains. Especially in the Swedish case, extending the invitation to use their space by the Lutheran majority parish to two minority groups could be viewed as a form of redistribution of resources. It could also extend the majority confession's banality, legitimizing the whole project, justifying the operation of marked religious communities, and providing a sense of security, however limited, for the authorities. Regardless of the degree to which this interpretation is adequate, both spaces add a new example of religious coexistence that could be considered justifying the role of religious communities in developing social cohesion. Both projects present religion as a potential place where cross-border coalitions may be built.

While quite diverse, I would argue that these "additive" multi-faith spaces also play into the logic of legible religion, although to a lesser extent than the

63 For a discussion of the notion of Abrahamic religions and some of its problems, see Aaron W. Hughes, *Abrahamic Religions: On the Uses and Abuses of History* (Oxford: Oxford University Press, 2012).

institutional spaces. While each comes from a different set of goals and intentions, their features support some principles of legibility described in earlier chapters. The extra-institutional spaces with a negative design support the notion of individualization of religious identity. They add an alternative that follows the same legible tropes that the subtracting spaces. However, it does not impose them. Access is granted by a "translation" into their terms, in line with Habermas as discussed in Chapter 3. They are also not an expression of the state's approach per se. Rather, they show how ingrained legible religion principles are in a broader consciousness.

The extra-institutional spaces with positive design, on the other hand, differ more significantly from the previously described examples. They are more in line with the notion that religion can be functionally relevant. They view religion as a significant source of identity and therefore are less in line with Marx than with Comte, as discussed in Chapter 1. They represent a functional outlook on religion as a source of social cohesion. Crossing religious boundaries, they show that all involved religious traditions can be in line with specific civil values, such as tolerance, inclusion, or openness. The House of One has explicit ties to the state. As shown by *Guds Hus*, they can even be learning sites for others.

2.5 *The Many Faces of Legibility*

By combining the distinction into institutional and extra-institutional with those of positive and negative design, I differentiated between the spaces that add and subtract.

Several features characterize spaces that subtract. The most typical ones are (1) usually the only spaces where religion can be practiced within the confines of the institution (exclusive), (2) they result from a managerial action, introduced in a top-down approach (top-down), (3) they express a specific policy towards religion, either as its direct implementation, indirect reproduction, or architectural adaptation (centralized), and (4) they are bound to a particular institutional context and constrained by it (institutionalized). They are then institutionalized, exclusive, top-down, and centralized. Finally, as most of them employ a negative design, their materiality and placement express a preference towards specific religiosity, one that is individual, private, internalized, iconoclastic, cognitive, and prayer-oriented.

Spaces that add are quite different in their features: (1) these spaces exist outside of the secular institutions and are not constrained by the institutional logic, (extra-institutional) (2) they all have a supplementary character—they are one choice among many, adding to the existing rather than the only facility available within a specific space, (supplementary) (3) the presented examples showed that they result from grassroots negotiations, either brought entirely from the bottom-up or from the local leadership, rather than a result of the top-down planning (grassroots), and (4) they are local, responding to the needs and background of a particular community (local). Thus, they are extra-institutional, supplementary, grassroots, and local.

Based on their design, one can differentiate two types of spaces that add: those that follow a negative design and those that follow the positive one. The negative spaces support the individualization of religious identity, offering new alternatives to the existing ones. However, the negative design in their case also expresses a preference for the individual, private, internalized, iconoclastic, cognitive, and prayer-oriented religiosity—even if their supplementary character weakens the impact of that preference. In contrast, spaces that follow the positive design aim to exemplify peaceful coexistence and appreciation of diversity. By that, they are posited as vehicles for social cohesion.

If analyzed from the perspective of the legible religion framework, these different roles that multi-faith spaces play highlight the previously outlined approaches to religion: control and either indifference or rejection, on the one hand, and functionalization on the other. Within the spaces that subtract, control dominates. Religion is tightly controlled by being confined in multi-faith spaces. Religions that fit into the legible framework or are willing to translate their broader observance into its constraints are treated with indifference. The dynamics of banal and unbanal sometimes allow the majority confession to introduce their own confessional spaces next to the multi-faith ones, although that depends on the context. All other religions are rejected or at least under suspicion. The spaces that add have milder effects. Those following the positive design offer new alternatives, expressing, but not imposing, a legible preference. In the case of spaces with positive design, a functional approach leads, framing religion as a potential "hero" of social cohesion.

Of course, not all spaces look like those described in this section. These generalizations allow us to look for tendencies in approaching religion behind multi-faith spaces. Nevertheless, these tendencies do not remain uncontested. An extra-institutional context already demonstrated quite a divergence based on the four examples presented, and more could be developed. Similarly, in the institutional context, one can find examples that do not fit neatly into the above-described typology, for example, Room of Silence in Utrecht, which follows a moderately positive design, or places that provide several rooms side by side.[64]

64 Francisco Díez de Velasco, *Multi-belief/Multi-faith Spaces: Theoretical Proposals for a Neutral and Operational Design*, RECODE Working Paper Series (Augsburg, 2014), https://www.recode.info/wp-content/uploads/2014/01/FINAL-26-D%C3%ADez-de-Velasco_fin.pdf.

Not all multi-faith spaces also express any legible preference. For example, my visit to the Yarl's Wood Immigration Detention Centre[65] provided me with a perspective on an alternative. There, a multi-faith team of ten chaplains created a whole contemplation center—a series of spaces in which each faith received a separate room specifically adapted to the needs of its users and accompanied by personalized spiritual care and communal activities. The chaplains aimed to create a vibrant faith community and were quite proud of these attempts. One of them, Reverend Larry Wright, writes in a blog post:

> In our society where religion is essentially a private affair we do not feel confident to talk of matters of belief; in Yarl's Wood the reverse is true. Most detainees have an active and vibrant faith and their detention intensifies their religious experience. In detention they do not suffer the distractions of every day life; there is more time to think, pray, reflect and seek answers to their situation. Yarl's Wood can feel like a school of prayer, indeed it is a place where prayer is powerfully present. With a large African population the exuberance, passion, and sheer volume of the worship is something to behold. Our weekday services are accompanied by drumming, dancing, clapping and tambourines, also tears of despair and joy. It is also a place where the prayer spaces are sought out for their silence and serenity. They provide a sacred area where the fearful and anxious may sit for long periods in silent awareness of God, heartfelt prayer or contemplate their scriptures. In such an environment they experience a deepening dependence upon God and seek divine reassurance and enfolding.[66]

This is of course a self-report of one of the chaplains who organize religious life in that institution and thus presents a subjective understanding of the situation. Nonetheless, it points to different thinking behind Yarl's Wood chaplaincy provisions. Instead of reducing religion only to the aspects deemed relevant by the administrative representative of the institution, religion is viewed as an inherent part of everyday life. The self-description does not contain any mention of control or functionalization, which suggests that, at least in this sphere, they are lacking, creating a sphere of freedom in an institution that otherwise

65 Since 2020, the Centre is used for other purposes than detention due to years of rising criticism. See, for example, Danny Shaw, "Yarl's Wood: Years of misery and controversy," *BBC News*, 10th of June 2015, https://www.bbc.com/news/uk-33043395.

66 Larry Wright, "Faith in Dention," *This is Church*, 2005, http://www.thisischurch.com/christian_teaching/sermon/faithindentioneaster2005.htm.

epitomizes control. There seems to be an openness to religion, both in terms of individual and collective dimensions, and variety of forms. The expression "school of prayer" suggests that there is also an exchange of experiences and space for mutual learning.

Thus, not all multi-faith spaces have to operate in the dynamics of control and functionalization, banal and unbanal, marked and unmarked. As mentioned in the introduction, while legible religion may be hegemonic, it is not uncontested. It may be imbricated in our consciousness to the point that many of our efforts seem to be guided by it, yet alternative approaches still exist and thrive in the most unexpected places.

3 Multi-faith Spaces Embody Legible Religion

After many chapters of theoretical considerations, I have finally arrived at the concrete analysis of multi-faith spaces in this chapter. In the beginning, I have presented the two earliest examples of contemporary multi-faith spaces as the Temple of Religion and the UN Meditation Room, arguing that they set a standard for future spaces. Then, I have discussed the development of chaplaincy as a vehicle for taking multi-faith spaces into the mainstream. At first concerned with carving out space for religion within secular institutions as a response to the narratives of secularization, chaplains turned to multi-faith spaces as an alternative to confessional chapels during a shift to the return of religion. With institutionalization, however, multi-faith spaces broke free from chaplains and, in many cases, followed a standardized model.

Although multi-faith spaces are typically bound to an institutional context, this term also encompasses spaces from a non-institutional context. Thus, I argued that there is a need for a more precise typology to understand the tendencies of thinking about religion behind multi-faith spaces. By combining the differentiation of institutional and extra-institutional spaces and, building on Crompton, those that follow a positive and negative design, I have distinguished between spaces that add and those that subtract.

Spaces that add were extra-institutional, supplementary, grassroots, and local. Depending on their design, they supported individualization of religious identity (negative design) or functional treatment of religion as an agent of social cohesion (positive design). Spaces that subtract were institutionalized, exclusive, top-down, and centralized. Their exclusive character meant that their preference imposed, rather than simply proposed, a specific vision of religiosity that was allowed in the confines of these institutions: one that was individual, private, internalized, iconoclastic, cognitive, and prayer-oriented.

Around the considerations of the definition of multi-faith spaces, following the title of the extensive research project, I have mentioned that these spaces operate as symptoms and agents of social change. After the above considerations, this description could be more precise. Many multi-faith spaces operate as symptoms and agents of legible religion. Symptoms because they follow the preferences and approaches inherent in this conceptual framework. Agents because they either directly impose them, as with spaces that subtract and that institute control, or strengthen them, as with spaces that add.

As Kühle and Reintoft Christensen pointed out, the context of public institutions is especially important. Through that context, individuals encounter the state. In many cases, chaplains play an intermediary role between individuals and the state represented by the institutional management. However, chaplains may not always be involved, as other parties develop the increasing number of multi-faith spaces, for example, architects, building managers, and institutional management. Nonetheless, the interaction with intra-institutional multi-faith spaces gives individuals a clear impression of how the state approaches religion.

The intra-institutional context is also important because it has greater constraints and potentially generates more significant tensions. These tensions sometimes resulted in widely publicized controversies, discussed in the next chapter. While this chapter showed how the framework of legible religion impacts the spaces themselves, the next chapter will show how it shapes broader consciousness and is constitutive of broader social reality. The discussion of chaplains as the middle persons and the example of Yarl's Wood IDC demonstrated that the people involved and the environment around the spaces may be as crucial as the materiality of the spaces. How they are perceived is not inconsequential either.

CHAPTER 5

Regulating Religion in Public

The Importance of Context

At the beginning of the previous chapter, I described the main argument of this part of the book: that most multi-faith spaces embody the legible religion framework. In the previous chapter, I discussed two claims inherent in this broader argument by studying the history, design, and typology of multi-faith spaces. First, I argued that the materiality of the most typical multi-faith spaces expresses a preference for individual, private, internalized, iconoclastic, cognitive, and prayer-oriented religiosity. Second, by combining a design approach with contextual placement, I differentiated between the spaces that add and those that subtract, showing that different types of spaces express the legible approaches of control, indifference, and functionalization.

While such a typology may help analyze the potential effect of multi-faith spaces, I did not yet account for other factors that influence their perception. Multi-faith spaces do not exist in a vacuum. Quite the opposite; they operate in a social reality in which layers upon layers of interpretation shape how they are understood by those who approach them: from users, through managers, to politicians and policy makers. In this chapter, I am interested in the interrelation of legible religion and the context, policy, and perception of multi-faith spaces in higher education institutions in Western Europe. I argue that the conceptual framework of legible religion impacts the shape of the spaces themselves and the policies and perceptions surrounding them. On the one hand, the legible preference, as discussed in chapters 1 and 2, shapes the institutional policies in supporting one type of religiosity over others. On the other hand, the dynamic of banal and unbanal, and the interaction of the modalities of Christianity, secularism, and religious pluralism as discussed in Chapter 3, provide multiple meanings which can be imposed on the spaces regardless of their materiality.

The chapter will begin with several cases of conflicts around multi-faith spaces in three European countries. To allow for a comparison between cases, I have focused on one type of spaces to analyze their perception: university multi-faith spaces that follow the most typical, intra-institutional negative design. These cases will exemplify how relatively similar rooms may be perceived differently, depending on factors unrelated to their materiality.

These spaces, supported by additional examples when needed, will prove illustrative in the second part of this chapter. There, I will investigate where these differences in perception come from. I will analyze the naming, institutional context, policy approaches, and the dynamics of banality as they affect the university multi-faith spaces. This will conclude the analysis of multi-faith spaces and their relation to the conceptual framework of legible religion.

1 The Perception of Multi-faith Spaces

University multi-faith spaces in Europe usually exemplify a typical arrangement. Most often following a negative design, university spaces can be taken as a magnifying glass to approach the problems of multi-faith spaces because of the character of their users, management, and their role from the state's perspective. First, their primary users must commit for long periods, usually several years, to study in the specific space. Students spend much more time at the university campuses, going to classes, studying by themselves, socializing, and sometimes even living in the on-campus dormitories. This makes universities the primary space for students' habitation. Second, the university culture provides a space for different constellations of groups and communities. It encourages activism. Articulating needs and complaints is also perhaps more common at universities than at other institutions. Third, universities play a formational role, which causes a greater interest in exercising influence and control, both for internal management and the larger political discussions. Public universities, as state institutions, especially play the role of an interface between the individuals and the state as discussed in the earlier chapter. Finally, universities should point towards future directions, being the beacons of innovation. The public eye closely follows the developments inside them. They are both the testing ground and the battlefield where policy battles are fought.

The following cases from three European countries show where the lines of contestation are drawn and how differently similar spaces may be perceived. I have selected the cases to present a breadth of approaches and perspectives from different levels and users: from students, through university staff and management, to politicians and government officials. The cases will show that each of these stakeholders imposes their own meaning on the spaces and that their context is crucial in the process.

1.1 *Case 1: Protests in the United Kingdom*

In early spring 2010, a group of Muslim students started to pray on the streets of London in protest over the closure of their prayer room at the City University. The room was closed because of several attacks on Muslim students in November of the preceding year. The students were harassed in front of the building with the prayer room in what the police described as racist incidents.[1] A new multi-faith space replaced the former prayer room.

Multiple sides emerged in the debate. On the side of the university management, vice-chancellor Julius Weinberg stated that the provision of a dedicated room for a particular religious group of students was against the secular character of the institution and its values of non-discrimination.[2] The university spokeswoman pointed out that the university consulted Muslim scholars when arranging the new space and followed the examples of other higher education institutions. Additionally, the university made its great hall available for Friday prayer meetings.[3]

The users' voices were more divided. Some Muslim students were comfortable with the change and willing to use the provided room. Others, however, viewed the replacement as unjustified. The president of the university's Islamic Society, Saleh Patel, argued that the needs of some students were not considered. As he argued, Muslim students were forced to pray outside. He viewed it as most detrimental to female Muslims. As he said, the "prayer room used to be a place where they were comfortable and able to take off their veils."[4]

According to the report of *Times Higher Education*, the students declared three fundamental problems with the space. First, they viewed the multi-faith space as inadequate for prayer, as "a vast number of Muslim scholars throughout history believe it is impermissible for Muslims to offer prayers in a place where [a god] other than our Lord, Allah, is worshipped."[5] Second, they viewed the multi-faith space as impractical, providing space for up to 40 people, which was insufficient for the ritual observance of all Muslim students who had to use it for prayers at least three times per day at set hours. Third, the need to share the space between different faiths and societies would, in their view, inevitably lead to restriction of their activities "to the detriment of their beliefs and practices, naturally [leading to] a breakdown of good relations."[6]

The case of London City University exemplifies the effects of subtraction discussed in the previous chapter. A top-down replacement of a confessional

---

1 Stephen Bates, "Police investigate gang attack on Muslim students in London," *The Guardian*, 9th of November 2009, https://www.theguardian.com/uk/2009/nov/09/racist-attacks-students-city-university.

2 Poonam Taneja, "Prayer facility row at university," *BBC News*, 1st of April 2010, http://news.bbc.co.uk/2/hi/8598455.stm, news.bbc.co.uk

3 Melanie Newman, "Muslim students continue street protest over closure of prayer room," *Times Higher Education*, 16th of March 2010, https://www.timeshighereducation.com/news/muslim-students-continue-street-protest-over-closure-of-prayer-room/410874.article.

4 Taneja, "Prayer facility row at university."

5 Newman, "Muslim students continue."

6 Newman, "Muslim students continue."

space with a multi-faith space led to fierce opposition from some of its users, despite other accommodations, including the consultations of Muslim scholars and the provision of a bigger space for Friday prayer meetings. The imposition of inter-faith collaboration on the students was met with complete rejection by some of them, both on theological and pragmatic grounds. On top of that, it included the specific dynamic of the marked Islamic presence, aggravating the problem even further.[7] This led to the clashing of two visions with no space for negotiation—the university management's self-understanding as secular and non-discriminatory, and the Islamic Society's notion of being discriminated against, both in terms of religion and gender (showed by the comment on the lack of comfortable space for female Muslim students).

1.2 *Case 2: Closures in Germany*

In early 2016, some German universities began to close multi-faith spaces. In February, *Der Raum der Stille* at the Technical University of Dortmund was closed. The room had been an example of a typical negative design, with pastel green walls, light carpet, and sparse IKEA furnishings, including two armchairs and a bookshelf. Apart from a few cloths with abstract patterns and a nature motive on a roll-up, the room was devoid of symbolism or decoration. However, it had been split into two separate spaces by room dividers. The divisions in the space were contested—some female students complained that Muslim men instructed them only to use the smaller space in the room. The presence of prayer rugs and a Quran in the room was interpreted as violating the rules forbidding the placement of any religious symbols in the room. Eva Prost, the university press officer, said, "An attempt to create a supra-religious meditation room has failed … There will be no new attempt."[8]

After the closure of the room, the contestation increased. Four hundred students signed a petition protesting the decision and accusing the rectorate of discrimination. Because security was mentioned as the primary reason for

---

7 The clash between the university and the Islamic Society continued for years. See Jerome Taylor, "Muslim students take legal advice after City University shuts down Friday prayer meeting," *Independent*, 22nd of February 2013, https://www.independent.co.uk/news/uk/home-news/muslim-students-take-legal-advice-after-city-university-shuts-down-friday-prayer-meeting-8507166.html; Secunder Kermani, "City University London locks Muslim prayer room on Fridays," *BBC News*, 22nd of February 2013, https://www.bbc.com/news/uk-england-london-21542041; NUS Connect, "CULSU: Right To Pray," 2016, accessed 12th of December, 2021, https://www.nusconnect.org.uk/articles/culsu-right-to-pray.

8 Alexander Jürgs, "Kulturkampf um den „Raum der Stille" an der TU Dortmund," *Welt*, 12th of February 2016, https://www.welt.de/vermischtes/article152169223/Kulturkampf-um-den-Raum-der-Stille-an-der-TU-Dortmund.html.

closure, many Muslim students felt they were under general suspicion, put under the umbrella of radical Salafism and terrorism. It referred to the closure of a similar room in Bochum in 2012 due to suspicions of indoctrination and links to al-Qaeda of some of its users. Some of the Muslim students began to receive threatening and insulting emails. Even those who agreed with the decision, like the chairman of the university's General Student Committee (*Allgemeiner Studierendenausschuss der Technischen Universität Dortmund*), Moritz Kordisch, found the approach lacking. He said that "It is no longer about solutions, it is just about damage limitation."[9]

Similar moves followed at the Technical University of Berlin. There, the room was closed as an implication of the church—state separation and the changing conditions. The university president, Christian Thomsen, stated that the mosques were now much more accessible and, even if not within walking distance, they were just a couple of bus stations away.[10] A Muslim student interviewed by *Süddeutsche Zeitung* responded to the news by choosing a pragmatic solution—to pray wherever he could find a secluded or quiet space. In response, president Thomsen said, "One or two students praying in front of an office don't bother me," underlining that this is a part of "our pluralistic society."[11]

Not all universities closed their spaces entirely at that time. At the University of Duisburg-Essen, the former prayer room has been closed in favor of a multi-faith space. The published announcement stated that the university planned such replacement due to the shortage of space, denying that it was motivated by rumors or complaints about its users.[12] The announcement pointed out that the prayer room was set up in a different urban context when a smaller number of mosques were available in the city. The university no longer viewed it as possible to "create separate spatial facilities for all worldviews and beliefs." Thus, it had to introduce a multi-faith room instead.[13]

9 Jürgs, "Kulturkampf."

10 Raphael Warnke, "No space for Allah as German unis close prayer rooms," *The Local Germany*, 11th of March 2016, https://www.thelocal.de/20160311/no-place-for-allah-as-german-unis-close-prayer-rooms/.

11 Matthias Kohlmaier, "Kein Platz für Allah an deutschen Unis," *Süddeutsche Zeitung*, 9th of March 2016, https://www.sueddeutsche.de/bildung/studium-kein-platz-fuer-allah-an-deutschen-unis-1.2897802.

12 Such complaints were reported in the media, see Focus, "Studenten beklagen Einschüchterung Universität Essen schließt muslimischen Gebetsraum," *Focus*, 13th of February 2016, https://www.focus.de/regional/essen/studenten-beklagen-einschuechterung-universitaet-essen-schliesst-muslimischen-gebetsraum_id_5280048.html.

13 Universität Duisburg-Essen, "Erklärung der Hochschulleitung. Schließung des Gebetsraums," 2016, accessed 12th of December, 2021, https://www.uni-due.de/de/presse/meldung.php?id=9291.

Similarly, the replacement caused protests from the affected Muslim students. Unlike in London, however, the Islamic Society was willing to use the Room of Silence for prayer.[14] However, this was forbidden by the rules established by the University Senate and the Rectorate. They wrote in an announcement that the room of silence was not meant as a prayer room. Collective prayer, artifacts, and ritual acts were strictly forbidden. The room was only available for still and silent prayer or contemplation.[15]

Like London, each closure of a university prayer space led to protests by Muslim students. Interestingly, this was the case both if the closed space was a confessional prayer room, as in Duisburg-Essen, or a "Room of Silence," a negative multi-faith space, as in Dortmund and Berlin. The university policy provided different outcomes in each case. In Dortmund, the closure was presented as a counteraction to fundamentalism and led to the stigmatization of Muslim students. In Berlin, it was a reconsideration of church—state separation, but with pragmatic accommodation of individual needs. In Duisburg-Essen, it was presented as a form of catering to all. Yet, the constraining rules developed around the space led to polarization between the university and the Islamic Society. Duisburg-Essen was one of the starkest examples of a distinction between banal and unbanal religiosity—it allowed only the former, and expressed a Protestant bias by positioning internal, silent prayer as the proper activity for religious people.

All universities implied secularism in their decisions, even if implicitly as in Duisburg-Essen. By that, they took a specific position in the debate on the degree of neutrality required of universities. This has been captured by the spokesman of the University of Cologne, Patrick Honecker. The University of Cologne, unlike the earlier three examples, planned to open a new "Room of Silence." As Honecker stated,

> As a university we are always caught between ideological neutrality and freedom of religion. However, you must see that there are people subject to certain compulsions in the practice of their religion—for example Muslims. For that they need an appropriate room.[16]

---

14 Der Westen, "Nach Schließung von Gebetsraum an Uni Essen: Islamische Studenten wollen „Raum der Stille" für Gebete nutzen," *Der Westen*, 17th of October 2018, https://www.derwesten.de/staedte/essen/gebetsraum-uni-essen-islamische-studenten-id215578697.html.

15 Ulrike Bohnsack, "Sitzung vom 2. März 2018," Universität Duisburg-Essen, 2018, accessed 12th of December, 2021, https://www.uni-due.de/2018-03-13-senatssitzung-maerz.

16 Kohlmaier, "Kein Platz für Allah."

The University of Cologne, like the TU Dortmund, the TU Berlin, and the University of Duisburg-Essen, also noticed the need for ideological neutrality. For them, however, it had to be balanced with the principle of religious freedom and response to the needs of specific groups. For the University of Cologne, a new multi-faith space was an adequate response.

1.3 *Case 3: Debates in Denmark*

In the same year of 2016, after over 12 years of existence, a small "retreat room" (*retræterum*) at the Humanities Campus of Copenhagen University stirred up controversy. It was a typical negative multi-faith space, including religious texts on the shelf and a patterned carpet on the floor. Marie Krarup, the MP of the Danish People's Party, known for its "tough on immigration" stance, accused the room of a hidden purpose. While multi-religious in theory, it was supposed to be a "hidden mosque" present at a public institution. She wrote in a social media post on the 9th of December:

> The prayer room at the Amager Campus of the University of Copenhagen. It is called "Retreat Room," and there should be room for all religions. But for whom is it really intended? Well … On Tuesday, I will meet the minister for consultations when I ask him to close all prayer rooms at educational institutions. The rooms are really Islamist and provide Islam with a privileged position that it should not have in Denmark. Denmark is a Christian country.[17]

Krarup initiated several parliamentary debates and governmental inquiries into the matter. In the debates, two diverging positions developed between the Danish People's Party (DPP) and the Danish government. The DPP viewed formally neutral contemplation spaces as a rejection of the Danish Christian roots in the name of political correctness. They interpreted these spaces as a denial of one's own needs in favor of the others. They also viewed them as a place of danger for Islamic indoctrination and social pressure.[18] This, in the DPP's view,

---

17 Bederum på Københavns Universitet Amager. Det hedder "Retræterum" og der er plads til alle religioner. Men hvem er det mon reelt indrettet til? Hm. …. På tirsdag har jeg ministeren i samråd, hvor jeg vil bede ham lukke bederum på uddannelses-institutioner. Rummene er reelt islamisme og giver islam en særstilling, som islam ikke skal have i Danmark. Danmark er nemlig et kristen land, quoted in Jens Haag, "Marie Krarups Kritik Af Retræterummet På KUA Er Vanvittig Forfejlet," *Uniavisen*, 15th of December 2016, https://uniavisen.dk/marie-krarups-kritik-af-retraeterummet-paa-kua-er-vanvittig-forfejlet/.

18 Christian Langballe and Bertel Haarder, "§ 20-Spørgsmål S 242 Om Religionsneutrale Bederum På Hospitalerne." 18th of November. Copenhagen: *Folketingen*, 2016. https://www.ft.dk/samling/20161/spoergsmaal/s242/index.htm

was a part of the encroaching Islamization of Denmark and required a swift governmental reaction.[19] At the same time, Christian Langballe, another DPP MP, presented a different line of argumentation. He viewed retreat rooms as an atheist invention that went against both Christians and Muslims. As he said, "Muslims do not mind Christian education and sometimes like to go to hymn singing or Christian services."[20]

The Danish government at the time agreed with some problems highlighted by the DPP but did not share their methods. They did not see anything wrong with multi-faith spaces in principle. Instead, they argued that such issues should be decided on a lower level, based on the principle of subsidiarity. The Minister of Education and Research, Søren Pind, pointed out that each institution should be responsible for its own arrangements instead of being instructed by central regulation.[21] The Minister of Integration, Ingrid Støjberg, accused preceding governments of a lenient migration policy which led to the growing presence of Muslims in Denmark. Thus, she agreed with the need to increase efforts in integration. She asserted that newcomers and their descendants had to adapt to the Danish foundational values and freedoms. Symbols that expressed a worldview that went against these foundations did not, in her view, promote integration. Thus, according to Støjberg, symbols such as headscarves, niqabs, or burqas expressed an oppressive view of women, which went against the fundamental value of gender equality. However, Støjberg disagreed with the DPP on the need for a centrally legislated ban on religious symbols. Instead, she argued that it was the responsibility of each individual Dane to engage in negotiation daily. Only in some cases, she argued, institutions should act. Even in those cases, the reaction should remain at a local level. For example, in the case of an educational institution in Lynby, where there was a discussion concerning the acceptability of niqab in the classroom, the school, in Støjberg's view, adequately stepped in. Instead of hiding behind a piece of legislation, the ability to step in was viewed by her as a source of strength for the Danish society.

1.4 *Similar Spaces, Different Perception*

These examples from three different countries show that what happens around multi-faith spaces is as important as what happens inside them. Factors beyond materiality influence their perception. Despite relative similarities in design

19 Marie Krarup and Ulla Tørnæs, "§ 20-spørgsmål S 259 Om at undgå islamisering i uddannelsesinstitutionerne," (24th of November, Copenhagen: Folketingen, 2016). https://www.ft.dk/samling/20161/spoergsmaal/s259/index.htm.

20 Langballe and Haarder, "§ 20-spørgsmål S 242."

21 Krarup and Tørnæs, "§ 20-spørgsmål S 259."

and placement in the presented cases, multi-faith spaces created widely different responses. For some Muslim students at London City University, changing a dedicated prayer room into a multi-faith space contradicted their needs. It pushed them outside of the university space regarding their religious observance. For the university management, it seemed a sensible decision considering xenophobic attacks and enforcement of the rules of non-discrimination. In Dortmund, university management interpreted religious artifacts in the space and contestations of the multi-faith space as a complete failure. Many students viewed the room's closure as an expression of discrimination. In Berlin, the university vice-chancellor viewed such rooms as no longer necessary, preferring students to pray in any suitable place. In Duisburg-Essen, a confessionally inclined prayer space was removed because of a shortage of space. A multi-faith space was introduced as a pragmatic solution for catering to 130 nations. A dedicated multi-faith space was planned in Cologne, especially with Muslims in mind. Finally, in Denmark, a multi-faith space was viewed as a "hidden mosque" by some, an atheist invention by others, and a space for local negotiation according to the government.

The described cases are concerned with similar spaces arranged according to the negative model, which attempts to create a neutral space following the "unity by exclusion" principle. They exclude any visible manifestations of religiosity. The broad range of the responses shows that the negative design of these spaces does not fully decide what they represent in the eyes of the beholder. Instead of being neutral, they provoke quite strong reactions. The spaces themselves and the discussions at hand defined the responses. Their presence became the subject of negotiations, both at the local and higher levels. It became a part of the broader struggle for control over religion. The marks of the legible religion can be noticed at first glance. In most cases, it is clear that religion is perceived as something dangerous, that requires careful effort to handle and restrict. The impact of the interplay of the modalities of Christianity, secularism, and religious pluralism is also visible. The Danish example shows it best—Krarup relied on the "civilizationist" combination of secularism and Christianity against religious pluralism, Langballe combined Christianity and religious pluralism against secularism, while the Danish government, although verbally embracing Christian roots, doubled down on religious pluralism and the local negotiation as the way to go. The analysis of naming, institutional and policy context, and the impact of the dynamic of banal and unbanal will present factors that contribute to how multi-faith spaces are perceived and what role they play in different European societies.

2 The Naming of Multi-faith Spaces

The typology of spaces that add and those that subtract has been helpful in the analysis of the materiality of different multi-faith spaces and their potential effect. However, in analyzing the operations of multi-faith spaces in their broader social setting, this typology needs to be supplemented with others. First, I need to inspect further how multi-faith spaces are named. In this section, I offer three arguments. First, various names for multi-faith spaces highlight the multiple roots and intentions behind them. Second, names do not define how multi-faith spaces are used, as expressed by a mismatch between their official and unofficial names. Third, names can function as rhetorical devices in public debates, where a conscious replacement of one term with another is meant to direct the perception of the spaces.

Henrik Reintoft Christensen, Ida Marie Høeg, Lene Kühle, and Magdalena Nordin differentiate three traditions of multi-faith spaces, each with its own motivations, following similar lines to those discussed in the previous chapter. The first one takes its roots in the UN Meditation Room, which is "clearly part of a trend involving ecumenical or 'supra'-religious projects which attempted to transform religious expressions by integrating insights from Eastern spirituality."[22] The second, which could see Temple of Religion as its predecessor, aimed at the coexistence of different faith traditions, and came to Europe via the United Kingdom from other Anglo-Saxon countries. Finally, the third resulted from a reaction of Christian chaplains to the perceived secularization and includes rooms that grew from traditional chapels in places like shopping malls, city centers, or airports, as exemplified by *Andachtsraum* in Vienna and the Room of Silence in Utrecht. This categorization is complimentary to the previously mentioned distinctions of positive and negative, intra-institutional and extra-institutional, as well as spaces that add and those that subtract—it differentiates multi-faith spaces based on the original intentions behind them, rather than their placement, shape, or effect.

Reintoft Christensen and colleagues point out that this is a historical rather than a contemporary account. The authors admit that "while it is possible to distinguish among these three traditions historically and analytically, in reality they have merged."[23] That is why today, the differentiation is no longer as helpful in analyzing the materiality of multi-faith spaces. These multiple roots

22 H. R. Christensen et al., "Rooms of Silence at Three Universities in Scandinavia," *Sociology of Religion* 80, no. 3 (2018), 303, https://doi.org/10.1093/socrel/sry040.

23 Christensen et al., "Rooms of Silence," 304.

testify to multiple intentions hiding behind these spaces and may suggest different reception among different audience groups. Traces of these different origins can be spotted in the six cases described at the beginning.

Reintoft Christensen and colleagues created a typology of shared religious spaces based on two axes concerned with the implied use of the space. First, they differentiate how the rooms are positioned: are they meant for collective or individual use (even if they often are used for both)? Second, they differentiate religious, spiritual, and secular spaces. Based on this, they propose six idealized types of spaces, fitting a name to each of them: three individual, *prayer room* (religious), *contemplation room* (spiritual) and *room of reflection* (secular), and three collective, *multi-faith room* (religious), *meditation room* (spiritual), and *recreational lounge* (secular).

The different terms, while used as pure "categories of analysis" by Reintoft Christensen and colleagues, and in practice "often used interchangeably" have, as they write themselves, "different connotations: terms like chapel or prayer room carry Christian connotations of space (even if also used by other religions), while some of the other terms may emphasize a neutral place as a deliberate reaction 'to perceived religious bias'."[24] This is confirmed by the previously mentioned *multi-faith* [*spaces*] exhibition. It notes that:

> MFS have many names, sometimes conscientiously discussed, at other times arrived at through inheritance or decree. Commonly names are formed by combining an adjective or qualifier such as: r*eflection, quiet, silent, multi-faith, interfaith, rest, contemplation, prayer, reconciliation, worship, wellbeing, living, serenity,* with a noun such as: *lounge, space, chapel, chaplaincy, room, center.*
>
> A detailed consideration of the many connotations presented by these terms has led to increasing neutrality and abstraction; evidenced in titles such as *The Space* or *Open Room.* Nonetheless, inertia can also be powerful, as even after conversion or gradual adaptation many MFS are still referred to as 'chapels'. Inevitably, the opposite is also possible, with some MFS being formally re-named in the obvious *absence* of any change of form or usage.[25]

Thus, it is not always clear from where these spaces get their name. There is much wishful thinking around naming, often with a desire to change reality

24 Christensen et al., "Rooms of Silence," 305.

25 Ralf Gregor Brand, Andrew Crompton, and Chris Hewson, "Multi-faith Spaces—Symptoms and Agents of Religious and Social Change," *University of Manchester and University of Liverpool*, 2012, accessed 17 September 2021, http://cargocollective.com/wwwmulti-faith-spacesorg, Naming section.

with a simple change of terms. Sometimes this results in a mismatch. While top-down approaches try to neutralize the space's meaning through increasingly abstract names, the users of the space, or at least those who encounter it daily, seem to take a pragmatic approach.

While different names might exemplify specific intentions behind the rooms, they surely do not define their usage:

> It is unwise to presume patterns of usage from a name alone. One is as likely to find a *Prayer Space* utilised for a range of activities, as a *Reflection Room* largely reserved for Islamic prayer. Whilst thought typically goes into the original naming decision, there are inevitably more types of space in existence than terms available to describe them. Indeed, an effort is often required to compel an MFS to resemble its name, aided by managers and users.[26]

The mismatch between the name and the usage again underlines the wishful thinking behind the former. This does not make it inconsequential. It may disclose the intentions of the space's founders. Even if the actual usage does not change between a confessional prayer room and a multi-faith space, the change of the name may cause the space's rejection, as in London. Or it may influence the regulations, as in Duisburg-Essen.

Additionally, the connotations behind the naming play a significant role in public rhetoric. Trying to underline the specific character of the room, different speakers changed the term used in the reference to the spaces from its actual name: thus, for example, the press officer at the TU Dortmund described the Room of Silence, *Raum der Stille*, as a "supra-religious meditation room" (*überreligiösen Meditationsraum*), the Danish People's Party, on the initiation of Marie Krarup, referred to the UCPH's Retreat Room (*retreaterum*) as a prayer room (*bederum*) instead, while the University of Duisburg-Essen started its change by turning a prayer room (*Der Gebetsraum*) into a room of silence (*ein Raum der Stille*) in official communication.

These communication strategies suggest that multi-faith spaces are not only defined by the intention, materiality, and practice, as Reintoft Christensenand colleagues suggest, but indeed exist "in the eye of the beholder" as the definition from the *multi-faith* [*spaces*] exhibition suggests. Everyone can read an intention into them. It may result from, for example, wishful thinking or purposeful strategy. These readings are defined by several external circumstances, which may lie behind the changing perspectives on these spaces and explain

26 Brand, Crompton, and Hewson, "Multi-faith Spaces," Naming section.

why some of them could have found themselves in the middle of controversy after decades of arguably seamless functioning.

To sum up, as Reintoft Christensen and colleagues argue, multi-faith spaces originated from several intentions. While over time, these directions merged into one, paving the way for the emergence of "typical" multi-faith spaces, these multiple intentions still influence how the spaces are perceived. This can be observed in how they are named, both officially and unofficially. The naming can also be used as a rhetorical device to suggest how multi-faith spaces should be interpreted. Again, one can see a specific dynamic in the approach to the spaces, shaped by the presuppositions and interpretive assumptions brought by the beholder. However, these presuppositions are not set in stone and can be influenced by certain institutional factors, which I will discuss in the next section.

3 The Institutional Context of Multi-faith Spaces

Naming is only one factor in divergent perceptions of multi-faith spaces. Local institutional context contributes as well. Below, I will discuss three main variables that influence such perceptions. First, direct managers have different levels of understanding, skill, and interest, which affects the shape and way in which spaces are run. Second, the population of end users also plays a role, as a smaller, more uniform, or more stable community may allow for adaptations and negotiations that would otherwise be impossible.[27] Third, the institutional policy towards the space itself, or religion more broadly, especially as an explicit set of rules, will curtail what can be done in the space and how it can be understood.[28]

Within the context of universities, these three variables pose significant challenges. At different universities, different entities *manage* different spaces.

---

27 For more on negotiation with different stakeholders, see Terry Biddington, *Multi-faith Space: History, Development, Design and Practice* (London: Jessica Kingsley Publishers, 2020), 95–96.

28 While these are the main factors, others can also have a significant impact; for example, sources of funding. Going beyond university spaces, one could consider the example of the Millennium Dome in Greenwich, London. In the original plans, one prayer room was planned inside the facility, to be run by a multi-faith team of chaplains. However, as the funding for the Dome came from the National Lottery, its association with gambling made it unsuitable for use by Muslims and necessitated the creation of a separate room outside the facility itself. See Sophie Gilliat-Ray, "From 'Chapel' To 'Prayer Room': The Production, Use, and Politics of Sacred Space in Public Institutions," *Culture and Religion* 6, no. 2 (2005): 293, https://doi.org/10.1080/01438300500226448.

As mentioned, chaplains play a significant role in their development and maintenance. However, they operate in different configurations, from majority religion chaplain teams[29] to multi-faith chaplaincies.[30] Sometimes these spaces are taken out of the custody of such professionals and placed in the hands of, for example, student organizations[31] or institutional administrative staff, such as university building managers.[32] These entities have different levels of understanding of the end users of the spaces, different interests, and differ in terms of how much freedom to act they have. This affects the perception of the space, how well it is adapted to the needs of the end users, and how skillfully these needs are also organized, structured, and scheduled.

These managers must also work with a highly diverse group of *end users*. The population of public institutions is highly fluid and changes constantly—it is impossible to find a solution that fits all in a "particular community" because that community will quickly change. Even in the university context, where the term rhythm could impose stability, the university's openness in terms of student exchanges, visits, or public events means that there is no population regularity. Thus, in the time of global population movements, every institution, at any time, can be potentially visited by a representative of one of the nearly infinite religious options or beliefs. Denominationally inclined student organizations could provide support in that matter, but they are often representatives of the whole part of the population that belongs to a particular faith. That can lead to significant tensions, as it disregards diversity within the group. The population changes also mean that the "ownership" of the space is fluid and can change within hours on a busy day.

---

29 For example, the multi-faith space at the Amager Campus of the University of Copenhagen has been established on a multi-faith initiative but has been managed by Christian student priests, see Christoffer Zieler, "UCPH has an exceptionally high number of prayer rooms," *University Post*, 2017, https://uniavisen.dk/en/ucph-has-an-exceptionally-high-number-of-prayer-rooms/.

30 For example, the multi-faith space, and the multi-faith activities, are managed by a whole multi-faith chaplaincy led by the Dean of Spiritual Life at the Winchester University, see University of Winchester, "Our Chaplaincies," 2021, accessed 12th of December, 2021, https://www.winchester.ac.uk/accommodation-and-winchester-life/student-life/spirituality/our-chaplaincies/.

31 For example, Vrije Universiteit Amsterdam, where the university's multi-faith space is managed by the NEWconnective student platform for meaning, see Vrije Universiteit Amsterdam, "Multi-faith space," 2021, accessed 12th of December, 2021, https://vu.nl/en/about-vu/more-about/stilteruimte-vu.

32 For example, Lund University, where, despite of the existence of the University's Multi-faith chaplaincy (see Svenska Kyrkan Lunds Domkyrkoförsamling, "Studentprästerna i Lund," 2021, accessed 12th of December, 2021, https://lundsdomkyrka.se/larande-motesplatser/studentprasterna/), the University's *Stilla Rum* are managed by the university building managers.

While the changing population makes local negotiations quite difficult, managers are much more constrained by the *institutional policies* towards religion. The freedom of action provided to them is extremely important, as even the greatest skill, highest knowledge, and wealth of good will are insufficient if they cannot be put to work. The same applies to the users—strict rules on how they should practice their religiosity may cause frustrations in individuals and tensions between different groups, especially if there are differences in privileges. Sophie Gilliat-Ray writes that:

> Regardless of how sacred spaces have come into being, they have qualities and characteristics that make them in some ways quite different to conventional places of worship. Although space is a resource wherever it is located—and is thus subject to the politics of property and ownership—sacred spaces in public institutions are slightly different on account of the fact that they are 'housed' within another institution that has its own politics. This can significantly affect the kind of negotiations and contests that surround the space.[33]

This comment refers us back to the division between the spaces that add and those that subtract. The intra-institutional placement of multi-faith spaces puts much greater pressure on them to perform the role that users and onlookers expect. That pressure can be intensified by the strict rules surrounding any of the stakeholders involved in the negotiations concerning them.

We need to consider several factors when analyzing the impact of institutional policy on multi-faith spaces, as exemplified in the cases at the beginning of this chapter. First, as mentioned in the previous chapter, these spaces are usually exclusive within the European context. They constitute the only space where religion can take place. Religious practice outside them can be explicitly banned, implicitly discouraged, or simply uncomfortable and out of place. The approach expressed by the President of TU Berlin, Christian Thomsen, who argued that he is not bothered by one or two students praying anywhere they find a quiet place, is rather uncommon. This prevents any supplementarity of multi-faith spaces and turns them into essential facilities. Those who follow a set schedule of religious practices are forced to occupy them, even if this means clashes with other users. Second, because of this exclusivity, multi-faith spaces function as entities of control. Religion can be more easily controlled and regulated by being contained in a particular space, making the regulations

33 Gilliat-Ray, "From 'Chapel' To 'Prayer Room'," 297.

concerning the room of interest to different stakeholder groups. These regulations allow for the central planning of religious practice. Third, this makes multi-faith spaces a potential ground for battles over high-level principles. The cases at the beginning of the chapter demonstrated some of the main principles in play: non-discrimination, church—state separation, supra-religiosity, ideological neutrality, religious freedom, or even responsibility for integration and creation of a particular sense of nationhood. Thus, while the design of multi-faith spaces exemplifies the implicit expectations that the framework of legible religion institutes, its main elements are explicitly involved in developing institutional policies towards religion in general and multi-faith spaces in particular. Finally, this means that the institutional policy results from a particular constellation of the modalities introduced in Chapter 3. There, I have discussed the interplay of three modalities and their coalitions in response to the return of religion narrative: Christianity, secularism, and religious pluralism. All three of them are at play in institutional policies. A closer look at two examples will visualize this further.

Aarhus University, the second-largest Danish University in the north of Jutland province, may serve as the first example. It shows that institutional policies are not always apparent at the outset. In many cases, they are implicit and difficult to pin down. Sometimes there is no official institutional policy, but there are interpretive guides like leaflets. Reintoft Christensen and colleagues describe the policy approach at Aarhus University in the following words:

> At the local level, Aarhus University (DK) has no actual policy for shared rooms. The room is located in the Student House, which is an organization closely associated with the university, but not formally part of it, and its relation with the university is therefore ambiguous. The room is administered by the university chaplains who have their office next to the room. The church of Denmark employs them, and the chaplain webpage is not hosted by the university (whose domain is au.dk). Nevertheless, the webpage uses an URL that signals an affiliation to the university (www.studenterpraest-au.dk). On the other hand, the chaplains' emails are university emails: "[name of chaplain]@au.dk." There may be historical reasons for these ambiguities, but when seen in connection with the lack of an actual policy, they signal a less than whole-hearted embrace of religion at the university. From the information leaflet, we can identify the kind of religion that is welcome in the room of silence. The leaflet, which is a small version of the poster on the door to the room, describes the room as a place where "you do not need to perform and deliver ... you are always welcome to use the room, as long as you respect the silence of

> others. The room is open during the day and evening, and is open for all regardless of religious belonging."[34]

The situation in Aarhus shows interesting dynamics. First, as mentioned by the authors, specific signals suggest that religion might not be entirely welcome on the university premises. Second, the room exercises control, encouraging practice that respects the silence of others, that is, practice that is individual, private, silent, internal, and not relying on external manifestations, the marks of the legible religion discussed before. Third, the ambiguity towards the status of the room and chaplaincy suggests potential tensions in terms of church—state relations, ideological neutrality, and religious freedom. Finally, the three modalities are all in play. Religious pluralism plays a role as this space is open to all regardless of religious affiliation. Christianity plays a role, as the main chaplains are from the majority confession and are paid by the Danish Church. Secularism plays a role in the placement and the ambiguous embracement of the room, as well as in the leaflet's content.

In contrast with Aarhus University's soft approach, the University of Hamburg may serve as an example of an explicit institutional approach written into a set of rules. *Verhaltenskodex zur Religionsausübung an der Universität Hamburg* describes in detail how religious practice should be conducted at its premises. This code of conduct contains two parts: the code itself, which provides the broader rationale behind the approach and its main principles, and a set of implementation provisions that move onto the level of individual rules.

The first part discusses the university's role as a secular institution committed to plurality in which religious content must meet scientific standards. The university guarantees freedom of religion to its staff and students, both in its positive (freedom to) and negative (freedom from) versions. The exercise of this freedom is delimited by respect for the other's convictions. The code rejects religiously motivated pressure towards a behavior viewed as correct within religious groups. The authors of the code underline that the university's academic mandate constraints the exercise of religion. Because of respect and tolerance, conflicts that arise from beliefs and their exercise are supposed to be constructively resolved, if it is compatible with the scientific mandate, with a presupposition that all involved in a said conflict recognize the primacy of research, teaching, and education, as well as renounce any denominational or non-denominational priority.

---

34 Christensen et al., "Rooms of Silence," 10–11.

Interestingly, the university recognizes the difficulty of its position in terms of end users. As the code reads, "The plurality of religious and non-religious ways of life in the university makes it impossible to orient research and teaching to all forms of religious organization in everyday life."[35] However, as far as possible, the code introduces an obligation of consideration for, for example, religious holidays or dietary regulations. In the final point, the code puts all university members in charge of implementing its principles:

> University members champion these principles. Teaching staff and others responsible for guaranteeing that academic pursuit proceeds smoothly will receive practical instruction on exercising the right to ban or expel persons from the premises, effectively prohibiting the impairment or endangerment of the primacy of research, teaching, and education at the University, and creating a climate of respect and tolerance.[36]

The footnotes to part one provide further details to the main content, shedding more light on the constraints on religious behavior. Thus, footnote 1 adds that the celebration of religious holidays is supposed to be limited only to the rooms provided and should not be attended by groups that do not belong to the university. Footnote 4 differentiates between students and teachers in terms of religiously motivated clothing, which is not rejected outright but may be problematic for staff as they have more restrictive demands for neutrality. The same footnote points out that the primary dedication of the rooms should be respected, and thus while silent prayer may take place in the library, loud and demonstrative prayer should not occur there. Religious behavior should be limited to non-disruptive acts or take place in specially dedicated rooms. However, footnote 8 establishes a certain "rule of good will" in providing the space for religious exercise:

> [8] Within its means the University attempts to provide all religious groups with the resources required for religious expression (Room of Contemplation, alternative offers in the case of compulsory religious precepts, to be supplemented if necessary with hand-outs on nearby cemevi, churches, mosques, synagogues, temples, etc.) providing that the University's mission and the freedom of all its members are duly recognized.

35 The President of Hamburg University, "Code of Conduct for Religious Expression," Hamburg University, 2021, accessed 18th of October, 2021, https://www.uni-hamburg.de/en/uhh/profil/leitbild/verhaltenskodex-religionsausuebung.html.

36 The President of Hamburg University, "Code of Conduct for Religious Expression."

> This requires waiving claims to unauthorized use of university resources and facilities to express your own religious beliefs as well as the willingness to resolve conflict constructively. The University reserves the right to ban or expel persons from all rooms that it provides.[37]

While part one leaves an opening for different activities and establishes a good will principle by the university management, part two, the implementation provisions, is more restrictive. The ordering of these provisions is quite suggestive. All provisions are either negative, prohibiting something, or restrictive, allowing for something under limited conditions. The first provision begins by prohibiting discrimination in the Room of Silence, exemplified by gender-based divisions. The second provision emphasizes that religious celebrations can take place only in the room of silence as it is the only appropriate space for various forms of religious expression. The third provision indicates that the unauthorized use of other university resources or facilities for religious expression is strictly prohibited. The fourth provision states that the ritual acts are only permitted if no other user of the space perceives them as a form of forced confrontation with the religion of the other, which is exemplified by the strictly prohibited ritual of washing feet in sanitary facilities or praying out loud. The fifth provision allows for religious symbols if it does not hinder engagement in communication, teaching, or examination. The sixth and seventh provisions indicate that there is no alignment of the university schedule to either daily religious routines or religious holidays that are not also public holidays. The eighth provision bans religiously motivated pressure. The ninth provision rejects any gender discrimination towards the teaching or administrative staff, while the tenth provision imposes responsibility for providing dishes congruent with dietary requirements on those running canteens and cafeterias.

Again, the example of Hamburg shows the importance of the four factors underlined above. First, the exercise of religion is restricted to authorized places. While silent prayer is permitted outside of the set bounds, any other exercise of religion should follow authorization and the rule of good will. The room of silence is mentioned as the primary place, while others are viewed as supplementary in special circumstances. Second, the whole code is an exercise in the control of religion, while the room of silence is a subset of this broader pattern. Third, several high-level principles known from the framework of legible religion are explicitly stated, such as non-discrimination, ideological

37 The President of Hamburg University, "Code of Conduct for Religious Expression."

neutrality, or religious freedom. Interestingly, one can also see some other legibility elements; for example, the expression of the primacy of civil values before any religious affiliation, with scientific principles overshadowing religious beliefs, and the demand for neutrality by the university staff. Finally, secularism and pluralism are explicitly mentioned at the beginning of the code. Christianity has a smaller impact than in the Danish example. Yet, it is implicitly at play; for example, alignment to public holidays in the university schedule, giving those from majority Christian confessions a certain advantage in celebrating their religious holidays over those who belong to minorities.

While Aarhus provides a glimpse of the implicit notions of religiosity, Hamburg offers a full-scale view of the assumptions inherent in their vision of religion on campus. Even if one approaches its first part generously and assumes that its general principles try to provide an overarching and more inclusive vision for religious interactions, implementing these principles does not leave much space for doubt about the vision of religion behind it. In the approach of the Executive University Board, religion appears as a potential problem that needs to be handled at the outset by strict control, limitations, and prohibitions. Representatives of non-majority traditions cannot reliably count on special accommodations for, for example, their religious holidays, while their dietary requirements are relegated to the level of individual cafeterias, *de facto* leaving it in the hands of individuals to negotiate such adaptations. The multi-faith spaces, suggestively named "spaces of silence," are turned into essential facilities, the only ones where visible expressions of religiosity can occur. The individuals are also put under the supervision of others, as their perception decides what is, and what is not, allowable. Gender discrimination is mentioned both at the beginning and end, posing it as an especially problematic aspect of religious conduct. Such a type of institutional policy, even with the best managers of the multi-faith space, restricts their space for action to such a large extent that they cannot in any meaningful way address the arising problems.

Of course, not all universities introduce such detailed regulations. Hamburg University is an extreme example of explicit rules, in which the level of control is much higher than elsewhere. Usually, the rules and guidelines are more pragmatic, as exemplified by, for example, the University of the West of England Bristol's provisions, which are concerned with the maximum number of people allowed in the space, rules on footwear, security, food consumption, and the booking of the room.[38] Approaches like this are somewhere in the middle between the complete lack of regulations and the HHU level of detail.

38 UWE Faith & Spirituality, "Guidance for Use of Multi-Faith Space," University of the West of England Bristol, 2021, accessed 22nd of April, 2021, https://www.uwe.ac.uk/-/media

To summarize, after looking at motivations and naming, in this section, I have considered the impact that direct management, the population of end users, and the institutional policies have on the perception of multi-faith spaces. While the first two factors pose potential challenges to the functioning of such rooms and thereby an element to consider from the perspective of good practice, the institutional policy goes beyond that. As argued, because multi-faith spaces are most often either exclusive or primary places for the exercise of religion, they are places that allow for the exercise of control over that religion. In turn, the policy towards the multi-faith spaces becomes an important ground for the operations of legible religion. As the examples of Aarhus and HHU show, the elements of legibility in the policies include central-level planning, the approach to religion as a potential threat, the reductive view of religion as individual, private, internalized, iconoclastic, cognitive, silent, prayer-oriented, and syncretic towards the civil values, and the interplay of the modalities of secularism, religious pluralism, and Christianity. However, as these are just two examples, I will now look at the broader picture by referring to the broader studies of policies at different universities.

4 The Policy Approaches to Multi-faith Spaces

In the previous section, I inspected two examples of institutional policies in detail. In this section, I will move to the trends in policy approaches. I will differentiate three types of policies. Two embrace the framework of legible religion: a *single vision model,* which is continuing engagement with religion based on premises of secularization, and a *service-oriented model,* which is more open to religion, but treats it primarily in functional terms as a form of capital. In contrast, a third approach, which I call a *holistic model,* breaks with legibility and aims to create conditions for negotiation between different stakeholders.

/uwe/documents/life/health-wellbeing/multi-faith-space-guidance.pdf. For comparison, see also St. George's University of London, "Protocol for the multi-faith and quiet contemplation room," 2013, accessed 22nd of April, 2022, https://www.sgul.ac.uk/about/governance/policies/documents/Agreed-Protocol-May-2015-Rochelle-Rowe-1.pdf. University of York, "Protocol for the use of multi-faith space at the University of York," 2021, accessed 22nd of April, 2022, https://www.york.ac.uk/media/studenthome/studentsupporthub/Protocol%20for%20the%20Multi-Faith%20Space%20(VS3.0%20Dec%2021).pdf; Umeå University, "Multi-faith space," 2022, accessed 22nd of April, 2022, https://www.umu.se/en/student/we-can-assist-you/group-rooms-and-other-spaces/multi-faith-space/#:~:text=The%20Multi%2Dfaith%20space%20is,regardless%20of%20faith%20or%20beliefs.

4.1 *The Axes Of Pragmatism and Public Religion*

Jonathan D. Smith analyzed different policy approaches in "Multi-faith muddle: trends in managing prayer spaces at UK universities." Smith proposed a typology of policies at British universities based on two axes. One axis is concerned with the *pragmatic* approach to these spaces. It considers to what extent the best practices on multi-faith spaces usage are in place. It also inquires to what extent there is a real, rather than a merely nominal, interest in the end users. On the plus side, Smith describes the provision of adequate resources, well-trained staff, user-centered design, and ongoing consultations with end users. On the minus side, Smith positions a legalistic approach and lack of consistency.

The other axis is characterized as a *public religion*. It considers whether campus is open to religion and welcomes its different manifestations or whether the university treats religion as a mainly private concern. It refers to the broader policy context. On the plus side, Smith puts engagement with public religion, an understanding of campus as a space of religious interaction, the perception of religion as a resource, and broad engagement with religion. On the minus side, Smith introduces the exclusive accommodation for private religion, a secular/neutral campus, and the perception of religion as a problem or distraction. It limits engagement with religion to a strictly legal response.

Smith argues that a position on the plus side of both axes results in lesser and more infrequent conflicts, while a position on the minus side has the opposite effect. The more the university policy positively employs the principles of pragmatism and public religion, the closer multi-faith spaces are to the needs of the users. Smith writes:

> Taking a broad approach to engaging public religion, a common practice is to provide for many types of multi-faith spaces: a designated room (or rooms) for Islamic prayer, adjoining spaces that are bookable rooms for faith societies, and non-bookable rooms for multi-faith private prayer and reflection. In this way accommodating for private prayer is joined with activities between faith societies to support interaction outside of individual religious practice. Student societies often share management of prayer spaces with chaplains or students' unions, which can create shared ownership.[39]

---

39 Jonathan D. Smith, "Multi-faith spaces at UK universities display two very different visions of public religion," *Religion and Global Society*, 12th of August 2016, https://blogs.lse.ac.uk/religionglobalsociety/2016/08/multi-faith-spaces-at-uk-universities-display-two-very-different-visions-of-public-religion/.

Thus, a position on the plus side of both axes includes accommodation for different practices and needs, such as individual prayer or contemplation and collective meetings, adequate adaptations to those with set observance times, space for mono-, multi-, and inter-faith engagement, and engagement of multiple stakeholders in the management of spaces.

The universities whose policies entail an approach oriented towards the negative sides of both axes are on the other side of the spectrum. Smith continues:

> Another trend springs from a narrower view of religion on campus, which enforces a multi-faith policy in each and every space, at least in principle. Considering limited space and resources, limiting religious accommodation to a single, multi-faith space could make sense. A legal perspective on religion raises concerns about spaces designated for one religious group or gender as possibly breaching equality law. This concern is often accompanied by concerns about radicalisation or isolation of Muslim students, with managers attempting to address concerns that rooms on campus would be 'taken over' by Muslim students. This is particularly the case in areas with large Muslim populations, where managers might assume that Muslim students can pray in local mosques. A narrow approach to religion often accompanies limited resources dedicated for religious students, making it difficult to support staff members needed to manage multi-faith spaces and to consult with users.[40]

Smith admits this model is founded on reasonable worries, such as a lack of space and resource limitations, legal constraints, concerns over radicalization, isolation, or domination of certain groups. However, he points out that the means that such approaches employ do not serve their ends. This type of policy demonstrates the constraining factors described earlier. Enforcement of a top-down policy on each space leads to increased tensions between different visions of the role religion should play. Limitations in staff and resources directed toward religion and arbitrary rejection of certain types of religiosities only deepen the problems.

4.2 *Single and Multiple-Visions Models*

Based on Smith's considerations, Visions could differentiate two ideal models of policy approaches to religion on campus, based on their position on

40 Smith, "Multi-faith spaces."

pragmatism and public religion axes. Those positioned on the negative side of both axes bring, in Smith's words, "negative media coverage, clashes between students of different faiths and beliefs forced to share prayer spaces, campaigns and public pray-ins on campus, and accusations of radicalization by think-tanks and government ministers."[41] I call this a *single vision model* because it centrally enforces one vision of religion's role on campus. This policy response could be viewed as resulting from the secularization narratives and implementation of the principles of secularism. It views religion as a problem to be controlled and a danger to be curbed.

On the positive side of both axes, Smith finds universities that adapt to the multiplicity of existing needs by providing spaces for different types of religious observance rather than forcing a single vision with an exclusive space for a specific type of religiosity. This model could be described as a *multiple visions model* because it accommodates multiple visions and negotiations.

However, I argue that this model needs further consideration. While Smith discusses the motivation behind the *single vision model*, he leaves this aspect out of consideration of the other approach. I argue that even if a university policy aims to engage with public religion and takes all pragmatic precautions, what stands behind that choice can affect the perception of the spaces. Motivation is crucial and allows us to differentiate two models out of what seems like one model in Smith's analysis.

First, a *service-oriented model*, which views religion instrumentally, for example, as a tool for increasing student numbers. Tony Acland and Waqar Azmi write that:

> The provision of Muslim prayer rooms in a secular institution may be easily lost in a resource-conscious university. However, there is one economic argument which might persuade institutions to make efforts to improve services and facilities for ethnic minorities. A number of universities compete to increase their overseas student admissions, with markets particularly buoyant in countries with Muslim populations. Provision of such facilities, accurately advertised, could result in increased overseas admissions.[42]

---

41 Smith, "Multi-faith spaces."

42 Tony Acland and Waqar Azmi, "Expectation and reality: ethnic minorities in higher education," in *Race and Higher Education*, ed. Tariq Modood and Tony Acland (London: Policy Studies Institute, 1998), 84.

A positive outlook on religion and catering to a broad range of student needs can influence their university choice. It can be an element of marketing strategy, resulting in increased revenue and prestige.

However, in such approaches, religion is still treated in the framework of legibility. Functionalization replaces the need for control. Religion remains separated from other spheres of activity, even if the university policy rejects the strictly secular character of its campus. In this approach, religion is treated as capital and engaged only in catering to the needs of the institutional clients and as a commodity that enriches the university. It is also still considered primarily individual, benefiting individual students. Such an approach could be a response to the return of religion narrative, viewed in a utilitarian fashion as a potential force for social cohesion, student development, and translated into the languages of wellness and growth. The fluidity in changes between the *single vision* and *service-oriented model*s testifies to their close connection. A six-year review of policies at the selected British universities showed the policies change in both directions.[43]

Second, the approach embracing pragmatism and public religion may result from a different choice. It can follow a rejection of the secular/religious binary and aim for a complete overhaul of the understanding of religion, in what I call a *holistic model*. This could be observed in the example of the University of Winchester, which, instead of keeping chaplaincy as a separate unit of the university, introduced "spirituality"[44] among the university's core values. Alongside the regular multi-faith team of chaplains,[45] the university created an office of the Dean of Spiritual Life within its senior management. The university also initiated a whole program of interweaving contemplative activities for students (contemplative student community) and staff (Winchester Institute for Contemplative Education and Practice).[46]

As the university's website states:

> We celebrate our Anglican Christian foundation and welcome people of all faiths and none. In a world in which religion is often associated with exclusivity and anti-intellectualism, we seek to model ways of being religious which are inclusive and intellectually robust.

43 Smith, "Multi-faith spaces."

44 The term is not defined in any specific way beyond the long quote in the text below.

45 University of Winchester, "Our Chaplaincies."

46 University of Winchester, "Your Spiritual Journey," 2021, accessed 12th of December, 2021, https://www.winchester.ac.uk/accommodation-and-winchester-life/student-life/spirituality/spiritual-journey/.

> We believe that everyone expresses their spirituality through a unique collage of values, disciplines, and practices. Working and studying here will give you a chance to experience and reflect on the creativity, beauty, and compassion in life—together, we aim to explore the mystery of life and grow in wisdom and love.
>
> Our passion is to see staff and students grow as a whole person. It is safe to try new things here, to stand up for what you believe in. You will be supported to engage with the big and deep questions of life, to bring about change and really make a difference. We seek to challenge and develop staff and students' thinking, enabling them to develop in wisdom for a fulfilling life as well as the knowledge they need for a successful career. Our staff and students will have the resilience and resourcefulness to seize the opportunities and face the challenges of life.
>
> Many of our students choose Winchester because of the way we take spirituality seriously.[47]

One can see similarities with other policies in this description. Student admissions are still mentioned, indicating the influence of the legible approach. By speaking of Anglican Christian foundations and people of all faiths and none, one can also see an interplay of two of the three modalities: Christianity and religious pluralism. However, I would argue that Winchester's policy takes a step away from the reductionism of legibility. It wants, at least in principle, to embrace religion in all its guises, without the need for control or functional justification. Instead of being strictly separated from other activities, religion is acknowledged as potentially present in all endeavors, including the core tasks of the institutions, such as teaching, involving both students and staff, and raised to the level of senior management.

The model proposed by Winchester is further away from a typically European approach and closer to the American one, where multi-faith facilities, "besides providing worship space for different religions, … have created opportunities for education and awareness of religious pluralism and spirituality."[48] This approach neither rejects religion based on secularism nor seeks to

47 University of Winchester, "Spirituality," 2021, accessed 12th of December, 2021, https://www.winchester.ac.uk/accommodation-and-winchester-life/student-life/spirituality/.

48 Johanson and Laurence, "Multi-Faith Religious Spaces on College and University Campuses," 62. Stanford Memorial Church at Stanford University campus, may serve as an example of this approach. See Stanford University Office for Religious & Spiritual Life, "Memorial Church & Companion Spaces," 2021, accessed 12th of December, 2021, https://orsl.stanford.edu/who-we-are/memorial-church-companion-spaces.

differentiate good religion from bad, following approaches of control, indifference, or functionalization. Instead, it views religion as an inherent part of individual and social life and does not constrain it in a particular space. It does not prevent providing a space for worship. Nor does it preclude seeing potential challenges, nor the positive role of religion in the lives of individuals and communities or its educational value. Rather, instead of resisting religion, it wants to resonate with the needs of people involved in the institution's life. In this context, potentially, multi-faith spaces may still function, but more in line with extra-institutional spaces, as a supplement or an alternative to the existing options.

The difference between the *service-oriented* and *holistic* approach is significant. The *service-oriented model* still follows the approach of legible religion. It approaches religion as something that needs to be made manipulable through reduction. Such reduction is forced onto multi-faith spaces. I argue that while the *single vision model* and its strict control are challenged by the tensions they generate, *the service-oriented model* functionalizing religion on campus still has the potential to miss the actual needs of users and, in terms of the mismatch between the expectations and reality, slide into the other model, as at many British universities. In contrast, the *holistic model* in its ideal version involves all relevant stakeholders, such as students and university staff, to negotiate the role of religion on campus.

4.3 *A Subtle Difference*

The difference between the *service-oriented* and *holistic models* may seem subtle. The actual use of the multi-faith spaces might clarify that difference. Alexander-Kenneth Nagel and Mehmet Kalendera studied guestbooks in German Rooms of Silence and Gardens of Religions to offer insight into the visitors' self-reported understanding of these spaces. Nagel and Kalendera found out that the guestbooks are used for three primary purposes, which may indicate how spaces are used:

> First, … guestbooks provide a platform for practices of *singularisation* which delineate the religious or spiritual self in relation to an anonymous public. In this regard, they become a medium for the formation and negotiation of religious identity similar to internet forums, but less interactive and more contextualised. Second, and in a similar vein, guestbooks are being used as media of mission and proselytisation as some authors put a religious tradition on display in a persuasive and advertising fashion. Third, and more related to interventionist practices, the books can become media of spiritualist communication across the

> transcendence line and mediate between the world of the dead and the living or the present and the absent. In contrast to the first aspect, the material nature of the book is not a restriction, but an enabling factor for this sort of medialisation.[49]

The guestbooks highlight a broad range of uses and understandings of one's place in the broader plurality of beliefs and worldviews. In each of these, a particular form of inter-faith contact is signified. Through singularization, individuals position themselves within that plurality. With proselytization, they see themselves as active agents in inter-faith contact, whose task is to bring greater uniformity. By spiritual communication, they engage the transcendent, leaving a permanent, public trace of such engagement.

While the service approach, with its top-down perspective, can address individual users' needs and provide them with a space to interact with each other, it does not necessarily provide them with tools for such interaction. Viewing religion as a functional element of campus puts the responsibility for these interactions primarily on either the institution's management or the middle-people, such as chaplains. In a constantly changing population, these interlocutors have a challenging task. When conflicts or proselytization arise and interreligious engagement is forced onto users, contradicting the wishes of the management, the eruption of tensions may proceed quickly.

Instead, the *holistic model* sees negotiation as an inherent part of the process. Because of that, it needs to equip stakeholders with the ability to engage in such negotiation. Thus, it may introduce opportunities for individuals to learn the tools of such negotiation, or at least create ambassadors in different stakeholder groups who are supposed to facilitate this process (for example, in Winchester, the contemplative pedagogy and community networks). It also does not view religion as only an individual matter but as an element of community. It points to the fundamental character of inter-faith engagement as something that occurs not only in particular containers and situations but also in everyday situations in university classrooms and student community activities. Of course, this is still not a guarantee of success. This model may not be enough to address all problems. The course of its implementation is critical and prone to many obstacles. Nonetheless, at least in principle, it is ready to address the problems that other models ignore.

49 Alexander-Kenneth Nagel and Mehmet Kalender, "Guestbooks in multi-faith spaces as (inter-)religious media," *Religion* 50, no. 3 (2020): 389, https://doi.org/10.1080/0048721X.2020.1756068.

4.4 *Three Policy Models*

To summarize, I have discussed three main policy approaches to religion on campus that influence how multi-faith spaces function and are perceived. Smith's typology allowed us to differentiate two basic models: a *single vision model*, in which religion is exclusively confined to one type of space regardless of users' needs, and a *multiple-vision model*, which opens the university to religion and adapts to the needs of users. The latter approach was further split into two models based on motivation. As I argued, while more inclusive, a *service-oriented model* still embraces the legible religion framework. It replaces control of a religion with its functionalization. While the *single vision model* responds to the narrative of secularization, the *service-oriented model* responds to the return of religion. Both models are resistant to religion by separating it from other spheres of activity.

The third *holistic model* takes a step away from legibility and involves all stakeholders in negotiation instead. This model arguably has a greater potential for dealing with potential problems lying behind the multi-faith spaces. The broader implications of this model will be further discussed in the next chapter.

Before I do that, however, there is one more element that needs to be considered in how multi-faith spaces are perceived. By now, I have discussed the effect of local elements on the perception of multi-faith spaces, from naming to institutional policy. The remaining element of the puzzle concerns the broader, extra-institutional context. Most importantly, I need to inspect how the difference between the banal and unbanal shapes the imposition of meanings on multi-faith spaces.

5 The Dynamics of Banality and Multi-faith Spaces

The regulations and environment outside of the institution are as crucial as that inside it. The historical background described in the first two chapters and the political surroundings discussed in Chapter 3 play a significant role in defining the spaces and how they are perceived. Both are extremely important in defining which religiosity is viewed as acceptable and what is considered neutral. Gilliat-Ray writes that:

> shared multi-faith spaces in public institutions 'open to people of all faiths, and none' are emerging out of a religious history predominately shaped by Protestant Christianity, and with this history come particular ideas and assumptions about what constitutes religion and religious

> practice. In many facets of public religion, from civic ceremonies to chaplaincy, minority faith traditions are struggling to achieve participation, recognition, or 'equality' (sometimes very successfully), but these efforts take place within a framework created by a history and tradition of which they were not a part. Thus, questions remain as to just how 'equal' they can be.[50]

Gilliat-Ray speaks about the influence of Protestant Christianity. Indeed, the types of religious observance favored by the materiality of multi-faith spaces, as discussed in the previous chapter, would confirm that thesis. However, as I argued at the end of Chapter 2, Roman Catholicism is not inconsequential. The Catholic chaplains introduced the first multi-faith spaces in Utrecht and Vienna. The modality of Christianity would not be so successful if a significant part of the picture were missing. Both Protestantism and Catholicism shape the content of legibility and are shaped according to that content themselves.

In Chapter 3, based on Oliphant's account, I have introduced the distinction between banal and unbanal religion. As I argued, banal religion has been adapted to legibility requirements. In such a reduced version, often masked as cultural, religion may operate in the public sphere. It can seamlessly disappear into the background, remaining unmarked. Both Protestant and Roman Catholic Christianity have that privilege, at least if they accept legibility constraints in a particular case.[51] The privilege of indifference is not given to religions that never went through such an adaptation. Quite the opposite; they are considered nominal and marked as potentially dangerous, requiring constant oversight, control, and, in some circumstances, even prohibition.

The cases from the beginning of this chapter demonstrate this dynamic well. No comprehensive analysis is required to see a clear pattern arising from these cases. It is difficult not to notice that Islam plays a particular role in each of them and is often targeted by the actions. It is singled out as an unbanal presence. In London, the Islamic Prayer Room is turned into a multi-faith space because of a racist incident aimed at Muslim students. In each of the four German universities, the Muslim presence plays a significant role. The instructions of Muslim men and the presence of the Quran and prayer mats are

50 Gilliat-Ray, "From 'Chapel' To 'Prayer Room'," 304–05. While Gilliat-Ray acknowledges the Protestant Christian roots, it is worth rememebering that most of the first MFS were introduced by the Catholic chaplains, who viewed their introduction as carving out the space for religion within the broader public institutions.

51 For example, by taking a political stance on issues such as abortion or welcoming refugees.

viewed as the failure of the supra-religious room in Dortmund. It also brings comparisons to al-Qaeda and Salafist-related incidents at other universities. The easier accessibility of mosques is among the reasons behind the closure of the prayer room in Berlin. Prayer mats, rituals, and collective gatherings are banned from the newly planned place in Duisburg-Essen. Muslims and their daily ritual schedule exemplify the rationale behind creating a new multi-faith space in Cologne. The whole Danish debate focuses on the Muslim presence in Denmark, with the simultaneous accusations of multi-faith spaces being the "hidden mosques," and incomprehensible to Muslims. Even if one carefully follows the provisions at the University of Hamburg, nearly all provisions are concerned with Muslims apart for the mention of the Star of David as an acceptable visible symbol.

This unbanal presence is contextually constructed. Again, in Chapter 3, I proposed that the return of religion means an increased presence of non-legible religiosity. In recent years, Muslim visibility increased significantly. Partly that is because of their increased population in many European countries and the need for more systematic catering to their needs. More importantly, however, Islam is presented as not adapted to the conditions of legibility. On the one hand, at least in some of its branches, it relies on external manifestations of religiosity, like head-covering. On the other, it is accused of not acknowledging that civil belonging takes primacy before religious affiliation.

Jocelyne Cesari describes the tendency in approaching Islam as "securitization," which she defines as a "multifaceted process through which the normal rule of law is suspended in favor of exceptional measures justified by extraordinary situations that threaten the survival of the political community."[52] If securitization is successful, certain phenomenon is redefined as a significant challenge to public safety and the survival of a given community. According to Cesari, this happened in Europe[53] after the events of 9/11 and the commencement of the War on Terror, which is exemplified not only by the acts directly aimed at Islamic extremism and terrorism but also by the broader legislative and rhetoric[54] changes in areas such as immigration or restrictions on Islamic

52 Jocelyne Cesari, "Securitization of Islam in Europe: The Embodiment of Islam as an Exception," in *Why the West Fears Islam* (New York: Palgrave Macmillan, 2013), 83.

53 Cesari gives examples from the UK, France, the Netherlands, and Denmark.

54 Which was discussed on the example of Samuel Huntington in Chapter 3.

practices and activities.[55] This extends down to the smallest expressions of religious affiliation, such as dress code or shaking hands.[56]

Such an approach singles out Muslims as "the alien." Securitization operates on the same principles as legible religion. It analytically differentiates Islam and Muslims as specific categories and reduces them to what seems essential from a public perspective—a global ideology and a threat. Securitization enforces the dynamic of banal and unbanal. It views any expression of affiliation with Islam as powerful, loaded, and thus dangerous. Thus, it marks these expressions as incompatible with the public sphere, even if similar behaviors of others go unnoticed. The latter are simply not viewed as significant from an administrative perspective.

The unbanality of Islam is so great that Muslims become physically separated in many cases, with the material separation of the multi-faith prayer spaces and Muslim separate spaces. Gilliat-Ray argues that:

> in many public contexts, sacred space has been produced for the exclusive use of Muslims, and often the 'economics of people' are at issue. However, there is also a sense in which Muslims are sometimes being constructively 'relegated' to their own separate spheres, setting up a dichotomy between Muslims, and all other faith groups. Sometimes they are relatively passive subjects of this relegation, and sometimes, perhaps as a result of prejudice, they understandably become more active agents in their own separation.[57]

Muslim "otherness" sets them against the three main modalities of post-secular legibility: secularism, religious pluralism, and Christianity. In London, the secular character of the institution is underlined as a justification for turning an Islamic prayer room into a multi-faith space, which causes protests by the university's student society. The secular is using the religiously plural to control

---

55 For example, the Swedish debate on free religious schools (*religiösa friskolor*). See, for example, Elisabeth Gerle, *Mångkulturalism—för vem? Debatten om muslimska och kristna friskolor blottlägger värdekonflikter i det svenska samhället* (Nora: Nya Doxa, 2002) and the collections of articles in the major Swedish newspapers: Svenska Dagbladet, "Debatten om religiösa friskolor," Svenska Dagbladet, 2022, accessed 12th of March, 2022, https://www.svd.se/story/debatten-om-religiosa-friskolor; Dagens Nyheter, "Religiösa friskolor," 2022, accessed 12th of March, 2022, https://www.dn.se/om/religiosa-friskolor/.

56 Jocelyne Cesari, "Securitization of Islam and Religious Freedom," *Berkley Forum*, 13th of September, 2018, https://berkleycenter.georgetown.edu/posts/securitization-of-islam-and-religious-freedom.

57 Gilliat-Ray, "From 'Chapel' To 'Prayer Room'," 301–02.

and restrict the actions of Islam. Similar justifications can be found in German and Danish cases as well. In the Danish example, however, the Christian cultural heritage is also viewed as threatened by Islam, which is why multi-faith spaces, as "hidden mosques," must be rejected. Each of the modalities is set as the "local standard" which now, confronted with an unbanal Islamic presence, needs to respond. Thus, Muslims are treated either as a danger (in most of the above cases) or as a challenge for social cohesion (as, for example, in Cologne).

The last of Gilliat-Ray's comments reminds us that Muslims are not only passive but also active agents. Setting the unbanal against the banal creates a certain dynamic of polarization, which is visible in some cases. That is why multi-faith spaces are viewed as, in some ways, offensive and, in the London example, as rejecting the needs of Muslims. That some Muslims are treated as representatives of the whole community only increases frustration and brings connotations of the accusations of, for example, Salafism, as at Dortmund.

And yet, as the Danish example shows, words such as Muslims, Islam, and their cognates often become rhetoric devices, which allow for the use of these figures in contradictory ways. These rhetorical uses, through their mediatized dissemination, become as important as the actual presence. They allow for the reduction of Muslims into one, flat phenomenon that bears the dangerous characteristics of "Islamization," social pressure, or gender oppression.[58] However, they also allow for such statements as "Muslims enjoy listening to Christian hymns." All such ideas are then, by proxy, imposed onto the spaces that are in any way associated with Muslims through use, by that shaping the perception of multi-faith spaces.[59]

The Danish example also shows more sophisticated ways of influencing the multi-faith space's existence, design, use, and perception. By introducing the notion of subsidiarity, the Danish government tried to relegate the responsibility for implementing its policies onto individuals and particular institutions. However, as I will discuss in the following chapter, the application of subsidiarity was only partial. While responsibility was relegated to a lower level, the directions of the actions were clearly drawn by the government ministers. Both

58 Just like in the cases of veiling, body covering, shaking hands, and many others.

59 Interestingly, this imposition of meaning does not have to correspond to reality. As mentioned above, in 2017, the Danish Ministry of Education send out a questionnaire to the primary and secondary educational institutions to check which of them have a prayer room. In the free-text responses, these institutions more often mentioned the use by Christian groups, rather than Muslims. Yet, Christian groups remained unmarked, while even sporadic Muslim use was noticed in the broader debate. Undervisnings Ministeriet, Short Information vedr. aktindsigt i undersøgelse om bederum på offentlige uddannelsesinstitutioner, fra undervisningsministeren. Bilag 2.

Pind and Støjberg did not hide their agreement with the Danish People's Party MPs regarding the responses to Muslim presence. They differed in the means they wanted to employ. While Støjberg stated that she does not want the institutions to hide behind pieces of legislation, her expectations towards these institutions were clear—an imposition of "Danishness" on all newcomers, and rejection of, for example, headscarves, niqabs, or burqas as incompatible with that.

The degree to which the unbanality of the Muslim presence, together with the historical and political context surrounding it, plays a role in the perception of multi-faith spaces, is clearly visible in the fact that most of the spaces mentioned in the introductory part of this chapter functioned for a decade until their "problematic character" was spotted.

As argued at the beginning of this section, the extra-institutional context significantly impacts how multi-faith spaces are perceived and approached. The dynamic of banal and unbanal marks some religions as potentially challenging, threatening, or detrimental to social cohesion, as exemplified by the securitization of Islam.[60] The interplay of secularism, religious pluralism, and Christianity impacts the institutional policies towards multi-faith spaces and broader discussions, conflicts, and political interventions concerning them. As indicated at the beginning of the chapter, multi-faith spaces do not operate in a void, but are surrounded by layers of meaning.

6 Perception and Context Matter

At the beginning of this second part of the book, I argued that multi-faith spaces, or at least their large share, constitute the embodiment of the legible religion. The last two chapters analyzed the history, the materiality, the effect, the naming, as well as the intra and extra-institutional context of multi-faith spaces to support this argument. The first chapter underlined the legible preference visible in different models of multi-faith spaces. It highlighted the concrete effects of the programs that, in early versions, were proposed by thinkers such

60 It must be noted that the distinction of banal and unbanal is used here as a heuristic tool. It is aimed to show the reductive tendency in approaching analytically defined and differentiated religions and classifying them based on that reductive tendency. The critique of the distinction is not meant to relativize some issues, such as gender equality, saying that "everything goes." Rather, it is meant to show the selectiveness and arbitrariness in approaching the same behaviour or approach when it is done by a representative of a certain category, for example, a Muslim, and when it is done by a member of the privileged class.

as Comte and Marx. The materiality of the most typical multi-faith spaces expressed an individualizing preference towards religion in line with some of the proposals discussed based on Marx. It supported religiosity that is individual, private, internalized, iconoclastic, cognitive, and prayer-oriented. It also showed how ingrained in the broader consciousness this approach became, as such design was presented as neutral. Even spaces that did not follow the same preference tended to treat religion in a functionalizing manner as a tool for social cohesion or coexistence, more in line with the approaches discussed based on Comte.

This chapter showed how reductions of legibility shape the perception of multi-faith spaces. It focused on the most typical, negative, intra-institutional spaces. These spaces are more significant from the perspective of legibility than extra-institutional ones because, as shown by Kühle and Reintoft Christensen, most individuals encounter the state via public institutions. Therefore, they are primary expressions of the state's approaches to a given subject, including religion. I chose university spaces to achieve standardization in the analysis.

Several conclusions can be drawn. First, the analysis of several cases showed that multiple competing meanings could be read into spaces with relatively similar materiality. Second, the analysis of how multi-faith spaces are named showed conflicting intentions behind these spaces and a mismatch between those intentions and the actual use. It also found that names can impose meaning onto spaces. Third, the institutional context analysis showed that the perception of multi-faith spaces is affected by pragmatic variables like space managers and the population of end users, and the implicit or explicit institutional policy towards religion. The analyzed policy examples expressed an interplay of the three modalities described in Chapter 3: secularism, religious pluralism, and Christianity. They confirmed the preference expressed by the materiality of these spaces. Both also exercised a degree of control over religion as something potentially challenging.

Fourth, the broader analysis of policy approaches differentiated between policies that responded to the two types of narratives described in Chapter 2. A *single vision model* constitutes a response to the narrative of secularization, secularizing the university campus, and enforcing a single vision of religion onto a single type of multi-faith spaces. A *multiple visions model* responds to the narrative of the return of religion, embracing religion on campus, and pragmatically adapting to the needs of its stakeholders. I differentiated the latter policy approach further, presenting two models according to the motivation behind adopting the approach. A *service-oriented model* looked at religion from a functional perspective, focusing on the superficially useful aspects of the legible religion framework. A *holistic model* rejected central planning and involved all stakeholders in negotiating what religion should be.

Fifth, and finally, I have discussed the influence of the wider extra-institutional context on the perception of multi-faith spaces. The analysis of the dynamic of banal and unbanal showed how adaptation to legibility confers the privilege of remaining unmarked, while the lack thereof raises the visibility and can mark a specific religion as potentially dangerous. The singling out of Islam because of its securitization helps explain why multi-faith spaces are, in some situations, strictly associated with Muslim use.

To sum up, multi-faith spaces exemplify the operations of legible religion. They show that this framework operates both constitutively, by influencing how different agents think about religion, and normatively, through concrete regulations and policies. In most cases, they express a strict religious/secular boundary. The shape and context of many of them present a reductive approach to religion as something that either can be manipulated to adapt to the functional needs of the state and its institutions, for example, social cohesion, or as something dangerous that requires strict control. Policies towards multi-faith spaces demonstrate the impact of the narratives of secularization and the return of religion. In the preference expressed by their most typical materiality, one can see the elements of religiosity that emerged in the development of secularism and were proposed by thinkers such as Comte or Marx. One can also notice the impact of both Protestant and Roman Catholic Christianity. Finally, in how they are perceived, one may see the dynamic of banal and unbanal and the interaction of three modalities: secularism, Christianity, and religious pluralism.

By far, the book focused on the critical description of legible religion. Throughout the five chapters I attempted to demonstrate and illustrate its emergence, development, and operations. Equipped with the understanding of legible religion in theory and practice we can now move on to two final questions. First, if a legible approach is indeed hegemonic, is that a problem? Second, if it is a problem, what are the alternatives? As I already noted, some spaces and institutions contested the foundational assumptions of the legible approach. The chaplaincy team at Yarl's Wood IDC and the University of Winchester attempted to create novel solutions. Even in governmental approaches, there were traces of potentially different approaches, although often trampled by the imposition of meanings, for example, the notion of subsidiarity in the Danish debate. These elements will guide me in responding to the two final questions in the last chapter of this book.

CHAPTER 6

Encountering Religion in Public

On the Need to Promote Practical Knowledge and Resonance

In the earlier parts of this book, I described a conceptual framework that I summed up with the term legible religion. This is a framework in which an analytically distinguished phenomenon of religion is reduced in a top-down manner only to the features deemed important from the administrative perspective. Such an approach, influenced by both the narrative of secularization and the narrative of the return of religion, has a dual effect. It acts normatively by restricting, with explicit rules, what is possible within a given administrative framework. It also influences broader ways of thinking about religion by spreading its reductive view at large among citizens, thus reshaping social consciousness and reality. As discussed in chapters 2 and 3, this leads to a dual way of thinking about religion: either as a potential threat that requires strict control or as a potentially functional category, useful for such purposes as social cohesion or provision of public services. In some conditions, a religion that adapted itself to the legible preference may also warrant indifference, a privilege lacking for religions that did not follow the same adaptations.

In an analysis of multi-faith spaces in chapters 4 and 5, I discussed the operations of the legible religion framework in practice. Normative inclinations are operative in the actions of individual agents, such as space managers, institutional leadership, or governmental officials, and in concrete, explicit policies, as described in leaflets and codes. The consciousness-shaping effect was much broader. By accepting the institutional logic, chaplains created spaces that allowed only for a specific religiosity. Other stakeholders, from users to politicians and policymakers, read or imposed meaning onto the spaces, regardless of the intention behind them. Different spaces presented the two main approaches to religion: either a potential threat that needs to be controlled, an understanding exemplified by the most typical, negative intra-institutional spaces; or, functionally, an understanding exemplified by positive extra-institutional spaces or spaces at universities that followed a service-oriented approach. We also saw the singling out of Islam and its "securitization" in conflicts and discussions about multi-faith spaces, highlighting the dynamic of banal and unbanal religion.

 | DOI:10.1163/9789004714366_008

Some readers may wonder, "so what?" Why should we be interested in the legible approach to religion? What are the practical implications of describing such a conceptual framework and analyzing its operation on the example of multi-faith spaces?

As hinted earlier, I argue that the legible approach is, at least in its current form, problematic because it is too reductive to respond adequately to the challenges posed by a religiously plural society. As exemplified by the most typical multi-faith spaces, there is a mismatch between what they promise (inclusivity and equality) and what they provide (exclusive preference for specific types of religiosity and uses of religion). And as exemplified by broader discussions about these spaces, this is true for rooms at public institutions and our societies more broadly. In that sense, multi-faith spaces stand for much larger problems in the approach to religion today.

Tackling these problems, this chapter is divided into two parts. First, I will develop the argument concerning the problematic character of the legible religion framework by returning to Scott's broader account of legibility and Hartmut Rosa's notion of institutional controllability to identify the main problems with this approach. The second part will discuss possible directions that could support replacement, or supplementation, of the legible approach. I will argue that the search for solutions could start in several areas: subsidiarity, conflict transformation, encounter, inter-faith praxis, and religious literacy.

1 Defining the Problem

1.1 *Between Legibility and Mētis*

In *Seeing Like a State*, Scott describes multiple examples of legible frameworks, from centrally designed forests and cities to forcefully collectivized farms. Concluding his analysis, Scott argues that the core mechanisms of legibility—central-level administrative reductions and simplifications—are unable to account for the complexity of reality. If significantly disruptive, they may lead to the decline or even destruction of the affected phenomena. Scott writes:

> Any large social process or event will inevitably be far more complex than the schemata we can devise, prospectively or retrospectively, to map it.
>
> …
>
> [Similarly,] the necessarily thin, schematic model of social organization and production animating the planning [is] inadequate as a set of instructions for creating a successful social order. By themselves, the

> simplified rules can never generate a functioning community, city, or economy.[1]

Scott underlines at the end of the quote that if all conduct is constricted within the boundaries of simplification, it cannot create a functioning social order.

And yet, as the reader might remember from Chapter 1, Scott argues that legible reductions are necessary for any modern administration to function. Administrative legibility is not a problem on its own. It becomes problematic when it disrupts the processes that it does not account for and that are nonetheless necessary. Thus, only a reduction that suppresses complexity is problematic. Scott argues that formal order relies on the very informal processes it tends to leave out of its simplifications. Leaving them out may provide a broader perspective and be administratively helpful. However, if these informal processes are removed as a side-effect, the entire formal order may become dysfunctional.[2]

Scott exemplifies the operations of this principle based on the "work-to-rule" strike (*grève du zèle*). In such an action, workers strike by closely adhering to all regulations and job descriptions instituted by the company representatives and doing nothing that goes beyond them. As a result, productivity drops, and production significantly slows down or stops altogether.

Administrative legibility, especially if supported by ideological accounts and the coercive power of the state, can achieve similar results. The worst, most destructive results Scott observes in authoritarian states. However, they are not limited to these states and are often the result of a genuine wish to improve the conditions of human life. Thus, negative consequences do not require ill will or despotic tendencies, although they are strengthened by them.

In the context of this book, this means that when the reduction of religion to its legible version goes beyond purely administrative use and becomes normative, it will significantly disrupt social reality. It will reshape phenomena classified as religious. Ultimately, it may lead to a dysfunctional social order. It does not require malice or authoritarian inclinations. But the effects are significantly strengthened when supported by ideological accounts, for example, secularization.

To further nuance his argument, Scott differentiates between scientific explanation and practical knowledge, or as he summed them up, *technē* and *mētis*. *Technē* is a type of knowledge that aims to be generalizable, freed from

---

1 James C. Scott, *Seeing like a State: How Certain Schemes to Improve the Human Condition Have Failed* (New Haven: Yale University Press, 1999), 309–10.

2 Scott, *Seeing like a State*, 310.

the particularity of a given situation, context, guesswork, or contingency. *Technē* is universal, settled knowledge that

> arises from the fact that it is organized analytically into small, explicit, logical steps and is both decomposable and verifiable. This universality means that knowledge in the form of *technē* can be taught more or less completely as a formal discipline. The rules of *technē* provide for theoretical knowledge that may or may not have practical applications. Finally, *technē* is characterized by impersonal, often quantitative precision and a concern with explanation and verification.[3]

Thus, *technē* is a legible type of knowledge—reality stripped of everything that is not strictly pertaining to the chosen goal and ordered into manageable steps. It is also generalizable and universal, applicable regardless of the individual circumstances and context.

Mētis, in contrast, is highly contextual, devised only to be useful for a particular context based on personal and communal experience. Scott writes:

> Mētis is most applicable to broadly similar but never precisely identical situations requiring a quick and practiced adaptation that becomes almost second nature to the practitioner. The skills of mētis may well involve rules of thumb, but such rules are largely acquired through practice … and a developed feel or knack for strategy. Mētis resists simplification into deductive principles which can successfully be transmitted through book learning, because the environments in which it is exercised are so complex and nonrepeatable that formal procedures of rational decision making are impossible to apply.[4]

Mētis does not fit well into the requirements of legibility. It is localized, requires practice instead of an overarching administrative perspective, and does not transfer well between contexts.[5] While *technē* operates on universal rules, *mētis* focuses on rules of thumb. *Technē* is the knowledge of analytical scholars and administrators. *Mētis* is a matter of skill and the domain of practitioners.

---

3 Scott, *Seeing like a State*, 320.

4 Scott, *Seeing like a State*, 315–16.

5 Compare with the conscious resistance and hidden language of the underprivileged described by Scott in *Domination and the Arts of Resistance. Hidden Transcripts* (New Haven and London: Yale University Press, 1990).

Scott argues that the legible approach tends to favor *technē* while discarding *mētis*. Uncertain factors are operationalized in ways that allow them to enter formulas of *technē* and, preferably, fitted into an excel sheet: the nation's development as GDP, public opinion as poll numbers, values as psychological inventories.[6] By that, however, it runs the risk of either missing the crucial characteristics in the simplification process or proposing a measure that is so complex as to be highly unpragmatic.

While in some contexts, *technē* can be extremely successful, improving upon *mētis* greatly (for example, by replacing variolation with vaccination), in conditions that are characterized by high levels of variability, the central-level generalizations, and simplifications, according to Scott, miss the elements that are inherent in *mētis*: context, the requirements of the concrete situation and locality, partisan interests, and plasticity.[7]

While the distinction between universal and particular knowledge, norms, and rules has been extensively discussed in ethics,[8] Scott reflects on their distinction in the context of the state. He does not indicate a clear preference for either of these. He argues that both have their time and place. Instead, Scott underlines the tendency to disregard one of these dimensions in favor of the other, regardless of the intention. While administrative simplifications are necessary in modern state organisms, they cannot come at the cost of the informal processes on which the formal order relies.

I argue that legible religion leads to the challenges described by Scott. As described in previous chapters, this framework limits religion only to administratively distinguished areas, forcibly removing everything else. Within the public sphere, religion can only operate either in a banal form which often means the removal of its symbolic power, or as a force for social cohesion based on the specified civil values. Negative intra-institutional multi-faith spaces embody this approach most explicitly—they force the internalization and privatization of faith to the extent that it misses the perspective of individual

6 Scott, *Seeing like a State*, 322.

7 Scott, *Seeing like a State*, 322.

8 See, for example, Stanley Hauerwas, *A Community of Character* (Notre Dame: University of Notre Dame Press, 1981); Alasdair MacIntyre, *After Virtue* (Notre Dame: University of Notre Dame Press, 1981); Michael Sandel, *Liberalism and the Limits of Justice* (Cambridge: Cambridge University Press, 1982); Robert N. Bellah, *Habits of the Heart* (Berkeley: University of California Press, 1985); Jeffrey Stout, *Ethics after Babel: The Lanuages of Morals and Their Discontents* (Boston: Beacon Press, 1988); Jeffrey Stout, *Democracy and Tradition* (Princeton: Princeton University Press, 2005); Alasdair MacIntyre, *Ethics in the Conflicts of Modernity. An Essay on Desire, Practical Reasoning, and Narrative* (Cambridge: Cambridge University Press, 2016).

needs and limits all other informal processes, such as intergroup contact and encounter, thereby unintendedly increasing, rather than decreasing, tensions.

However, as I discussed on the example of the multi-vision policy approaches, the limitations are imposed not only explicitly via the space. The legible pronouncements also reshape the way we think about reality, that is, they are consciousness-shaping. The theory developed by a German sociologist, Hartmut Rosa, will support us in better understanding these processes.

1.2 *Between Resistance and Resonance*

As a sociologist, Rosa is interested in how people constitute their relationship to the world. He argues that for late-modern people, the attitude towards the world is characterized by aggression, conquest, and the need for control, what Rosa sums up under the term "resistance." The world requires our constant intervention to not lose what we already have and to improve our life by bringing more world into our reach. Rosa writes:

> The sociocultural formation of modernity thus turns out to be, in a way, doubly calibrated for the strategy of making the world controllable. We are structurally compelled (from without) and culturally driven (from within) to turn the world into a point of aggression. It appears to us as something to be known, exploited, attained, appropriated, mastered, and controlled. And often this is not just about bringing things—segments of world—within reach, but about making them faster, easier, cheaper, more efficient, less resistant, more reliably controllable.[9]

Rosa points out that this resistant approach is conditioned both externally and internally. On the one hand, social structures externally direct us towards resistance. On the other hand, culture reshapes our thinking by reframing each element of reality either in terms of acquisition, functionalization, or control. However, Rosa notes, they do not only condition us to rethink how we approach them, but actively reshape reality to make them more in line with such an approach.

Rosa visualizes it with the metaphor of endless to-do lists. We see the world and ourselves as tasks to be tackled, from control over our body (weight that needs to be changed or controlled, wrinkles that need to be reduced, blood pressure that needs to be lowered, a daily number of steps that needs to be surpassed) to the conquest of the environment (mountains climbed, sights visited

---

9 Hartmut Rosa, *The Uncontrollability of the World*, trans. James C. Wagner (Cambridge: Polity Press, 2021), 14.

and photographed) and people (number of people in the network raised, lovers conquered).

If one relates Rosa's considerations to the legible religion framework, one can see such a dynamic clearly. Culturally, the ingrained narratives reshape our consciousness to perceive religion as a separate category that can be either viewed functionally, for example as a tool for social cohesion or an element of personal development, or as a potential danger, something that needs to be tightly controlled. The existing structures only strengthen these attitudes. Many multi-faith spaces and policies around them are the clearest example of that—they embody these two approaches to reality.

The attempt at making the world controllable, Rosa writes, can be divided along four dimensions. Different phenomena must be made (1) visible, (2) reachable or accessible, (3) manageable, and (4) useful. According to Rosa, all these dimensions are entrenched in modern social institutions, from science and technology to economic development, legal regulations, and political-administrative apparatuses.[10] This may not result in complete control over the world. Quite the opposite, the results may be contrary to expectations. Rosa concludes:

> My theory is that this institutionally enforced program, this cultural promise of making the world controllable, not only does not "work" but in fact becomes distorted into its exact opposite. The scientifically, technologically, economically, and politically controllable world mysteriously seems to elude us or to close itself off from us. It withdraws from us, becoming mute and unreadable. Even more, it proves to be threatened and threatening in equal measure, and thus ultimately constitutively uncontrollable.[11]

Examples of these dynamics were visible in the British and German cases described in the previous chapter. The more control over religion the universities introduced, the greater tensions seemed to be generated. An imposition of strict regulations concerning religious practice led to protests, alienation, and vilification of groups of students, and the rise of inter-group tensions.

Rosa argues that the more one attempts to control reality, the more closed and muter it becomes. There is a mismatch between promise and practice. The need for controllability encounters constitutive uncontrollability. The institutional impositions only constrain the room for maneuver but do not change

10 Rosa, *The Uncontrollability of the World*, 15–18.

11 Rosa, *The Uncontrollability of the World*, 19.

what Rosa calls *Unverfügbarkeit* following Rudolf Bultmann, the radical elusiveness of the world. This mismatch leads to severe, unexpected consequences: alienation instead of adaptive transformation, reification instead of revivification, the world becoming illegible instead of comprehensible etc. Rosa points out that "Modernity has lost its ability to be *called,* to be *reached.*"[12] Thus, forceful institutional attempts alienate individuals and groups, reify them instead of providing them with life, and create a sense of loss and lack of comprehensibility. Paradoxically, insistence on controllability instead of increasing reachability decreases it.

The ability to be called and reached needs to be regained, in Rosa's view. Thus, as an alternative to controllability and resistance in approaching the world, Rosa proposes an approach summed up under the term "resonance."[13] This term, originally from physics, describes a relationship in which two entities mutually stimulate each other, just like a string of the guitar creates resonance in the instrument's wooden body. Rosa argues that resonance is a mode of relation defined by four characteristics. First, resonance means that one is affected in an encounter with a particular phenomenon (being affected)—in contrast, in an aggressive approach, a book can be read without affecting the reader, a person can be met without being noticed, leading to mute relationships. Second, resonance means that one is not only affected, but also responsive. One responds emotionally as a separate being, using one's own voice in what Rosa called self-efficacy. Third, the resonant relationship of affect and emotion effectuates a change in the people involved in a resonant relationship, leading to an adaptive transformation. Rosa emphasizes that a resonant relationship requires a middle stance between being fully open and fully closed—one must be open enough to be affected but closed enough to recognize one's own identity and voice. Fourth, resonance is uncontrollable—one can create conditions or enter a setting in which a resonant experience or relationship can happen, but resonance cannot be guaranteed.[14]

It must be noted, however, that, similarly to Scott's evaluation of legibility, Rosa does not reject all attempts at making reality reachable or even controllable. He does not believe resonance is the only type of relationship that needs to be adopted. He views mute or reifying relationships as helpful for some endeavors, such as science, technology, administration, and many others. He

12 Rosa, *The Uncontrollability of the World*, 28.

13 Rosa, *The Uncontrollability of the World*, 32.

14 Rosa, *The Uncontrollability of the World*, 32–37. Rosa's model of Resonance has been developed in much greater depth in a larger volume: Hartmut Rosa, *Resonance. A Sociology of Our Relationship to the World*, trans. James C. Wagner (Cambridge: Polity Press, 2019).

notes that while rooted in mute relationships, these endeavors create conditions in which resonance can occur. Instead, Rosa criticizes the balance and preference imposed by the current model of the organization of society. In his view, mute relationships cannot be the norm, and resonance an exception (delimited only to spheres like art and spirituality). Thus, the current relationship of resistance and resonance, controllability and uncontrollability, needs to be inverted. Quite the opposite, resonance should be the norm, and muteness the exception. The constitutively resonant structures should create areas in which specific endeavors that require mute relationships could be developed, not the other way around.[15]

The same could be said about Scott's account. Reality should not be reshaped to fit the requirement of legibility. Quite the opposite; legibility should be used cautiously, not to suppress the crucial elements that are not included in its simplifications and allow for the operations of *mētis* when practical and pragmatic. While *technē* encourages mute relationships, which implement a centrally devised plan, *mētis* promotes resonant approaches that adapt to the concrete context and particular situation.

Both conclusions, when referred to religion, would mean that there is nothing wrong per se with administrative simplifications of religion or a mute understanding of religion as an object. Both can be useful in specific situations; both can have their uses. The problem lies in the balance between the legible and the real, between the resistance and the resonance. When legible approaches overhaul complexity, and when resistance dominates approaches to phenomena classified as religious, social reality is disrupted, and constitutive uncontrollability strikes back.

1.3 *Legible Religion and Its Fallacies*

What do these broader frameworks of Scott and Rosa offer to this book's analysis of legible religion and multi-faith spaces? We can draw several conclusions.

First, the simplified, centrally devised vision of religion created by legible religion does not account for the world's complexity. It most often lacks the adaptation to context, the requirements of the concrete situation and locality, or plasticity, and it does not account for particular, partisan interests.[16]

15 Rosa, *Resonance*, 441.

16 Legal realists tend to speak about the "law in the books" and the "law in practice," pointing out that the former does not necessarily correspond to the latter, as practice will entail extra-juridical elements that cannot be accounted for just based on the assessment of what is the law. See Roscoe Pound, "Law in Books and Law in Action," *American Law Review* 44, no. 1 (1910). For discussion see Jean-Louis Halperin, "Law in Books and Law in Action: The Problem of Legal Change," *Maine Law Review* 64, no. 1 (2011). In a similar way,

As discussed on the example of multi-faith spaces, the relatively similar solution can have completely different results depending on the particular context, from bringing accusations of being a hidden mosque to being rejected by Muslims as an attack on their rights; from being viewed as an imperative in Cologne, to, as I encountered during my visit to Ireland, being received with fear when a multi-faith space replaced a Catholic chapel during the remodeling of one of the Dublin hospitals.

Second, this framework represents a mute, resistant approach to religion, as something that should be controlled, rather than something that introduces a resonant relationship of affection, emotion, and transformation. Both features of legible religion are not problematic in themselves. As noted by Scott and Rosa, neither legibility nor resistance is problematic *per se*. Both administrative simplification and a mute relationship to the world may have their use, time, and space. However, they should not operate as the primary approach to which reality has to yield. Legibility, on its own, cannot create a functioning community. Mute relationships lead to alienation and reification. When conflicts arise, different sides seem to embrace this mode as primary, and become mute to each other, neither able to be called nor reached by the other sides. That is why, in the typology of policies towards multi-faith spaces, I further nuanced the distinction between *single vision* and *multiple visions models*. I split the latter into a *service-oriented* and a *holistic model*. While a *service-oriented model* offers greater flexibility of adaptation, it still promotes a mute, resistant relationship to the religiosity of others. The *holistic model*, at least in principle, provides conditions for resonant relationships.

Third, the tendency of legible religion to establish a hegemonic status, supported by the dominant and ideologized narratives of, first, secularization and, later, the return of religion, is problematic and brings both normative and consciousness-shaping consequences. Normatively, it potentially leads to the suppression of crucial elements of the affected phenomena, and people who take part in them, categorized as religious. It also constrains the employment of practical knowledge, *mētis*, in situations concerning it. Constitutively, legible religion imposes a preference for a specific religiosity onto reality, differentiating between "good" and "bad" religion, and reshapes general attitudes

one could speak about "religion in the books" and "lived religion." Even if well informed by the generalized knowledge of religion as, for example, developed by religious studies, the administrators engaged in legibility will not be able to account for all elements not accounted for in the books. For more on the notion of lived religion, see David D. Hall, *Lived Religion in America: Roward a History of Practice* (Princeton: Princeton University Press, 1997).

towards religion along the lines of resistance: either as a potential threat that needs to be controlled or as a tool for expanding our share of the world, a functional tool for expanding Westernness, promoting civil values or strengthening social cohesion. Following the four dimensions of controllability proposed by Rosa, legible religion differentiates between marked religion, one of interest to the administrator, and unmarked religion, one that can be treated with indifference, and aims to make that marked religion (1) visible by bringing attention to all of its expressions, (2) reachable, by confining it to specific spaces and/or circumstances, (3) manageable, by simplifying and generalizing it, and (4) useful, whenever deemed functional. Such an approach conditions, both structurally and culturally, a mute relationship to reality, which results in a growing, frustrating mismatch between the aim for control and the constitutive uncontrollability of the world.

To sum up, I have reviewed the limits of legibility and the dangers of reductive impositions reshaping reality. Building on Scott, I discussed Rosa's ideas on the institutional need for controllability and its clash with the constitutive uncontrollability of the world. I then applied their broader discussions to the concrete analysis of legible religion and multi-faith spaces. However, both Scott and Rosa diagnosed not only a problem but also proposed solutions or at least directions in thinking about solutions. The primary task of this book is diagnostic, but, like these two scholars, I would like to discuss potential directions that could allow us to move beyond the fallacies of legible religion. By necessity for a study such as this one, my suggestions will have to remain a sketch.

2 Finding a Solution

How can one move beyond the fallacies of legible religion? I argue that there is a need to focus on both words included in the term 'legible religion' to answer this question. First, as argued before, legibility, if supported by ideological accounts and the state's coercive power, reshapes reality under its dictate. Part of the solution, then, needs to consider reducing the impact of areas in which central-level, reductive legibility, with its insistence on control, operates. Second, there is a need to attend to the notion of religion, deconstructing the normative assumptions behind it and proposing alternative approaches in their place.

The reconsideration of religion and the normative assumptions behind it have been the main focus of this book, as a contribution to the growing field of critical religion. The contributors to this field of study, for example, Nongbri or Cavanaugh, discussed in Chapter 1, have increasingly emphasized that there is no such thing as a transhistorical, transnational phenomenon of religion, but that this is an analytical concept developed for specific purposes. Thus, not only the administrative use of this term, but any application of this term to reality, is not neutral but potentially constitutes an imposition of meaning on phenomena labeled as religious, based on the context and circumstances in which this term was created.

Moreover, it is not always clear why some elements are labeled religious while others are not. Chapters 3 and 5 pointed out that some potentially religious elements are banalized by referring to them as cultural (primarily concerning Christianity) or philosophical (for example, Buddhism). Thus, some scholars have called for rethinking the social and political uses of the term religion,[17] while others proposed rejecting this category altogether.[18]

While I agree that there is a need to rethink the use of religion as a socio-politico-legal category, this book has shown that such a rethinking cannot

---

17 For example, Svenungsson writes: "I think that a critical attention to the affinities between various forms of experience could be particularly helpful in breaking up reductive and distorting categorizations of human behavior, customs and practices into 'religious' and 'secular'. One may, for instance, draw attention to the fact that experiences related to bodily integrity may be a significant uniting factor for both Muslim women's and transgender persons' requests vis-à-vis public baths. Or, to refer to a slightly different domain, one could reflect on the affinities between experiences that some subjects would define as 'religious' and others as 'aesthetic'—for example, the sense of wonder experienced when confronted with an artistic masterpiece or when overwhelmed by the beauty of a cathedral. This is, of course, not to say that the one experience could be reduced to the other or that complex experiences could be distilled down to more fundamental 'pure' experiences. On the contrary, what makes an experience an experience in the more compound sense is precisely the specific interpretative framework in which it is inserted, which is also why one subject's 'religious' experience of, say, a Bach concert, is certainly not identical to another subject's 'aesthetic' experience of the same concert. The point I am making, though, is that there are still enough common features in the two forms of experience to enable one subject to enhance the understanding of the other's experience. Drawing attention to phenomenologically similar experiences can in other words stir our imagination and help us think beyond established boundaries between religious and secular, rational and irrational, traditional and modern, and so on." Jayne Svenungsson, "The return of religion or the end of religion? On the need to rethink religion as a category of social and political life," *Philosophy and Social Criticism* 46, no. 7 (2020): 803–04, https://doi.org/10.1177%2F0191453719896384.

18 For example, political theorist Cécile Laborde argues that in a liberal egalitarian state, religion is not a useful politico-legal category. She argues that the state should adopt a disaggregate conception of religion, in which religion should be broken into separate elements with protection or rejection addressed only at the elements warranting state's interest. See Cécile Laborde, *Liberalism's Religion* (Cambridge, MA and London, U.K.: Harvard University Press, 2017).

be simply done in a top-down manner and later enforced by the state, as it risks following the legibility trap once again. Similarly, splitting religion into separate elements and, from the state's perspective, focusing only on socially salient elements, may not necessarily solve legibility problems, as the choice of what is deemed relevant and what is not may follow the same biases as described before.[19]

In this final part of the book, I would like to focus on what could be done to move beyond the fallacies of legibility. Following alternatives proposed by Scott and Rosa, I argue that, normatively, there is a need to provide more scope for *mētis* while, from a consciousness-shaping perspective, one should focus on promoting the approaches to the world that are more resonant.

In practice, this could mean three main changes. First, and most importantly, on a normative level, to counteract the primacy of the simplifying tendency of legibility at the central level, states should embrace subsidiarity. They should do so not only formally but also in practice, and not only relegating responsibility but also agency, unlike in the Danish government's position during the debate on multi-faith spaces. Second, on a consciousness-shaping level, to counteract one side of the resistant view of religion, the states should reframe their approach to religion, moving away from the view of religion as inherently violent and dangerous. This requires a broader change of perspective on conflict—a replacement of conflict aversion with the notion of conflict transformation. Third, as the other side of the resistant approach—that is, the view of religion from the perspective of utility—cannot account for the complexity of religion, it should be replaced by the resonant notions of encounter and inter-faith praxis, supported by religious literacy.

2.1 *Subsidiarity*

The most straightforward antidote to the fallacies of central-level simplifications is to limit their amount, scope, and impact. The central-level simplifications should be limited only to those areas and cases where they provide a significant benefit over lower levels. They should be imposed onto reality to as small a degree as possible. Or, reversing the order, the decisions and regulations should be established at a level as low and adequate as possible.

This is the central premise of the so-called principle of subsidiarity, which assumes that the higher level authority should only perform the tasks that cannot be satisfactorily done by a lower level organization. In other words, the

19 For a discussion of potential risks of abolishing the concept of religion, see: Thomas Lynch, "Social construction and social critique: Haslanger, race, and the study of religion," *Critical Research on Religion* 5, no. 3 (2017), https://doi.org/10.1177/2050303217732133.

state should only intervene if all smaller and more immediate organizational units cannot do it effectively. Before advocating for this principle, we need to take a closer look at what it exactly entails.

According to John M. Finnis, while the roots of this concept go back to Aristotle's *Nicomachean Ethics*, the principle was clarified during the nineteenth century. Finnis argues, referring to thinkers like John Stuart Mill and Frederick William Maitland, that two visions of political organization emerged. On the one hand, as explicated in Maitland's 1903 Sedgwick Lecture, the French Revolution introduced a model comprising two entities: the individual and the state. In its most extreme versions, this view rejected all other types of organization, giving the state complete freedom to govern by itself. On the other hand, in opposition to this, there was a view, increasingly advocated by the emerging Catholic social teaching, that the state should allow for the free operation of families, trade unions, and other associations, interfering in their activities only in exceptional cases of abuse or collapse.[20]

The foundations for this approach were already laid in the earliest social encyclical, *Rerum Novarum*,[21] issued by Pope Leo XIII in 1891, later expanded upon by Pope Pius IX in *Quadragesimo Anno*,[22] and more recently straightforwardly confirmed and defined by John Paul II in issued in 1991 *Centesimus Annus*, which reads:

> *the principle of subsidiarity* must be respected: a community of a higher order should not interfere in the internal life of a community of a lower order, depriving the latter of its functions, but rather should support it in case of need and help to coordinate its activity with the activities of the rest of society, always with a view to the common good.[23]

This version of subsidiarity follows the most common understanding of the term—a vertical approach that asks at which level decisions should be made. It has been translated in some forms into legal systems of multiple countries

---

20 John M. Finnis, "Subsidiarity's Roots and History: Some Observations," *The American Journal of Jurisprudence* 61, no. 1 (2016): 138–40, https://doi.org/10.1093/ajj/auw006.

21 Leo XIII, "Rerum Novarum," (1891): paragraphs 12–14, 48–52. https://www.vatican.va/content/leo-XIII/en/encyclicals/documents/hf_l-xiii_enc_15051891_rerum-novarum.html.

22 Pius XI, "Quadragesimo Anno," (1931): paragraphs 78–81. https://www.vatican.va/content/pius-XI/en/encyclicals/documents/hf_p-xi_enc_19310515_quadragesimo-anno.html.

23 John Paul II, "Centesimus Annus," (1991): paragraph 48. https://www.vatican.va/content/john-paul-II/en/encyclicals/documents/hf_jp-ii_enc_01051991_centesimus-annus.html.

worldwide, from European states as diverse as Denmark,[24] Germany,[25] and Poland,[26], to Australia[27] or Nigeria[28] in other continents. An augmented vertical understanding is also employed by the Treaty on European Union, first introduced at Maastricht in 1992, and in the current, consolidated form reads in article 5 point 3:

> Under the principle of subsidiarity, in areas which do not fall within its exclusive competence, the Union shall act only if and in so far as the objectives of the proposed action cannot be sufficiently achieved by the Member States, either at central level or at regional and local level, but can rather, by reason of the scale or effects of the proposed action, be better achieved at Union level.[29]

If this rule is already in place, one could ask, why would I advocate for it here? First, the formal adoption of the principle does not necessarily mean that subsidiarity is adopted in practice. For example, describing the EU, arguably the most carefully studied example of formal subsidiarity, the principle is constantly presented as requiring further adoption effort.[30] For example, Till Olbrich and Rudolf Raye note that:

---

24 Joseph M. Lookofsky, "Desperately Seeking Subsidiarity Danish Private Law in the Scandinavian, European, and Global Context," *CICLOPs* 1 (2009).

25 Greg Taylor, "Germany: The subsidiarity principle," *International Journal of Constitutional Law* 4, no. 1 (2006), https://doi.org/10.1093/icon/moi054.

26 Marek Zubik, *Prawo konstytucyjne współczesnej Polski*, Studia Prawnicze, (Warszawa: C.H. Beck, 2021), 34–36.

27 Marco Balboni, "The global reach of the principle of subsidiarity: the case of Australia," *Commonwealth & Comparative Politics* 57, no. 2 (2019), https://doi.org/10.1080/14662043.2019.1574001.

28 Kangnikoé Bado, "Good governance as a precondition for subsidiarity: human rights litigation in Nigeria and ECOWAS," *Commonwealth & Comparative Politics* 57, no. 2 (2019), https://doi.org/10.1080/14662043.2019.1574015.

29 European Union, "Consolidated version of the Treaty on European Union," (2012): Article 5 point 3. https://eur-lex.europa.eu/legal-content/EN/TXT/?uri=celex%3A12012M%2FTXT. The principle is further supplemented and detailed in Protocol No. 2 to the treaty.

30 See, for example, Jean-Pierre Danthine, "Subsidiarity: The forgotten concept at the core of Europe's existential crisis," *Vox EU CEPR*, 12th of April 2017, https://voxeu.org/article/subsidiarity-still-key-europe-s-institutional-problems; Reinhold Lopatka, "Subsidiarity: Bridging the gap between the ideal and reality," *European View* 18, no. 1 (2019), https://doi.org/10.1177/1781685819838449; Roel Beetsma and George Kopits, "Is the EU ready to truly apply the subsidiarity principle?," *Vox EU CEPR*, 15th of June 2020, https://voxeu.org/content/eu-ready-truly-apply-subsidiarity-principle.

> Europe's leaders have been … clear that the principle remains to be implemented in practice. "More attention needs to be paid to the subsidiarity principle," says German Chancellor Angela Merkel. "We have to get to the point that what is better done locally or regionally is actually decided at that level," says EU Parliament President Martin Schulz. "Since the Maastricht Treaty, we have been talking about the correct application of the subsidiarity principle," says European Commission President Jean-Claude Juncker. "What we are doing, however, is not sufficient. Our speeches last longer than our efforts."[31]

Second, the adoption of the rule of subsidiarity does not mean the same thing in each case. In the Danish example from the previous chapter, the Danish government referred to the idea of subsidiarity extensively. They pointed out that it is the responsibility of each individual Dane to find ways of engagement with "the others," in this case, Muslims. The problem with this approach was that it only relegated responsibility while withholding agency at the national level. Even if the Danish government did not rely on legislation to force certain solutions, the government's expectations and the desired result were clear. The offered comments provided implicit, top-down guidelines. Instead of guiding, there is a need to equip both individuals and managers with greater religious literacy.

Finnis points out that not all conceptions of vertical subsidiarity lead to the same results. He criticizes the formulations of article 5 of the Treaty on European Union and the accompanying Protocol 5:

> None of these EU concepts—better (or worse or insufficient) efficiency for achieving presupposed "objectives" of some "proposed action"; deciding on the action "close to the peoples"—is adequate to stating or understanding the principle [of subsidiarity]. They remain within the framework of French revolutionary flattening out of social and political thought denounced by Maitland: the reduction of social realities and issues to "individual and state/Society."[32]

Finnis notes a crucial tension in different conceptions of subsidiarity. He points to the different understandings of how society should be structured,

31 Till Olbrich and Rudolf Rayle, "Whatever Happened to EU Subsidiarity?," *Project Syndicate*, 8th of December 2015, https://www.project-syndicate.org/commentary/eu-subsidiarity-treaties-important-by-till-olbrich-and-rudolf-rayle-2015–12.

32 Finnis, "Subsidiarity's Roots and History," 141.

and what constitutes the smallest social unit. In the quote, Finnis points to the flattening in line with the French Revolution that creates a bi-focal social order divided into two levels, individual and state or society, with different levels of operation of the latter (local, national, European). In such an understanding, centrally devised objectives should then be realized as close to the people as possible. An alternative understanding, proposed among others in the papal encyclicals, includes communities of different orders. This approach assumes a multi-focal social order, in which higher-level communities support the lower-level ones, each with their own function.

The first of these approaches still retains a degree of top-down approach. Michelle Evans and Augusto Zimmermann point out that subsidiarity could be understood as "a decentralizing principle, which favors decentralized over centralized decision-making."[33] The relegation of responsibility without proper agency, including the ability to set the agenda, does not lead to decentralized decision-making but the state's subsumption of lower order entities as "sub-contractors" of the state's plan. Contrary to that, the Roman Catholic notion of subsidiarity involves neither the relegation of responsibility only, nor the complete abandonment of lower levels by the higher ones, but comprises an offer of *subsidy* or, in other words, help and assistance to the proper level. Russell Hittinger writes that "Subsidiarity, therefore, is a principal derivative from social justice: namely, that when *subsidium* be given either by the parts to the whole or the whole to the parts the plurality of functions or *munera* should not be destroyed or absorbed."[34] Each part of society has its proper role and should support other parts of society.

Of course, this approach also has its problems. The flattening approach of the French Revolution was meant to emancipate individuals from the power of different communities and provide them with personal agency. While the Roman Catholic notion has been developed to balance the approaches of individualism and collectivism, it does not have all the answers on how to maintain the autonomy of the individual against the coercive power of the groups, for example with regard to gender-related questions.[35] In Roman Catholic social

33 Michelle Evans and Augusto Zimmermann, "The Global Relevance of Subsidiarity: An Overview," in *Global Perspectives on Subsidiarity*, ed. Michelle Evans and Augusto Zimmermann (Dordrecht: Springer, 2014), 4.

34 Russell Hittinger, "Social Pluralism and Subsidiarity in Catholic Social Doctrine," *Annales theologici* 16 (2002): 394.

35 For more on gender-related questions in the context of religious communities and freedom of religion or belief, see, for example, Susan Moller Okin, *Is Multiculturalism Bad for Women?*, ed. Joshua Cohen, Matthew Howard, and Martha C. Nussbaum (Princeton: Princeton University Press, 1999); Susan Frank Parsons, *The Ethics of Gender: New*

teaching, family is the central unit, what the *Compendium of the Social Doctrine of the Church* describes as "the first natural society" which also requires careful consideration in this context.[36] The core of the notion of subsidiarity—the decentralizing principle—is just a step towards dealing with some problems of legible religion. It does not solve all of them by any means.

Third, vertical subsidiarity cannot be the only understanding of the ordering of different social entities. It should be supplemented with its horizontal equivalent. Rosa Mulé and Günter Walzenbach argue that while Roman Catholic thought contributed to the debate with the notion of a proper hierarchical ordering of social units, the Protestant Reformed tradition introduced the complementary principle of "sphere sovereignty."[37] Lael Daniel Weinberger defines sphere sovereignty in the following words:

> Sphere sovereignty emphasises the importance of social pluralism on the horizontal axis. Regardless of whether the activity is taking place on a local level or a national level, sphere sovereignty emphasizes the distinction between different kinds of social activities and institutions—state and church, for instance. At any level of social activity, there are multiple manifestations of sociability and many kinds of organisations and associations, formed for a variety of ends. The sphere sovereignty vision is for a richly-textured society.[38]

Dimensions to Religious Ethics (Oxford: Wiley-Blackwell, 2001); Elisabeth Gerle, "Multicultural Society: Dilemmas and Prospects," in *Theology and the Religions: A Dialogue*, ed. Viggo Mortensen (Grand Rapids, MI: William B. Eerdmans Publishing Company, 2003); Elisabeth Gerle, "Various Interpretations of Human Rights for Women Challenges at United Nations Conferences," in *Human Rights Law: From Dissemination to Application. Essays in Honour of Göran Melander*, ed. Jonas Grimheden and Rolf Ring (Leiden: Martinus Nijhoff Publishers, 2006).

36 Pontifical Council for Justice and Peace, *Compendium of the Social Doctrine of the Church* (Vatican: Libreria Editrice Vaticana, 2005), Chapter 5, https://www.vatican.va/roman_curia/pontifical_councils/justpeace/documents/rc_pc_justpeace_doc_20060526_compendio-dott-soc_en.html; See also K. S. Wright, "The principles of Catholic social teaching: A guide for decision making from daily clinical encounters to national policy-making," *Linacre Q* 84, no. 1 (Feb 2017), https://doi.org/10.1080/00243639.2016.1274629.

37 Rosa Mulé and Günter Walzenbach, "Introduction: two spaces of subsidiarity?," *Commonwealth & Comparative Politics* 57, no. 2 (2019): 141, https://doi.org/10.1080/14662043.2019.1573991.

38 Lael Daniel Weinberger, "The Relationship Between Sphere Sovereignty and Subsidiarity," in *Global Perspectives on Subsidiarity*, ed. Michelle Evans and Augusto Zimmermann (Dordrecht: Springer, 2014), 57–58.

The idea of sphere sovereignty thus underlines two distinct elements that supplement the idea of vertical subsidiarity. On the one hand, it argues for the freedom of action for different spheres of activity regardless of the difference in levels. On the other, it encourages the broader participation of different stakeholders in developing a richly textured society.

Thus, by advocating for subsidiarity, I argue that there is a need to adopt it formally and practically by embracing a decentralization of decision-making. This needs to be done vertically, by relegating agency and aiding the lowest adequate level; and horizontally, by not concentrating the decision-making power in only one entity, regardless of levels.

Of course, the practicalities of such a solution require further consideration. How to assess which level is adequate, or which stakeholders should be engaged in which problems, are not easy to resolve and will require careful solutions. How to approach the tension between the autonomy of individuals and the rights of groups and communities? Here, I only want to suggest this as the potential direction for solving the problems of the approach of legible religion in particular, and problems of centralization more broadly. As the above-mentioned examples of subsidiarity show, however, subsidiarity should not be approached as a singular legal rule. In this form, it tends to malfunction. Instead, it should be treated as a principle and a constant process aiming at lowering centralizing tendencies. Its meaning should be a matter of constant negotiation and cultivation. Its operations should also be weighed in the context of individual autonomy. What could such a change achieve? It would promote both the implementation and development of *mētis* whenever the local context was employed, either in terms of a local organization, local government, or local institution. Engagement of both individuals and lower-level stakeholders in actual problem solving on a day-to-day basis could promote the development of pragmatic, contextually adequate solutions that would not require surviving the stress test of universalization. The engagement of a broader range of stakeholders in the decision-making process at the higher levels could protect them from reductive simplifications and the overt imposition of central-level simplifications.

2.2 *Misapprehension of Conflict*

The full implementation of the above-mentioned understanding of subsidiarity will result in the strengthening of multiple independent social entities with their own vertical and horizontal subsidiarity. This may lead to conflicts between them. As discussed in Chapter 1, conflict and sectarian violence are primary fears in thinking about religion. Cavanaugh described the common notion that there exists a transcultural and transhistorical phenomenon of religion that is essentially violent as the "myth of religious violence." If such an essentialist notion was true, it could justify the retention of decision-making power at the highest levels of the state.

Again, here the answer requires a double approach. On the one hand, the notion of religion needs to be deconstructed, showing that essentialism in thinking about religion is problematic. The first and the second part of this book followed in the footsteps of the growing field of critical religion, which underlines the socially constructed character of this notion and investigates the mechanisms of this construction. Such efforts should be continued, and their results need to be further disseminated and advocated for.

However, that religion is not "essentially violent" does not mean that the types of beliefs that are denoted by this term do not, on some occasions, result in conflict. Instead, the primary assumption proposed by people like Cavanaugh is that these types of profound beliefs do not differ from other types of beliefs or, as they are sometimes called, comprehensive conceptions of good in how conflict-generating they are. To say anything else would be to deny their seriousness. A replacement of the control of a religion with a broader control of comprehensive conceptions of good would not improve the current situation at all.

A different approach is needed. In her recent *Introduction to Christian Ethics,* Ellen Ott Marshall argues that conflict is not necessarily wrong, but it is a necessary by-product of existence and human changeability. She writes that

> to be human is to be in conflict ... Advancing the moral value of conflict is one way of affirming relationship *and* respecting autonomy. One of the pitfalls of relationality is that we obscure differences or downplay division in order to maintain the relationship. We say, "peace, peace when there is no peace" (Jer. 6:14). Autonomy can be a corrective to this effort at 'peacekeeping' because it recognizes others rather than silencing them and because it respects the agency of others rather than denying their power. On the other hand, one of the pitfalls of autonomy is that we tolerate differences without seriously engaging them or feeling accountable to them. ... That separate living keeps us from being accountable to others, and it keeps us from challenging others.[39]

Marshall points out that in our attempts at maintaining relationships with others, we tend to adopt the strategy of conflict-avoidance, which she views as

39 Ellen Ott Marshall, *Introduction to Christian Ethics. Conflict, Faith, and Human Life* (Louisville, Kentucky: Westminster John Knox Press, 2018), 6–7.

deeply problematic, as it underplays, or even denies, the agency of others. It also means that we deny seriousness to the dividing differences.

Marshall differentiates between conflict and violence. She argues that conflict is a necessary aspect of being human, and it can be a positive force for change. For example, when someone's rights are violated, an underplaying of difference is not helpful but contributes to the problem. Marshall criticizes both the idea of conflict avoidance and conflict management, the notion that conflict can be avoided or resolved by either underplaying the seriousness of differences or strictly controlling certain ideas. Indeed, as demonstrated in Chapter 5, the example of conflicts around multi-faith spaces could suggest that the exercise of strict control within and around them resulted neither in avoidance of conflict nor in its resolution. Instead, Marshall advocates for the idea of conflict transformation. In this approach, one does not view conflict as inherently wrong but as a potential means of resolving the structural causes behind it. If conflicts are common around a certain issue, this might point to a broader underlying problem; for example, the imbalance between banal and unbanal religiosity.[40]

Marshall's approach comes from her practical involvement in peace and conflict studies. Marshall wants to emphasize conflict's dynamic, contextual, and relational character. She points out that conflict should not be judged based on abstract principles, goals, or narratives but always in the concrete particularity of the situation. Thus, she ties into the notion of subsidiarity by pointing out where to locate the agency in solving the problems.

If conflict is an inherent part of human changeability, differences between people require constant and ongoing negotiation. They cannot be simply handled with centrally set rules, especially in cases concerning such fundamental issues as comprehensive conceptions of the good. Thus, they require the development of an understanding of how to engage in conflict constructively.

---

40 In many respects, Marshall followed the same line of argumentation as representatives of the so-called agonistic pluralism, for example, Chantal Mouffe. See, for example, Chantal Mouffe, *Agonistics: Thinking the World Politically* (London: Verso, 2013). However, as Mark Wenman pointed out in his description of agonistic democracy, *agonism* is comprised of three constitutive elements: "(i) a conception of constitutive pluralism, (ii) a tragic vision of the world, and (iii) a belief that conflict can be a political good." See Mark Wenman, *Agonistic Democracy* (Cambridge: Cambridge University Press, 2013), 28. However, Marshall focused primarily on the last of these points, which is also the case in this chapter. The other two are more problematic and would not necessarily fit into the vision of Christian ethics presented by Marshall, which might be the reason why she never referred to the concept. A proper consideration of these differences would require a separate discussion.

Nathan C. Funk and Christina J. Woolner differentiate three main approaches to thinking about religion and peace-making. First, there is what they describe as "traditional thinking," the notion that peace can be achieved only by engaging in some form of religious devotion.[41] The idea of a particular religion as a source of unity for the state could be considered a functionalized version of this approach. Second, they describe "hard secularism,"[42] that is, the idea that peace can be achieved only if religion disappears. Finally, there is the third, "flexible approach," the notion that acknowledges that religious claims are neither inherently problematic nor inherently positive.[43] They can both contribute to conflict generation and help resolve conflicts.[44] However, different religious traditions can offer a rich tapestry of resources for supporting the ongoing negotiations, from particular ideas on conflict transformation, through motivation and empowerment, to pedagogical resources.[45]

This last approach has been increasingly important with the development of the return of religion narrative. Atalia Omer points out that "the field of religion and the practices of peace has grown exponentially since policy makers

---

41 Nathan C. Funk and Christina J. Woolner, "Religion and Peace and Conflict Studies," in *Critical Issues in Peace and Conflict Studies*, ed. Thomas Matyok, Jessica Senehi, and Sean Byrne (Toronto: Lexington Books, 2011), 351.

42 Funk and Woolner, "Religion and Peace," 352.

43 Funk and Woolner, "Religion and Peace," 355.

44 For classical discussions of the subject, see Scott Appleby, *The Ambivalence of the Sacred* (Lanham, MA: Rowman and Littlefield, 2000); also Douglas Johnston and Cynthia Sampson, *Religion: The Missing Dimension of Statecraft* (Oxford: Oxford University Press, 1994); Jeffrey Haynes, *Religion in Global Politics* (London: Longman, 1998).

45 Religious traditions have a rich tradition of constructive conflict engagement, for example, Jewish notions of *hevruta* and *machloket* (for more, see, for example, Orit Kent, "Interactive Text Study: A Case of Hevruta Learning," *Journal of Jewish Education* 72, no. 3 (2006), https://doi.org/10.1080/15244110600990155; Devorah Schoenfeld, "Using Hevruta to Do and Teach Comparative Theology," in *Teaching Interreligious Encounters*, ed. Marc A. Pugliese and Alex Y. Hwang (Oxford: Oxford University Press, 2017); Gerald Steinberg, "Jewish Sources on Conflict Management: Realism and Human Nature," in *Conflict and Conflict Management in Jewish Sources*, ed. Michal Roness (Tel Aviv: Bar Ilan University, 2017).) and conflict resolution, for example, the Muslim idea of *Sulha* (for more, see, for example, Mneesha Gellman and Mandi Vuinovich, "From Sulha to Salaam: Connecting local knowledge with international negotiations for lasting peace in Palestine/Israel," *Conflict Resolution Quarterly* 26, no. 2 (2008), https://doi.org/10.1002/crq.227; Sharon Lang, "Sulha Peacemaking and the Politics of Persuasion," *Journal of Palestine Studies* 31, no. 3 (2020), https://doi.org/10.1525/jps.2002.31.3.52; Doron Pely, "Where East not always meets West: Comparing the Sulha process to Western-style mediation and arbitration," *Conflict Resolution Quarterly* 28, no. 4 (2011), https://doi.org/10.1002/crq.20028.). See also Eleazar S. Fernandez, *Teaching for a Multi-faith World* (Eugene, OR: Pickwick Publications, 2017).

and analysts "discovered" religion's political relevance and world-transforming outcomes in the aftermath of the Iranian Revolution of 1979 and 11 September 2001."[46] Such development, then, could suggest that the change in approach to the conflict-generating character of religion, and to the conflict per se, is already underway. However, again, here one encounters a significant impact of the framework of legible religion.

Omer sums up the developments concerning religion, peace, and conflict in two ways. First, she notes that two genres emerged, distinguishing between "good" religion, considering how it can be mobilized, and "bad" religion, considering how to contain it. Second, she points out that two subsequent generations of thinking about religion and peace emerged: the liberal and the neoliberal. As Omer argues, while the liberal generation was interested in the exceptionality of "religious actors" and their prophetic ability to speak truth to power, the neoliberal bureaucratized and operationalized religion as a utility. It reduces religion into concrete services and practices that can be pragmatically employed in conflict-resolution. "Religion and peace," she notes, "has been a field about practice to show the effectiveness and usefulness of religion as a tool and capital rather than a substantive scrutiny of religion, violence, and justice-oriented peace."[47]

Both developments show that the simple reformulation of religion in positive terms does not necessarily solve the problems of legible approaches. As the difference between the *service-oriented* and the *holistic* policy models showed in the previous chapter, a positive outlook on religion does not necessarily solve all problems. Religion can still be classified in a simplified way, into one of the categories of "good" and "bad," either in a utilitarian fashion or as a potential threat. Even if categorized as good it can still be treated as a simple utility and deprived of agency. In a way typical for administrative reductions, its complexity can be reduced only to the features deemed relevant.

Thus, Omer argues that the field of religion and practices of peace needs greater reflexivity and a change of approach. On the one hand, it needs to critically assess its own susceptibility to ideological, geopolitical, and theological agendas. On the other hand, instead of finding ways to operate in the existing system, it needs "to critically reflect about the shaping environment in order to transform it."[48] Instead of providing simple utility to the existing structures, it needs to constantly reassess them, define the problems that arise

46 Atalia Omer, "Religion and the Study of Peace: Practice without Reflection," *Religions* 12, no. 12 (2021): 1, 1069, https://doi.org/10.3390/rel12121069.

47 Omer, "Religion and the Study," 2–3.

48 Omer, "Religion and the Study," 14.

in their operations, including how they shape broader consciousness and the categories in which we think, and provide constructive solutions for their transformation.

To sum up, I argue that the idea of religion as inherently problematic and conflict-generating, requiring strict, high-level control and potential prohibition, needs to be deconstructed. Conflict avoidance and management need to be replaced with the notion of conflict transformation and ongoing negotiations. But the effort to reconsider religion in positive terms cannot rely on the other side of the legible religion framework. It cannot consider religion a simple utility either. Thus, the growing field of religion, conflict, and peace studies requires further reflection and decolonization in terms of its own ideological dependence and contribution to maintaining the status quo. At the same time, the view of religion as a potential resource in the negotiations also requires constant reconsideration and ongoing decolonization.

2.3 *The Importance of Encounter*

Gordon Allport's book, *The Nature of Prejudice*, is a foundational study of intergroup relations and the formation of perceptions. Allport rejects the notion that contact between different groups increases prejudice. Instead, he argues that the impact of contact depends on its type. While superficial contact may increase the levels of prejudice, serious and personal contact with the "other" can help alleviate it, provided that two additional prerequisites are satisfied: if it takes place in conditions of relatively equal status, and if it orients towards the pursuit of common goals.[49]

Allport's conclusions have been recently applied to contemporary interreligious relations by Hannah Strømmen and Ulrich Schmiedel in *The Claim to Christianity: Responding to the Far Right*. There, building on the work of Gert Pickel and Cemal Öztürk,[50] they argue that "statistically, the more Muslims

49 See Gordon Allport, *The Nature of Prejudice* (Boston, MA: Addison-Wesley, 1954), 261–81. An interesting example of this process was the unintended consequence of housing refugees at the Budapest Central Station during the early stages of 2015—a significant decrease in the number of xenophobes, followed by a sudden increase after the refugees were transferred outside of the country. See Bori Simonovits, "The Public Perception of the Migration Crisis from the Hungarian Point of View: Evidence from the Field," in *Geographies of Asylum in Europe and the Role of European Localities*, ed. Birgit Glorius and Jeroen Doomernik, IMISCOE Research Series (New York: Springer International Publishing, 2020), 162.

50 Gert Pickel and Cemal Öztürk, "Islamophobia Without Muslims? The "Contact Hypothesis" as an Explanation for Anti-Muslim Attitudes — Eastern European Societies in Comparative Perspective," *Journal of Nationalism, Memory & Language Politics* 12, no. 2 (2018), https://doi.org/10.2478/jnmlp-2018-0009.

there are in a country, the less likely it is that Islamophobic prejudices can be shaped and sustained among the population," although they admitted that there are notable exceptions from this trend.[51] Nonetheless, they note that contact, while not sufficient on its own, constitutes a strategic element in overcoming divisions both within and between religious communities.[52]

Allport's contact argument has been encapsulated in the turn to encounter of major faith communities in Europe.[53] For example, the Church of Sweden describes the years 2015–2016 as "a time of encounters" in their report on the work with asylum-seekers and new arrivals,[54] while in 2016, Pope Francis called "for a culture of encounter." As coverage of *L'Osservatore Romano* put it, the pope called for:

> not just seeing, but looking; not just hearing, but listening; not just passing people by, but stopping with them; not just saying "what a shame, poor people!", but allowing yourself to be moved with compassion; "and then to draw near, to touch and to say: 'Do not weep' and to give at least a drop of life."[55]

The pope noticed the nuanced distinction between what I could describe, following Rosa, as mute and resonant encounters. While in the former, one sees, hears, and passes others by, it does not entail a degree of interpersonal and intergroup contact that can help bring social cohesion. Only a resonant encounter, one in which parties get affected and emote, can bring about the transformation needed to bring about greater social cohesion. But, as argued

---

51 Hannah Strømmen and Ulrich Schmiedel, *The Claim to Christianity: Responding to the Far Right* (London: SCM Press, 2020) , 133. See also Gert Pickel and Alexander Yendell, "Islam als Bedrohung? Beschreibung und Erklärung von Einstellungen zum Islam im Ländervergleich," *Zeitschrift für Vergleichende Politikwissenschaft* 10, no. 3–4/2016 (2016), https://doi.org/10.1007/s12286-016-0309-6.

52 Strømmen and Schmiedel, *The Claim to Christianity*, 133–34.

53 For more on the theological and philosophical considerations of encounter see Matthias Petzoldt, "Encountering the Other: The Concept of Encounter in Philosophy and Theology," in *Dynamics of Difference: Christianity and Alterity*, ed. Ulrich Schmiedel and James M. Matarazzo Jr. (London: Bloomsbury T&T Clark, 2016).

54 Kristina Hellqvist and Andreas Sandberg, *A Time of Encounters. The Work with Asylum Seekers and New Arrivals in the Parishes of the Church of Sweden 2015–2016* (Uppsala: Svenska Kyrkan, 2018).

55 Pope Francis, "For a culture of encounter," *L'Osservatore Romano*, 23rd of September, 2016, https://www.vatican.va/content/francesco/en/cotidie/2016/documents/papa-francesco-cotidie_20160913_for-a-culture-of-encounter.html.

in this book, such transformation is not only a matter of individual change, but it requires tackling structural issues as well.[56]

Different policy approaches to religion on the university campus, described in the previous chapter, illustrate that. While the *single vision model* outwardly mutes any relationships between people of different faiths, the *multiple-vision model* can, in principle, provide space for encounter. However, the *service-oriented model* primarily provides space for mute encounters, as it only bases religious provisions on individual needs. Instead, the *holistic model* comes out from the fundamental assumption that negotiation is a necessary part of campus culture. By offering tools for such negotiation and by encouraging exchange between individuals and groups that goes beyond the established boundaries, it facilitates, although of course not warrants, resonant encounters.

In the broader social perspective, this difference could be described in envisioned inter-faith collaborations and their role in bringing about social cohesion. For a long time, the primary notion employed in such situations revolved around the so-called inter-faith dialogue. This notion assumes that by engaging religious leaders in a discussion, one can achieve greater engagement between communities in a typically Habermasian communicative approach. This, however, assumes strict boundaries between different traditions and representativeness of leadership, all remaining within the realm of a top-down understanding of religions and their apparent separation in a legible manner. It also skips the encounter on the individual level and orients the discussion to the cognitive level. Thus, it promotes primarily mute relationships rather than resonant ones.

A supplementary alternative to inter-faith dialogue, implementing Allport's conclusions, could include inter-faith praxis, understood as engagement in the work for common goals between individuals from different faith communities and motivations. If social cohesion and social transformation are the goal, individuals can work together towards a common goal instead of focusing on the dialogue. By being engaged at a grassroots level in joint projects based on a specific goal, they can start encountering each other, figuring out ways to act together despite their different backgrounds, and better understanding their different motivations. Inter-faith praxis allows for greater decentralization of agency, which could provide significant benefits. While broadly debated in the development studies, there is some evidence that decentralization leads to

56 See also Timothy Hanchin, "Encounter And/As Pedagogy For Catholic Higher Education In Our Time," *Religious Education* 114, no. 5 (2019), https://doi.org/10.1080/00344087.2019.1631975.

higher participation and social engagement levels.[57] By bringing individuals together to pursue common goals, the inter-faith praxis also facilitates individual encounters. But, again, it does not warrant them—as Rosa pointed out, resonance cannot be controlled nor imposed.

Such an approach also cannot completely replace more theologically inclined engagements. I am not claiming here that the theological differences do not matter. Inter-faith praxis has its benefits, but also limitations. A significant element of resonance in Rosa's approach included self-efficacy, that is, the ability to speak with one's own voice. Thus, inter-faith praxis requires a sustained development of each individual's theological identity, both through internal mono-religious formation, as well as theologically inclined inter-faith engagement, as exemplified (but not exhausted) by inter-faith dialogue.

As exemplified earlier by different campus policies, the encounter needs to be further facilitated by providing tools for common understanding and negotiations. The *holistic* policy model did not simply leave campus open to all kinds of religious engagement and interaction. Rather, as exemplified by the University of Winchester's policy, it took a proactive approach with different kinds of contemplative activities, education, and communities.

Similarly, as already pointed out in the context of religion and peace studies in the previous section, the utility perspective should not operationalize encounter as a tool for social cohesion or any other goal. Inter-faith praxis should not become a bureaucratized form of introducing contact between religious communities. While some degree of goal orientation might be helpful in translating the complex social processes into institutional support, it cannot overtake them. Again, resonance should be the norm, while muteness an exception.

The risks can be exemplified with the recent turn to the notion of "religious literacy." Religious literacy has been a crucial concept among the tools to facilitate encounters since the publication of Stephen Prothero's book under the same title. The knowledge about one's own tradition and that of others was viewed as necessary to function in a pluralist society. However, scholars increasingly pointed out that religious literacy can be as much of a legible tool as other administrative instruments.[58] It was criticized for its canon- and

57 Mark Robinson, "Does Decentralisation Improve Equity and Efficiency in Public Service Delivery Provision?," *IDS Bulletin* 38, no. 1 (2007), https://doi.org/10.1111/j.1759-5436.2007.tb00333.x.

58 Stephen Prothero, *Religious Literacy: What Every American Needs to Know-And Doesn't* (New York: HarperOne, 2007).

fact-orientation and confirmation of hegemonic perspectives.[59] If overtly reified and generalized, the knowledge inherent in the notion of religious literacy may promote mute relationships instead of resonant ones. It can provide a set of presumptions that will close off a relationship before it begins.[60] A broader and more competency-based perspective on literacy requires further development.

Literacy is also not sufficient. As researchers in educational psychology point out, while the number of literacies required for civil participation has been significantly increased in recent decades, they need to be supplemented by other soft competencies.[61] I saw that firsthand while developing A World of Neighbours Practitioners' Network,[62] an inter-faith network of migration practitioners in 22 European countries. In one of our conversations, a Muslim practitioner noted that soft skills were more crucial than an understanding of detailed sets of religious tenets in his practice. As he pointed out, it was not crucial for everyone in society to know about the dietary customs of Muslims from different traditions. That would require a vast cognitive effort and be unrealistic in the information-based world. An ability to acknowledge one's lack of knowledge and simply ask "Do you eat pork?" before serving a meal would be sufficient.

Thus, reframing Scott's argument, it could be suggested that a greater embrace of *mētis* might also be highly beneficial in the context of encounter and inter-faith praxis. While *technē* has its uses, it can enforce legibility, impose a reductive perspective, and mute relationships if overemphasized. Instead, a more localized solution in line with the notion of *mētis*, as simple as acknowledging one's lack of knowledge and asking, can be more adequate.

---

59 See, for example, articles in the anthology Alberto Melloni and Francesca Caddedu, *Religious Literacy, Law and History. Perspectives on European Pluralist Societies* (London and New York: Routledge, 2019); A good review of different policy models is available in: Kerstin von Brömssen, Heinz Ivkovits, and Graeme Nixon, "Religious literacy in the curriculum in compulsory education in Austria, Scotland and Sweden - a three-country policy comparison," *Journal of Beliefs & Values* 41, no. 2 (2020), https://doi.org/10.1080/13617672.2020.1737909.

60 For example, it can reproduce biased, simplified representations of a particular group, and present the world in clear-cult categories. See, for example, Kerstin von Brömssen and Christina Rodell Olgaç, "Intercultural education in Sweden through the lenses of the national minorities and of religious education," *Intercultural Education* 21, no. 2 (2010): 129–30, https://doi.org/10.1080/14675981003696263.

61 Katarzyna Bobrowicz et al., "Aiding Reflective Navigation in a Dynamic Information Landscape: A Challenge for Educational Psychology," *Front Psychol* 13 (2022), 88159, https://doi.org/10.3389/fpsyg.2022.881539.

62 "60 Practitioners in 22 Countries," 2022, accessed 12th of March, 2022, https://aworldofneighbours.org/network/.

To conclude, I argue that the turn to encounter, following Allport's contact argument, is an important element of overcoming prejudice and creating constructive forms of engagement within and between religious communities. A pragmatic form of such engagement is encapsulated in the notion of inter-faith praxis, the idea that people coming from different religious communities should start working towards a common goal and find out how to solve their theological differences in the process. While helpful, this approach needs to be supported by both a strong understanding of one's own identity and tools for engagement. These tools do not have to include highly detailed specialized knowledge but can be suggestions for how things can be solved in everyday, local conditions. Scott's understanding of *mētis* might be a helpful framework for reconsidering that. Such contact might be helpful in overcoming stereotypes and a simplified view of the world, and support more nuanced conversations and appreciation for complexity. However, encounters should not be limited to individual change. It needs to be supported by a structural transformation and move away from mute relationships as a standard.

2.4 *Toward a Decentralized, Holistic Public Sphere*

To summarize, the solutions to the fallacies of legible religion will need to follow two paths—a consideration of religion as a category, already broadly discussed among critical religion scholars, and a consideration of overcoming the consequences of legibility in practice.

Subsidiarity, conflict transformation, encounter, inter-faith praxis, religious literacy, and soft-skill-based competence—these were my proposals for how one could move away from the explicit and consciousness-shaping effects of the centralized, reductive legibility. None of these solutions provides a magical cure, and each requires careful balancing of different potential challenges and disadvantages. They all require further inspection, investigation, and consideration. These proposals support the conclusions made both by Scott and Rosa and promote *mētis* and resonant relationships.

All of them are meant as the building blocks of a different public sphere. Instead of a legible, deliberative public sphere with centralized sources of power, I argue for a decentralized, holistic public sphere in which pluralism is not strictly controlled but facilitated and constitutively rooted in resonant relationships. Such a public sphere does not prevent supplementary multi-faith spaces. They can be physical manifestations of the "mute exceptions" described by Rosa, places primarily devoted to stillness and silence in a negative design, or to encounter in a positive one. But it prevents exclusive multi-faith spaces, imposing one vision of what religion should be. Encounter and resonance would be the standard; silence, and muteness an exception. As I tried to suggest throughout the chapter, the spaces themselves are less important than what happens around them. They should be a result of the engagement with *mētis*, the local negotiation based on the needs, knowledge, skills, and competences of all their stakeholders.

3 Conclusion

This chapter completed the diagnostic aim of this book and sketched potential next steps, highlighting possible solutions to the outlined problems. The first section discussed why the approach of legible religion is so problematic. Scott's analysis demonstrated that legibility, while a useful administrative tool, becomes problematic when imposed on phenomena, as it reduces them to the point where some of their vital elements are lost. Rosa's work showed the tension generated by the clash between the institutionally imposed logic of controllability and the constitutive uncontrollability of the world. Based on their work, I argued that legible religion suppresses the complexity of affected phenomena, promotes mute relationships to the world, and does not allow for the operations of practical knowledge—what Scott described as *mētis*. While both scholars have been discussed extensively before in various contexts, the combination of their insights in the context of state approaches to religion helps us better understand the existing dynamics.

In search for solutions to these fallacies, in the second section, I argued that one needs to attend to both parts of the notion of legible religion—the essentialist understanding of religion as more than a heuristic category, and the ideas inherent in legibility.

Regarding the essentialist understanding of religion, I pointed to some recent calls to rethink or reject religion as a politico-legal category. While I agreed with them, I noted that they pose a risk of maintaining the top-down dynamics. On the one hand, they risk introducing a new conception of religion in place of the former, which would still have to be implemented by the state in a top-down manner. On the other hand, removing this concept altogether and turning the focus of the state only to what is deemed relevant does not remedy previous biases. Further consideration in these areas is needed, with the provision that it should not be simply changed through a top-down, centrally guided approach, as it might continue to follow the fallacies of legibility.

Regarding the challenges inherent in legibility, I proposed three potential solutions. First, I argued that the idea of vertical and horizontal subsidiarity might help counteract the centralizing and simplifying tendencies of legibility if implemented properly. Second, I argued that a changed understanding of conflict, to view it as a necessary part of social reality and potentially constructive force, could aid us in rejecting the notion that essentially approached religion, or, even if one rejects this notion, more broadly comprehensive conceptions of the good, need to be strictly controlled because of their conflict-generating character. Future research will require developing methods for constructive conflict engagement that could draw on existing religious traditions. Finally, I proposed that the functionalistic approach to religion, as, for example, a force for social cohesion, could be replaced with a more resonant approach to inter-faith praxis. This notion could still realize the broader goals of social cohesion without the constraints of a centrally devised agenda.

If these solutions are related back to the considerations of Scott and Rosa from the previous section, one can see the following advantages. The notion of subsidiarity has the advantage of allowing for the operations and development of *mētis.* Vertical subsidiarity forces lower-order organizations and individuals to engage in problems concerning them. Horizontal subsidiarity allows for the engagement of broader experience in developing practical knowledge. This is strengthened by both the ongoing character of conflict transformation and the ideas of inter-faith praxis. All three approaches also encourage resonance. They promote the encounter between different "others," providing, at least in principle, space for being affected, reacting with emotion, and being transformed.

In terms of multi-faith spaces and institutional policies, the vision offered by the University of Winchester, as prepared by Terry Biddington, the expert on the topic of multi-faith chaplaincy, may be inspiring. Instead of resisting religion at its campus, Winchester envisioned not only opening for encounters between students and staff of different beliefs but aimed to create special tools for facilitating them, from a contemplative pedagogy network for staff, through contemplative communities for students, to hiring specialized management, including the Dean of Spiritual Life and a multi-faith team of chaplains. It wanted to allow for religion to "take place" everywhere on campus and supplemented it with particular spaces devoted to religion, such as chapel, multi-faith space, or the planned contemplative center. By that, it introduced both vertical (allowance for many decisions to be made by the concerned individuals and groups themselves, both students and staff, with the higher-order aid of specialized management) and horizontal (by engaging a broad network of stakeholders in decision-making and conflict-resolution process) subsidiarity and created a framework for both conflict-transformation and inter-faith praxis. The future will show how that vision turned into practice, especially after the changes in the university management.

Of course, this does not mean that any of these proposals are magical solutions that, when applied, will cause the complete disappearance of any problems. The potential solutions presented here are just proposals on potential directions in thinking how to move beyond the fallacies of legible religion. Their implementation is a step in the process and hopefully will lead to (1) a more equal and less prejudiced society, (2) which does not bottle tensions until they explode, and (3) does not suppress complexity to detrimental social effects, accounting for complex networks of "believing, belonging, and behaving."[63] The detailing of these solutions is where future research is gravely needed.

---

63 Zoë Bennet et al., *Invitation to Research in Practical Theology* (London and New York: Routledge, 2018), 71. See also Katie Day and Sebastian Kim, "Introduction," in A Companion to Public Theology, ed. Katie Day and Sebastian Kim (Leiden: Brill, 2017).

EPILOGUE

Turning Grappa into Wine

Mark Carney, the former head of the Bank of England, recollecting his meeting with Pope Francis, wrote:

> A few summers ago when a range of policymakers, business people, academics, labour leaders, and charity workers gathered at the Vatican to discuss the future of the market system, Pope Francis surprised us by joining the lunch and sharing a parable. He observed that:
>
> *Our meal will be accompanied by wine. Now, wine is many things. It has a bouquet, colour, and richness of taste that all complement the food. It has alcohol that can enliven the mind. Wine enriches all our senses.*
>
> *At the end of our feast, we will have grappa. Grappa is one thing: alcohol. Grappa is wine distilled.*
>
> He continued:
>
> *Humanity is many things—passionate, curious, rational, altruistic, creative, self-interested. But the market is one thing: self-interest. The market is humanity distilled.*
>
> And then he challenged us:
>
> *Your job is to turn the grappa back into wine, to turn the market back into humanity. This isn't theology. This is reality. This is the truth.*[1]

If one replaces the word "market" with the word "religion," the papal words would come close to expressing the major conclusions of this book—that the word religion, especially in its legible version, does not account for the complexity of the world, and that there is a need for constant complexification of the approaches to the phenomena that hide behind it. I would only challenge the papal distinction between theology and reality. Based on the results of this book, I would argue instead that these two are closely related. Considering the administrative simplifications and reductions of religion, more, not less, theological engagement is needed. By way of conclusion, I argue that it is the primary job of public theologians in the twenty-first century to lead the efforts

1 Mark Carney, "'We are seeing a crisis in values' — an exclusive extract from Mark Carney's book," *The Guardian*, 13th of March 2021, https://www.theguardian.com/business/2021/mar/13/crisis-in-values-exclusive-extract-mark-carneys-book.

 | DOI:10.1163/9789004714366_009

of turning grappa back into wine. There is a need to create space and appreciation for the complexity of the phenomena labeled as religious.

This book attempted to delineate what such a process could look like within the European context. I began by noting an apparent mismatch between the heated responses to multi-faith spaces and their seemingly neutral character. As I argued throughout this book, they are, in fact, not neutral. Instead, as hypothesized at the beginning, multi-faith spaces represent a broad tendency in thinking about religion in the public sphere, which I called the legible religion framework, resulting in a mismatch between the promise that such spaces bring and the actual practice. Throughout the three parts of this book, I have explored how this framework emerged and achieved hegemony, how it has functioned in practice, and how to move beyond it. The first two parts fulfilled the main aim of the book. They analyzed and provided tools for understanding the contradictory responses to multi-faith spaces by critically examining the visions of religion behind them. The third part offered constructive pointers on how to deal with at least some of the highlighted problems.

Therefore, the book contributed to a better understanding of several areas of knowledge. First, by showing how administrative processes shape religion, religious diversity, and the boundary between the religious and the secular, this book contributed to the growing field of critical religion studies. Second, differentiating a particular European tendency provided a more sophisticated perspective on the development and operations of geographically- and culturally-conditioned secularities.[2] Third, this book proposed an alternative view of secularization and the return of religion that could constitute a potentially useful heuristic tool in rethinking the connection between religion and modernity. Fourth, by analyzing the history, materiality, and placement of multi-faith spaces, this book deepened comprehension of their impact. It combined results of previous research projects, such as the "Multi-Faith Spaces: Symptoms and Agents", with an analysis of previously unstudied spaces, and showed that they are highly consequential phenomena, whose design has an important bearing on the understanding of religion in the public sphere. Fifth, the differentiation between the multi-faith spaces that follow the legible religion framework and those that do not offered a more nuanced understanding of policy approaches to religion on the university campus and in the public sphere more broadly. Sixth, the analysis of the context in which multi-faith spaces operate deepened an understanding of how *épistémè* conditions the perception of seemingly neutral phenomena. Seventh, the empirical part of this book showed that the

2 As, for example, developed in the Multiple Secularities research group. See Monika Wohlrab-Sahr and Marian Burchardt, "Multiple Secularities. Towards a Cultural Sociology of Secular Modernities," *Comparative Sociology* 11 (2012), https://doi.org/10.1163/15691330-12341249.

conceptual framework of legible religion has a hegemonic status in defining attitudes toward religion. Finally, the last chapter underlined why such a hegemonic status is problematic and what are its main challenges. It also proposed a way forward and offered encouragement for further work in this direction.

Thus, this study constitutes the beginning rather than the end of an investigation into the impact of administrative attempts at making religion legible. The study of multi-faith spaces covers a small part of a much bigger picture. As my research has progressed, more and more fields proved to be promising avenues for further research on religion and legibility. For example, what role does religious education play in the hegemonic status of the legible religion framework? While concepts like religious literacy have been recently introduced as important elements of coexisting in plural societies,[3] what role do they play in establishing mute relationships?[4] What role does state funding for religious organizations play in the reification of legible religion?[5] What about popular culture? What role does legible religion play in healthcare, and how is patient well-being understood? These are just a few potential areas that could be addressed in future research.

Of course, as with any research, there are also limitations to this study. For example, the interest in a common European tendency meant that the study could not fully account for the particular mechanisms of legibility and the particular constructions of secularity in the respective countries and even in the respective public administration sectors. More detailed studies could follow, both individual and comparative, which could be supported by the proposed overarching approach. Individual thinkers could also be analyzed more in-depth regarding their influence on the formation of the framework. Multi-faith spaces are increasing in numbers and developing dynamically all over Europe, which means that the need to study them is by no means satisfied by this book alone.

There is a need to revive the complexity of the phenomena labeled as religious and continue both critical and practical engagement with the topic. As this book has shown, religion is not simply a category existing "out there" as a natural phenomenon. It is an analytical, artificial concept that is continuously constructed and re-constructed by a multitude of processes. This book emphasized

3 Stephen Prothero, *Religious Literacy: What Every American Needs to Know-And Doesn't* (New York: HarperOne, 2007).

4 See Alberto Melloni and Francesca Caddedu, Religious Literacy, *Law and History. Perspectives on European Pluralist Societies* (London and New York: Routledge, 2019); Kerstin von Brömssen, Heinz Ivkovits, and Graeme Nixon, "Religious literacy in the curriculum in compulsory education in Austria, Scotland and Sweden - a three-country policy comparison," *Journal of Beliefs & Values* 41, no. 2 (2020).

5 For example, see Ulf Bjereld, Daniel Lindvall, and Linda Svärd, *Statens stöd till trossamfund i ett mångreligiöst Sverige*, Statens Offentliga Utredningar (Stockholm, 2018). SOU 2018:18.

the administrative impact on that construction. It showed how different narratives, such as secularization and the return of religion, impact the broader consciousness, and how power dynamics shape the particular understandings of religion, the preference for particular religiosities, and the differentiation of distinct religions. It showed how these theoretical considerations result in concrete physical spaces and specific public debates. These concrete manifestations visualize the reductive capacity of administrative processes—that administrative efforts at defining religion are not only intellectual exercises but reshape the phenomena they consider. Failing to account for the great complexity of such phenomena, they potentially deprive them of features vital for non-administrative stakeholders and sometimes even administrative stakeholders as well.

Thus, there is an ongoing need for turning grappa into wine. Only then will the promise of religious equality and religious freedom be matched with their practice. Only then the gravity of multi-faith spaces will be decreased, as, instead of constituting an imposition, they will begin to play simply a supplementary role. The empty white room described at the beginning of the book will be serving only those who want to use it. While this task needs to be undertaken collectively by different stakeholders, I believe that public theologians could lead these efforts as the agents between their particular religious communities and the broader public who can thread the thin line between the priestly and prophetic roles. The exploration of the role of public theology in moving beyond the fallacies of legible religion constitutes another important direction for future research.[6]

---

6 Martin E. Marty, "Two Kinds of Two Kinds of Civil Religion," in *American Civil Religion*, ed. Russell E. Richey and Donald G. Jones (New York: Harper & Row, 1974) is credited with creating the concept of "public theology." See, for example, Katie Day and Sebastian Kim, "Introduction," in *A Companion to Public Theology*, ed. Katie Day and Sebastian Kim (Leiden: Brill, 2017), 3. The field of public theology has developed significantly since its inception, resulting in increasingly sophisticated discussions about its role. E. Harold Brietenberg Jr. offered a concise definition of the field as "theologically informed public discourse about public issues, addressed to the church, synagogue, mosque, temple or other religious body, as well as the larger public or publics, argued in ways that can be evaluated and judged by publicly available warrants and criteria E. Harold Brietenberg Jr., "To Tell the Turth: Will the Real Public Theology Please Stand Up," *Journal of the Society of Christian Ethics* 23, no. 2 (2003), 66, https://doi.org/10.5840/jsce20032325 . More recently, the field expanded, starting to include more publics and types of publicness and engagement. However, the administrative angles as discussed in this book remain understudied in public theology. This is where the future research is needed. For more, see Tracy, "Three Kinds of Publicness in Public Theology." Day and Kim, "Introduction," 4–6; Ulrich Schmiedel, "'Take Up Your Cross': Public Theology between Populism and Pluralism in the Post-Migrant Context," *International Journal of Public Theology* 13, no. 2 (2019), https:// doi.org/10.1163/15697320-12341569; Ulrich Schmiedel, "The legacy of theological liberalism. A ghost in public theology," in *T&T Clark Handbook of Public Theology*, ed. Christoph Hübenthal and Christiane Alpers (London: T&T Clark, 2022).

References

Acland, Tony, and Waqar Azmi. "Expectation and Reality: Ethnic Minorities in Higher Education." In *Race and Higher Education*, edited by Tariq Modood and Tony Acland, 74–85. London: Policy Studies Institute, 1998.

Acquaviva, Sabino S., and Renato Stella. *Fine Di Un'ideologia: La Secolarizzazione.* Rome: Borla, 1989.

Ahlm, Emma. *EU Law and Religion: A Study of How the Court of Justice Has Adjudicated on Religious Matters in Union Law.* Uppsala: Juridiska institutionen, Uppsala universitet, 2020.

Alcoff, Linda Martin, and John D. Caputo. *Feminism, Sexuality, and the Return of Religion.* Bloomington: Indiana University Press, 2011.

Aldrin, Viktor. *Skolavslutningar i Kyrkan och Spelet om Religion i Svensk Skola.* Skellefteå: Artos & Norma Bokförlag, 2018.

Allport, Gordon. *The Nature of Prejudice.* Boston, MA: Addison-Wesley, 1954.

Alvarez, José E. "State Sovereignty Is Not Withering Away: A Few Lessons for the Future." In *Realizing Utopia: The Future of International Law*, edited by Antonio Cassese, 26–37. Oxford: Oxford University Press, 2012.

Ando, Clifford. "Interpretatio Romana." *Classical Philology* 100, no. 1 (2005): 41–51. https://doi.org/10.1086/431429.

APA-OTS. "Seit 20 Jahren Gibt Es in Wien-Schwechat Die 'Flughafenkapelle'." *APA-OTS*, 3rd of July 2008. http://www.ots.at/presseaussendung/OTS_20080703_OTS0034.

Appleby, Scott. *The Ambivalence of the Sacred.* Lanham, MA: Rowman and Littlefield, 2000.

Arendt, Hannah. *Eichmann in Jerusalem: A Report on the Banality of Evil.* New York: Penguin, 1963.

Asad, Talal. *Formations of the Secular: Christianity, Islam, Modernity.* Stanford: Stanford University Press, 2003.

Asad, Talal. *Genealogies of Religion: Discipline and Reasons of Power in Christianity and Islam.* Baltimore: Johns Hopkins University Press, 1993.

Asch, Ronald G. "Religious Toleration, the Peace of Westphalia and the German Territorial Estates." *Parliaments, Estates & Representation* 20, no. 1 (2000): 75–89. https://doi.org/10.1080/02606755.2000.9522099.

Audi, Robert. "Liberal Democracy and the Place of Religion in Politics." In *Religion in the Public Square: The Place of Religious Conviction in Public Debate*, edited by Robert Audi and Nicholas Wolterstorff, 1–66. London: Rowman & Littlefield Publishers, Inc., 1997.

A World of Neighbours, "60 Practitioners in 22 Countries." 2022, accessed 12th of March, 2022, https://aworldofneighbours.org/network/.

Badinter, Robert. *Libres Et Égaux … L'émancipation Des Juifs Sous La Révolution Française (1789–1791)* Paris: Fayard, 1989.

Bado, Kangnikoé. "Good Governance as a Precondition for Subsidiarity: Human Rights Litigation in Nigeria and Ecowas." *Commonwealth & Comparative Politics* 57, no. 2 (2019): 242–59. https://doi.org/10.1080/14662043.2019.1574015.

Bailey, James R., and Wayne N. Eastman. "Positivism and the Promise of the Social Sciences." *Theory & Psychology* 4, no. 4 (2016): 505–24. https://doi.org/10.1177/0959354394044003.

Balboni, Marco. "The Global Reach of the Principle of Subsidiarity: The Case of Australia." *Commonwealth & Comparative Politics* 57, no. 2 (2019): 193–207. https://doi.org/10.1080/14662043.2019.1574001.

Balk Møller, Anna. "Der Er Behov for Alternative Ceremonirum i Danmark." *Politiken*, 18th of December 2018. https://politiken.dk/debat/kroniken/art6874853/Der-er-behov-for-alternative-ceremonirum-i-Danmark.

Balk Møller, "Ti År Med Frivilligt Arbejde. Giver Det Mening?," *Ceremonirum*, 26th of September, 2019, http://www.ceremonirum.dk/ti-aar-med-frivilligt-arbejde-giver-det-mening/.

Bates, Stephen. "Police Investigate Gang Attack on Muslim Students in London." *The Guardian*, 9th of November 2009. https://www.theguardian.com/uk/2009/nov/09/racist-attacks-students-city-university.

Baxter, Hugh. *Habermas: The Discourse Theory of Law and Democracy.* Stanford: Stanford Law Books, 2011.

Beard, Mary, John North, and Simon Price. *Religions of Rome. A History.* Vol. 1, Cambridge: Cambridge University Press, 1998.

Beattie, Tina. *The New Atheists: The Twilight of Reason and the War on Religion.* London: Darton, Longman and Todd Ltd, 2007.

Beaulac, Stéphane. "The Westphalian Model in Defining International Law: Challenging the Myth." *Australian Journal of Legal History* 8 (2004): 181–213.

Beck, Roger. *The Religion of the Mithras Cult in the Roman Empire.* Oxford: Oxford University Press, 2006.

Beetsma, Roel, and George Kopits. "Is the EU Ready to Truly Apply the Subsidiarity Principle?" *Vox EU CEPR*, 15th of June 2020. https://voxeu.org/content/eu-ready-truly-apply-subsidiarity-principle.

Bellah, Robert N. *Habits of the Heart.* Berkeley: University of California Press, 1985.

Bender, Courtney. "Abraham Centre/Parroquia Patriarcha Abraham." SSRC Forums, 2014, accessed 17th of November, 2021, http://forums.ssrc.org/ndsp/2014/08/04/abraham-centreparroquia-patriarcha-abraham/.

Bender, Courtney. "The Architecture of Multi-Faith Prayer: An Introduction." SSRC Forums, 2014, accessed 17th of November, 2021, http://forums.ssrc.org/ndsp/2014/08/04/the-architecture-of-multi-faith-prayer-an-introduction/.

Bender, Courtney. "Bet- Und Lehrhaus (the House of Prayer and Learning)." SSRC Forums, 2014, accessed 17th of November, 2021, http://forums.ssrc.org/ndsp/2014/08/04/bet-und-lehrhaus-the-house-of-prayer-and-learning/.

Bender, Courtney. "Temple of Religion, New York World's Fair (1939–1940)." SSRC Forums, 2014, accessed 17th of November, 2021, http://forums.ssrc.org/ndsp/2014/08/04/temple-of-religion-new-york-worlds-fair-1939-1940/.

Bennet, Zoë, Elaine Graham, Stephen Pattison, and H. Walton. *Invitation to Research in Practical Theology.* London and New York: Routledge, 2018.

Berger, Peter L. *The Desecularization of the World.* Washington, D.C.: Grand Rapids, MI: William B Eerdmans Publishing Co, 1999.

Berger, Peter L. *The Many Altars of Modernity.* Boston and Berlin: De Gruyter, 2014.

Berger, Peter L. "Secularisation Falsified." *First Things*, February (2008). https://www.firstthings.com/article/2008/02/secularization-falsified.

Berger, Peter L. "Secularism in Retreat." *The National Interest*, December 1, 1996. https://nationalinterest.org/article/secularism-in-retreat-336.

Berger, Peter L. "Some Second Thoughts on Substantive Versus Functional Definitions of Religion." *Journal for the Scientific Study of Religion* 13, no. 2 (1974): 125–33.

Berman, Harold J. *Law and Revolution. The Formation of the Western Legal Tradition.* Cambridge, MA and London, U.K.: Harvard University Press, 1983.

Bhargava, Rajeev. "Rehabilitating Secularism." In *Rethinking Secularism*, edited by Craig Calhoun, Mark Juergensmeyer and Jonathan VanAntwerpen, 92–113. Oxford: Oxford University Press, 2011.

Biddington, Terry. *Multi-faith Space: History, Development, Design and Practice.* London: Jessica Kingsley Publishers, 2020.

Biddington, Terry "Towards a Theological Reading of Multi-faith Spaces." *International Journal of Public Theology* 7, no. 3 (2013): 315–28. https://doi.org/10.1163/15697320-12341293.

Blankholm, Joseph. "Remembering Marx's Secularism." *Journal of the American Academy of Religion* 88, no. 1 (2020): 35–57. https://doi.org/10.1093/jaarel/lfz104.

Blanning, T. C. W. *The French Revolution. Class War or Culture Clash.* London: Macmillan Press, 1998.

Bobrowicz, Katarzyna, Areum Han, Jennifer Hausen, and Samuel Greiff. "Aiding Reflective Navigation in a Dynamic Information Landscape: A Challenge for Educational Psychology." *Front Psychol* 13 (2022): 881539. https://doi.org/10.3389/fpsyg.2022.881539.

Bobrowicz, Ryszard. "The Inverted Relationship: Constitutive Theory of Law and the Enforcement of Orthodoxy in Book XVI of the Theodosian Code." In *Law, Religion and Tradition*, edited by Jessica Giles, Andrea Pin and Frank S. Ravitch, 87–118. Cham: Springer Nature Switzerland AG, 2018.

Bobrowicz, Ryszard, and Emil Bjørn Hilton Saggau. "The Organisation of Prayer Rooms in Educational Institutions in Denmark—Moderate Secularism between Perception and Practice." *Nordic Journal of Religion and Society* 35, no. 2 (2022): 96–110. https://doi.org/10.18261/njrs.35.2.3.

Bobrowicz, Ryszard, and Mattias Nowak. "Divided by the Rainbow: Culture War and Diffusion of Paleoconservative Values in Contemporary Poland." *Religions* 12, no. 3 (2021): 170. https://www.mdpi.com/2077-1444/12/3/170.

Bobrowicz, Ryszard, and Jakob Wirén. "Cemeteries as Spaces of Interreligious Encounter? The Use of Different Types of Neutrality in the Context of Graveyards in Scandinavia." *International Journal of Public Theology* 17, no. 4 (2023): 581–601. https://doi.org/10.1163/15697320-20230106.

Böckenförde, Ernst-Wolfgang. "The Rise of the State as a Process of Secularization." In *Religion, Law, and Democracy*, edited by Ernst-Wolfgang Böckenförde, M. Künkler and T. Stein, 152–67. Oxford: Oxford University Press, 2020 [1967].

Bodin, Jean. *Les Six Livres De La Republique*. Paris: Chez Jacques du Puys, 1576.

Bohman, James, and William Rehg. "Jürgen Habermas." In *The Stanford Encyclopedia of Philosophy*, edited by Edward N. Zalta. Fall 2017. https://plato.stanford.edu/entries/habermas/#DiaBetNatRel.

Bohnsack, Ulrike. "Sitzung Vom 2. März 2018." Universität Duisburg-Essen, 2018, accessed 12th of December, 2021, https://www.uni-due.de/2018-03-13-senatssitzung-maerz.

Borén, Thomas, Patrycja Grzyś, and Craig Young. "Intra-Urban Connectedness, Policy Mobilities and Creative City-Making: National Conservatism Vs. Urban (Neo) Liberalism." *European Urban and Regional Studies* 27, no. 3 (2020): 246–58. https://doi.org/10.1177/0969776420913096.

Bottos, Davide and Elena Calabrò. "Nova Project - Multi Faith Space." Divisare, 2016, accessed 8th of October, 2021, https://divisare.com/projects/325458-davide-bottos-elena-calabro-nova-project-multi-faith-space.

Brand, Ralf Gregor, Andrew Crompton, and Chris Hewson. "Multi-faith Spaces—Symptoms and Agents of Religious and Social Change." University of Manchester and University of Liverpool, 2012, accessed 17 September 2021, http://cargocollective.com/wwwmulti-faith-spacesorg.

Brems, Eva, Corina Heri, Saila Ouald Chaib, and Lieselot Verdonck. "Head-Covering Bans in Belgian Courtrooms and Beyond: Headscarf Persecution and the Complicity of Supranational Courts." *Human Rights Quarterly* 39, no. 4 (2017): 882–909. https://doi.org/10.1353/hrq.2017.0053.

Brietenberg Jr., E. Harold. "To Tell the Turth: Will the Real Public Theology Please Stand Up." *Journal of the Society of Christian Ethics* 23, no. 2 (2003): 55–96. https://doi.org/10.5840/jsce20032325.

Brubaker, Rogers. "Between Nationalism and Civilizationism: The European Populist Moment in Comparative Perspective." *Ethnic & Racial Studies* 40, no. 8 (2017): 1191–226 https://doi.org/10.1080/01419870.2017.1294700.

Brubaker, Rogers. "Why Populism?." *Theory & Society* 46 (2017): 357–85. https://doi.org/10.1007/s11186-017-9301-7

Burchardt, Marian. *Regulating Difference.* Rutgers University Press, 2020. https://doi.org/10.36019/9781978809635.

Carney, Mark. "'We Are Seeing a Crisis in Values'—an Exclusive Extract from Mark Carney's Book." *The Guardian*, 13th of March 2021. https://www.theguardian.com/business/2021/mar/13/crisis-in-values-exclusive-extract-mark-carneys-book.

Carol, Sarah, and Ruud Koopmans. "Dynamics of Contestation over Islamic Religious Rights in Western Europe." *Ethnicities* 13, no. 2 (2013): 165–90. https://doi.org/10.1177/1468796812470893.

Casanova, José. *Public Religions in the Modern World.* Chicago and London: The University of Chicago Press, 1994.

Cavanaugh, William T. *Migrations of the Holy. God, State, and the Political Meaning of the Church.* Grand Rapids, MI and Cambridge, U.K.: William B. Eerdmans Publishing Company, 2011.

Cavanaugh, William T. *The Myth of Religious Violence. Secular Ideology and the Roots of Modern Conflict.* Oxford: Oxford University Press, 2009.

Cesari, Jocelyne. "Securitization of Islam and Religious Freedom." *Berkley Forum*, 13th of September, 2018. https://berkleycenter.georgetown.edu/posts/securitization-of-islam-and-religious-freedom.

Cesari, Jocelyne. "Securitization of Islam in Europe: The Embodiment of Islam as an Exception." In *Why the West Fears Islam*, 83–105. New York: Palgrave Macmillan, 2013.

Chamedes, Giuliana. *A Twentieth Century Crusade. The Vatican's Battle to Remake Christian Europe.* Cambridge, MA: Harvard University Press, 2019.

Chappel, James. *Catholic Modern. The Challenge of Totalitarianism and the Remaking of the Church.* Boston, MA: Harvard University Press, 2018.

Chartier, Roger. *The Cultural Origins of the French Revolution.* Translated by Lydia G. Cochrane. Durham and London: Duke University Press, 1991.

Christensen, H. R., I. M. Høeg, Lena Kühle, and Magdalena Nordin. "Rooms of Silence at Three Universities in Scandinavia." *Sociology of Religion* 80, no. 3 (2018): 299–322. https://doi.org/10.1093/socrel/sry040.

Cipriani, Roberto. "Secularization." In *Sociology of Religion. An Historical Introduction*, 167–78. New York: Aldine De Gruyter, 2000.

Clot-Garrell, Anna, and Mar Griera. "Las Salas Multiconfesionales En El Contexto Hospitalario Catalán: Negociaciones Y Tensiones En La Gestión De La Diversidad." *Salud Colectiva* 14, no. 2 (2018): 289–304. https://doi.org/10.18294/sc.2018.1534.

Collins, Peter, Simon Coleman, Janne Macnaughton, and Tessa Pollard. *NHS Hospital 'Chaplaincies' in a Multi-Faith Society. The Spatial Dimension of Religion and Spirituality in Hospital.* Durham University and NHS (Durham: 2007).

Colosimo, Anastasia. "Laïcité: Why French Secularism Is So Hard to Grasp." Institut Montaigne, 2017, accessed 11 December, 2021, https://www.institutmontaigne.org/en/blog/laicite-why-french-secularism-so-hard-grasp.

Comte, Auguste. *A General View of Positivism.* Translated by J. H. Bridges. London: Trübner & Co., 1865.

Comte, Auguste. *The Positive Philosophy of Auguste Comte.* Translated by Harriet Martineau. Volume 1, London: John Chapman, 1853.

Connolly, Kate. "'House of One': Berlin Lays First Stone for Multi-Faith Worship Centre." *The Guardian*, 27th of May 2021. https://www.theguardian.com/world/2021/may/27/berlin-lays-first-stone-for-multi-faith-house-of-one-worship-centre.

"Declaration of Human and Civic Rights of 26 August 1789." Conseil Constitutionnel, 2021, accessed 8 March 2021, https://www.conseil-constitutionnel.fr/en/declaration-of-human-and-civic-rights-of-26-august-1789.

Copson, Andrew. *Secularism: A Very Short Introduction.* Oxford: Oxford University Press, 2019.

Crompton, Andrew. "The Architecture of Multi-faith Spaces: God Leaves the Building." *The Journal of Architecture* 18 (2013): 474–96. https://doi.org/10.1080/13602365.2013.821149.

Crompton, Andrew. "The Tate Modern Multi-Faith Room: Where Sacred Space and Art Space Converge and Merge." LSE Blog "Religion in the Public Sphere", 2016, accessed 17th of March, 2022, http://eprints.lse.ac.uk/id/eprint/76477.

Crompton, Andrew, and Chris Hewson. "Designing Equality: Multi-Faith Space as Social Intervention." In *Religion, Equalities, and Inequalities*, 77–88. London and New York: Routledge, 2016.

Croxton, Derek. "The Peace of Westphalia of 1648 and the Origins of Sovereignty." *The International History Review* 21, no. 3 (1999): 569–91. https://doi.org/10.1080/07075332.1999.9640869.

Dagens Nyheter, "Religiösa Friskolor." 2022, accessed 12th of March, 2022, https://www.dn.se/om/religiosa-friskolor/.

Danthine, Jean-Pierre. "Subsidiarity: The Forgotten Concept at the Core of Europe's Existential Crisis." *Vox EU CEPR*, 12th of April 2017. https://voxeu.org/article/subsidiarity-still-key-europe-s-institutional-problems.

Davie, Grace. "Is Europe an Exceptional Case." *International Review of Mission* 95, no. 378–379 (2006): 247–58. https://doi.org/10.1111/j.1758-6631.2006.tb00562.x.

Day, Katie, and Sebastian Kim. "Introduction." In *A Companion to Public Theology*, edited by Katie Day and Sebastian Kim, 1–21. Leiden: Brill, 2017.

Department for Communities and Local Government. *Face to Face and Side by Side: A Framework for Partnership in Our Multi Faith Society.* London: Department for Communities and Local Government, 2008.

Der Westen. "Nach Schließung Von Gebetsraum an Uni Essen: Islamische Studenten Wollen „Raum Der Stille" Für Gebete Nutzen." *Der Westen*, 17th of October 2018. https://www.derwesten.de/staedte/essen/gebetsraum-uni-essen-islamische-studenten-id215578697.html.

Diez, Georg. "Habermas, the Last European. A Philosopher's Mission to Save the Eu." *Der Spiegel International*, November 25th 2011. https://www.spiegel.de/international/europe/habermas-the-last-european-a-philosopher-s-mission-to-save-the-eu-a-799237.html.

Dinham, Adam. "The Multi-Faith Paradigm in Policy and Practice: Problems, Challenges, Directions." *Social Policy and Society* 11, no. 4 (2012): 577–87. https://doi.org/10.1017/S1474746412000255.

Dobbelaere, Karel. *Secularization: An Analysis at Three Levels.* Brussels: P.I.E.-Peter Lang, 2002.

Doyle, William. *The French Revolution: A Very Short Introduction.* Oxford: Oxford University Press, 2019.

Dupuy, Pierre-Marie, and Vincent Chetail. *The Roots of International Law / Les Fondements Du Droit International.* Leiden: Brill, 2014.

Durkheim, Émile. *The Elementary Forms of the Religious Life.* Translated by Carol Cosman. Oxford: Oxford University Press, 2008.

Eatwell, Roger, and Matthew Goodwin. *National Populism: The Revolt against Liberal Democracy.* London: Pelican Books, 2018.

European Union. "Consolidated Version of the Treaty on European Union." (2012). https://eur-lex.europa.eu/legal-content/EN/TXT/?uri=celex%3A12012M%2FTXT.

Evans, Michelle, and Augusto Zimmermann. "The Global Relevance of Subsidiarity: An Overview." In *Global Perspectives on Subsidiarity*, edited by Michelle Evans and Augusto Zimmermann, 1–7. Dordrecht: Springer, 2014.

Fernandez, Eleazar S. *Teaching for a Multi-faith World.* Eugene, OR: Pickwick Publications, 2017.

Ferrari, Silvio. "Law and Religion in a Secular World: A European Perspective." *Ecclesiastical Law Journal* 14, no. 3 (2012): 335–70. https://doi.org/10.1017/S0956618X1200035X.

Finlayson, James Gordon. *Habermas: A Very Short Introduction.* Oxford: Oxford University Press, 2005.

Finnis, John. M. "Subsidiarity's Roots and History: Some Observations." *The American Journal of Jurisprudence* 61, no. 1 (2016): 133–41. https://doi.org/10.1093/ajj/auw006.

Focus. "Studenten Beklagen Einschüchterung Universität Essen Schließt Muslimischen Gebetsraum." *Focus*, 13th of February 2016. https://www.focus.de/regional

/essen/studenten-beklagen-einschuechterung-universitaet-essen-schliesst-muslimischen-gebetsraum_id_5280048.html.

Foster, Russell, Nick Megoran, and Michael Dunn. "Towards a Geopolitics of Atheism: Critical Geopolitics Post the 'War On Terror.'" *Political Geography* 60 (2017): 179–89. https://doi.org/10.1016/j.polgeo.2017.07.011.

Foucault, Michel. *The Archaeology of Knowledge*. London: Routledge, 1992.

Funk, Nathan C., and Christina J. Woolner. "Religion and Peace and Conflict Studies." In *Critical Issues in Peace and Conflict Studies*, edited by Thomas Matyok, Jessica Senehi and Sean Byrne, 349–369. Toronto: Lexington Books, 2011.

Furseth, Inger. "The Return of Religion in the Public Sphere? The Public Role of Nordic Faith Communities." In *Institutional Change in the Public Sphere. Views on the Nordic Model*, edited by Fredrik Engelstad, Håkon Larsen, Jon Rogstad and Kari Steen-Johnsen, 221–240. Warsaw and Berlin: De Gruyter, 2017. https://doi.org/10.1515/9783110546330-012.

Geertz, Clifford. *Local Knowledge: Further Essays in Interpretative Anthropology*. New York: Basic Books, 1983.

Gellman, Mneesha, and Mandi Vuinovich. "From Sulha to Salaam: Connecting Local Knowledge with International Negotiations for Lasting Peace in Palestine/Israel." *Conflict Resolution Quarterly* 26, no. 2 (2008): 127–48. https://doi.org/10.1002/crq.227.

Gerle, Elisabeth. *Mångkulturalism—För Vem? Debatten Om Muslimska Och Kristna Friskolor Blottlägger Värdekonflikter I Det Svenska Samhället*. Nora: Nya Doxa, 2002.

Gerle, Elisabeth. "Multicultural Society: Dilemmas and Prospects." In *Theology and the Religions: A Dialogue*, edited by Viggo Mortnesen, 31–45. Grand Rapids, MI: William B. Eerdmans Publishing Company, 2003.

Gerle, Elisabeth. "Various Interpretations of Human Rights for Women Challenges at United Nations Conferences." In *Human Rights Law: From Dissemination to Application. Essays in Honour of Göran Melander*, edited by Jonas Grimheden and Rolf Ring, 343–73. Leiden: Martinus Nijhoff Publishers, 2006.

Gilliat-Ray, Sophie. "From 'Chapel' to 'Prayer Room': The Production, Use, and Politics of Sacred Space in Public Institutions." *Culture and Religion* 6, no. 2 (2005): 287–308. https://doi.org/10.1080/01438300500226448.

Gilliat-Ray, Sophie. "'Sacralising' Sacred Space in Public Institutions: A Case Study of the Prayer Space at the Millennium Dome." *Journal of Contemporary Religions*, no. 20 (2005): 357–72. https://doi.org/10.1080/13537900500249921.

Gordon, Robert W. "Critical Legal Histories." *Stanford Law Review* 36, no. 1/2 (1984): 57–125. https://doi.org/10.2307/1228681.

Graham, Elaine. *Between a Rock and a Hard Place: Public Theology in a Post-secular Age*. London: SCM Press, 2013.

Gross, Leo. "The Peace of Westphalia, 1648–1948." *The American Journal of International Law* 42, no. 1 (1948): 20–41. https://doi.org/10.2307/2193560.

Guds Hus, "God's House. Where People Meet." 2020, accessed 12th of March, 2020, http://gudshus.se/en/.

Guds Hus, "Om Guds Hus." 2020, accessed 12th of March, 2020, https://gudshus.se/en/om-guds-hus/.

Haag, Jens. "Marie Krarups Kritik af Retræterummet på KUA er Vanvittig Forfejlet." *Uniavisen*, 15th of December 2016. https://uniavisen.dk/marie-krarups-kritik-af-retraeterummet-paa-kua-er-vanvittig-forfejlet/.

Haarscher, Guy. *Laickość. Kościół, Państwo, Religia.* Translated by Ewa Burska. Warszawa: Instytut Wydawniczy Pax, 2004.

Habermas, Jürgen. *An Awareness of What Is Missing: Faith and Reason in a Post-Secular Age.* Cambridge: Polity Press, 2010.

Habermas, Jürgen. "Glauben Und Wissen. Dankesrede." Friedenspreis des Deutschen Buchhandels, 2001, https://www.friedenspreis-des-deutschen-buchhandels.de/alle-preistraeger-seit-1950/2000-2009/juergen-habermas.

Habermas, Jürgen. "Notes on Post-Secular Society." *New Perspectives Quarterly* 25, no. 4 (2008): 17–29. https://doi.org/10.1111/j.1540-5842.2008.01017.x.

Habermas, Jürgen. *On the Pragmatics of Communication.* Edited by Maeve Cooke. Cambridge, MA: MIT Press, 1998.

Habermas, Jürgen. "Religion in Der Öffentlichkeit. Kognitive Voraussetzungen Für Den »Öffentlichen Vernunftgebrauch« Religiöser Und Säkularer Bürger." In *Zwischen Naturalismus Und Religion. Philosophische Aufsätze*, edited by Jürgen Habermas, 117–52. Frankfurt am Main: Suhrkamp Verlag, 2005.

Habermas, Jürgen. "Religion in the Public Sphere." *European Journal of Philosophy* 14, no. 1 (2006): 1–25. https://doi.org/10.1111/j.1468-0378.2006.00241.x.

Habermas, Jürgen. "Religion in the Public Sphere: Cognitive Presuppositions for the "Public Use of Reason" by Religious and Secular Citizens." Translated by Ciaran Cronin. In *Between Naturalism and Religion*, 114–148. Cambridge: Polity Press, 2006.

Habermas, Jürgen. *The Structural Transformation of the Public Sphere: An Inquiry into a Category of Bourgeois Society.* Cambridge, MA: MIT Press, 1998.

Habermas, Jürgen. *Theory of Communicative Action. Volume One: Reason and the Rationalization of Society.* Boston, MA: Beacon Press, 1984.

Habermas, Jürgen. "What Is Meant by a 'Post-Secular Society'? A Discussion on Islam in Europe." Translated by Ciaran Cronin. In *Europe: The Faltering Project*, 59–78. Cambridge: Polity Press, 2009.

Habermas, Jürgen. "Why Europe Needs a Constitution." *New Left Review*, no. 11 (2001): 5–26.

Habermas, Jürgen, and Joseph Ratzinger. *The Dialectics of Secularization: On Reason and Religion.* San Francisco: Ignatius Press, 2007.

Hall, David D. *Lived Religion in America: Roward a History of Practice.* Princeton: Princeton University Press, 1997.

Halldorf, Joel. *Gud: Återkomsten.* Stockholm: Libris förlag, 2018.

Halperin, Jean-Louis. "Law in Books and Law in Action: The Problem of Legal Change." *Maine Law Review* 64, no. 1 (2011): 46–76.

Hamel, Chouki El. "Muslim Diaspora in Western Europe: The Islamic Headscarf (Hijab), the Media and Muslims' Integration in France." *Citizenship Studies* 6, no. 3 (2002): 293–308. https://doi.org/10.1080/1362102022000011621.

Hanchin, Timothy. "Encounter and/as Pedagogy for Catholic Higher Education in Our Time." *Religious Education* 114, no. 5 (2019): 565–80. https://doi.org/10.1080/00344087.2019.1631975.

Harris, Sam. *The End of Faith: Religion, Terror, and the Future of Reason.* New York and London: W. W. Norton & Company, 2005.

Hauerwas, Stanley. *A Community of Character.* Notre Dame: University of Notre Dame Press, 1981.

Haynes, Jeffrey. "From Huntington to Trump: Twenty-Five Years of the "Clash of Civilizations."" *The Review of Faith & International Affairs* 17, no. 1 (2019): 11–23. https://doi.org/10.1080/15570274.2019.1570755.

Haynes, Jeffrey. *Religion in Global Politics.* London: Longman, 1998.

Haynes, Jeffrey. "Twenty Years after Huntington's 'Clash of Civilzations'." In *The Clash of Civilizations. Twenty Years On*, edited by J. Paul Barker. Bristol: E-International Relations, 2013.

Heckel, Martin. *Gesammelte Schriften.* Band v: Staat—Kirche—Recht—Geschichte. Tübingen: Mohr Siebeck, 2004. https://doi.org/9783161483202.

Heelas, Paul, and Linda Woodhead. *The Spiritual Revolution. Why Religion Is Giving Way to Spirituality.* Oxford: Oxford University Press, 2005.

Hekman, Susan. *Weber, the Ideal Type, and Contemporary Social Theory.* Notre Dame: University of Notre Dame Press, 1983.

Heller, Henry. "Marx, the French Revolution, and the Spetre of the Bourgeoisie." *Science & Society* 74, no. 2 (2010): 184–214. https://doi.org/10.1521/siso.2010.74.2.184.

Hellqvist, Kristina, and Andreas Sandberg. *A Time of Encounters. The Work with Asylum Seekers and New Arrivals in the Parishes of the Church of Sweden 2015–2016.* Uppsala: Svenska Kyrkan, 2018.

Hendrix, Scott H. "Loyalty, Piety, or Opportunism: German Princes and the Reformation." *Journal of Interdisciplinary History* xxv, no. 2 (1994): 211–24. https://doi.org/10.2307/206343.

Hill, David Jayne. *A History of Diplomacy in the International Development of Europe.* New York and London: Longmans, Green, and Company, 1906.

Hitchens, Christopher. *God Is Not Great.* New York and Boston: Twelve, 2007.

Hittinger, Russell. "Social Pluralism and Subsidiarity in Catholic Social Doctrine." *Annales theologici* 16 (2002): 385–408.

Holloway, R. Ross. *Constantine & Rome.* New Haven: Yale University Press, 2004.

Holyoake, George Jacob. *English Secularism. A Confession of Belief.* Chicago: The Open Court Publishing Company, 1896.

Holyoake, George Jacob. *The Last Trial for Atheism in England: A Fragment of Autobiography.* London: Trübner & Co., 1871.

Horii, Mitsutoshi. "Contextualizing "Religion" of Young Karl Marx: A Preliminary Analysis." *Critical Research on Religion* 5, no. 2 (2017): 170–87. https://doi.org/10.1177/2050303217690 8.

Horii, Mitsutoshi "Historicizing the Category of "Religion" in Sociological Theories: Max Weber and Emile Durkheim." *Critical Research on Religion* 7, no. 1 (2019): 24–37. https://doi.org/10.1177/2050303218800369.

House of One, "Guds Hus—Our Partner Project in Sweden." 2019, accessed 18th of November, 2021, https://house-of-one.org/en/news/guds-hus-%E2%80%93-our-partner-project-sweden.

House of One, "The Concept" 2019, accessed 18th of November, 2021, https://house-of-one.org/en/concept.

Hughes, Aaron W. *Abrahamic Religions: On the Uses and Abuses of History.* Oxford: Oxford University Press, 2012.

Huntington, Samuel Phillips. *The Clash of Civilizations and the Remaking of World Order.* London: Simon & Schuster, 1996.

Huntington, Samuel Phillips. "The Clash of Civilizations?." *Foreign Affairs* 72, no. 3 (1993): 22–49.

Hurd, Elizabeth Shakman. *The Politics of Secularism in International Relations.* Princeton and Oxford: Princeton University Press, 2008.

International Hildreth Meière Association, "New York 1939 World's Fair: Temple of Religion, Flushing, NY." 2021, accessed 17th of September, 2021, https://www.hildrethmeiere.org/commissions/new-york-1939-worlds-fair-temple-of-religion-arcade-facing-courtyard.

Istanbul Airport, "Prayer Rooms." 2021, accessed 17th of November, 2021, https://www.istairport.com/en/passenger/services/airport-services/prayer-rooms.

Itzcovich, G. "One, None and One Hundred Thousand Margins of Appreciations: The Lautsi Case." *Human Rights Law Review* 13, no. 2 (2013): 287–308. https://doi.org/10.1093/hrlr/ngs038.

Iversen, Hans Raun. "Secularization, Secularity, Secularism." In *Encyclopedia of Sciences and Religions*, edited by Oviedo L. Runehov A.L.C. Dordrecht: Springer, 2013.

Janis, Mark S. "Sovereignty and International Law: Hobbes and Grotius." In *Essays in Honour of Wang Tieya*, edited by Ronald St. John MacDonald. Leiden: Brill and Nijhoff, 1994.

Johanson, Karla, and Peter Laurence. "Multi-Faith Religious Spaces on College and University Campuses." *Religion & Education* 39, no. 1 (2012): 48–63. https://doi.org/10.1080/15507394.2012.648579.

John Paul II. "Centesimus Annus." (1991). Accessed 12th of December 2021. https://www.vatican.va/content/john-paul-ii/en/encyclicals/documents/hf_jp-ii_enc_01051991_centesimus-annus.html.

Johnston, Douglas, and Cynthia Sampson. *Religion: The Missing Dimension of Statecraft.* Oxford: Oxford University Press, 1994.

Jürgs, Alexander. "Kulturkampf Um Den „Raum Der Stille" an Der TU Dortmund." *Welt*, 12th of February 2016. https://www.welt.de/vermischtes/article152169223/Kulturkampf-um-den-Raum-der-Stille-an-der-TU-Dortmund.html.

Kabakcı, Enes. "Trajectoire Du Positivisme Comtien (1820–1857) De La Philosophie Positive a La Religion De L'humanite." *Sosyoloji Dergisi / Journal of Sociology*, no. 23 (2011): 137–64.

Kaminski, Matthew. "Another Face of Europe's Far Right." *Wall Street Journal*, 3rd of May 2002. https://www.wsj.com/articles/SB102037039985461320.

Kaya, Serdar. "State Policies toward Islam in Twenty Countries in Western Europe: The Accommodation of Islam Index." *Muslim World Journal of Human Rights* 14, no. 1 (2017): 55–81. https://doi.org/10.1515/mwjhr-2016-0003.

Kelly, Michael. "France's Laïcité: Why the Rest of the World Struggles to Understand It." *The Conversation*. (20 November 2020). Accessed 16 May 2021. https://theconversation.com/frances-la-cite-why-the-rest-of-the-world-struggles-to-understand-it-149943.

Kent, Orit. "Interactive Text Study: A Case of Hevruta Learning." *Journal of Jewish Education* 72, no. 3 (2006): 205–32. https://doi.org/10.1080/15244110600990155.

Kermani, Secunder. "City University London Locks Muslim Prayer Room on Fridays." *BBC News*, 22nd of February 2013. https://www.bbc.com/news/uk-england-london-21542041.

Kim, Sung Ho. "Max Weber." In *The Stanford Encyclopedia of Philosophy*, edited by Edward N. Zalta. Winter 2019. https://plato.stanford.edu/archives/win2019/entries/weber/.

Kleine, Christoph, and Monika Wohlrab-Sahr. "Research Programme of the HCAS "Multiple Secularities—Beyond the West, Beyond Modernities."" (2016). Accessed 12th of October 2021. https://www.multiple-secularities.de/media/multiple_secularities_research_programme.pdf.

Kluchert, Gerhard. "The Paradigm and the Parody. Karl Marx and the French Revolution in the Class Struggles from 1848–1851." *History of European Ideas* 14, no. 1 (1992): 85–99. https://doi.org/10.1016/0191-6599(92)90294-M.

Kohlmaier, Matthias. "Kein Platz Für Allah an Deutschen Unis." *Süddeutsche Zeitung*, 9th of March 2016. https://www.sueddeutsche.de/bildung/studium-kein-platz-fuer-allah-an-deutschen-unis-1.2897802.

Korioth, Stefan, and Ino Augsberg. "Religion and the Secular State in Germany." In *Religion and the Secular State / La Religion Et L'état Laïque*, edited by Javier

Martinez-Torrón and W. Cole Durham Jr., 320–30. Provo, UT: The International Center for Law and Religious Studies, Brigham Young University, 2010.

Krarup, Marie, and Ulla Tørnæs. "§ 20-Spørgsmål S 259 Om at Undgå Islamisering i Uddannelsesinstitutionerne." 24th of November. Copenhagen: Folketingen, 2016. https://www.ft.dk/samling/20161/spoergsmaal/s259/index.htm.

Kühle, Lena, and Heinrik Reintoft Christensen. "One to Serve Them All. The Growth of Chaplaincy in Public Institutions in Denmark." *Social Compass* 66, no. 2 (2019): 182–97. https://doi.org/10.1177/0037768619833331.

Laborde, Cécile. *Liberalism's Religion.* Cambridge, MA and London, U.K.: Harvard University Press, 2017.

LaCapra, Dominick. "Intellectual History and Its Ways." *The American Historical Review* 97, no. 2 (1992): 425–39. https://doi.org/10.2307/2165726.

Lang, Sharon. "Sulha Peacemaking and the Politics of Persuasion." *Journal of Palestine Studies* 31, no. 3 (2020): 52–66. https://doi.org/10.1525/jps.2002.31.3.52.

Langballe, Christian, and Bertel Haarder. "§ 20-Spørgsmål S 242 Om Religionsneutrale Bederum På Hospitalerne." 18th of November. Copenhagen: Folketingen, 2016. https://www.ft.dk/samling/20161/spoergsmaal/s242/index.htm.

Latreille, André, and Joseph E. Cunneen. "The Catholic Church and the Secular State: The Church and the Secularization of Modern Societies." *Cross Currents* 13, no. 2 (1963): 217–48.

Lee, Lois. *Recognizing the Non-Religious: Reimagining the Secular.* Oxford: Oxford University Press, 2015.

Lefebvre, Solange. "Secularism, Secularization, Public Theology, and Practical Theology." In *Catholic Approaches to Practical Theology*, edited by C. E. Wolfteich and A. Dillen, 207–224. Leuven: Peeters Publishers, 2016.

Leithart, Peter J. *Defending Constantine: The Twilight of an Empire and the Dawn of Christendom.* Downers Grove, IL: IVP Academic, 2010.

Leo XIII. "Rerum Novarum." (1891). Accessed 12th of December 2021. https:// www.vatican.va/content/leo-xiii/en/encyclicals/documents/hf_l-xiii_enc_15051891_rerum-novarum.html.

Lipsky, Michael. *Street Level Bureaucracy Dilemmas of the Individual in Public Services.* New York: Russell Sage Foundation, 1980. http://www.jstor.org/stable/10.7758/9781610447713.

Lookofsky, Joseph M. "Desperately Seeking Subsidiarity Danish Private Law in the Scandinavian, European, and Global Context." *CICLOPs* 1 (2009): 111–30.

Lopatka, Reinhold. "Subsidiarity: Bridging the Gap between the Ideal and Reality." *European View* 18, no. 1 (2019): 26–36. https://doi.org/10.1177/1781685819838449.

Lotnisko Chopina, "Chaplaincy." 2021, accessed 8th of October, 2021, https://www.lotnisko-chopina.pl/en/chaplaincy.html.

Luther, Martin. "Temporal Authority: To What Extent It Should Be Obeyed (1523)." In *Martin Luther's Basic Theological Writings*, edited by Timothy F. Lull, 655–703. Minneapolis: Fortress Press, 1989.

Lynch, Thomas. "Social Construction and Social Critique: Haslanger, Race, and the Study of Religion." *Critical Research on Religion* 5, no. 3 (2017): 284–301. https://doi.org/10.1177/2050303217732133.

Lyon, Alynna J. "Moral Motives and Policy Actions: The Case of Dag Hammarskjöld at the United Nations." *Public Intergrity* 9, no. 1 (2007): 79–95. https://doi.org/10.2753/PIN1099-9922090105.

MacIntyre, Alasdair. *After Virtue*. Notre Dame: University of Notre Dame Press, 1981.

MacIntyre, Alasdair. *Ethics in the Conflicts of Modernity. An Essay on Desire, Practical Reasoning, and Narrative*. Cambridge: Cambridge University Press, 2016.

Mahmood, Saba. *Politics of Piety: The Islamic Revival and the Feminist Subject*. Princeton: Princeton University Press, 2005.

Mahmood, Saba. *Religious Difference in a Secular Age: A Minority Report*. Princeton: Princeton University Press, 2015.

Mankefors, Linda. "Här Får De Neutrala Den Sista Vilan." *dt.se*, 23rd of September 2016. https://www.dt.se/artikel/har-far-de-neutrala-den-sista-vilan.

Marius, Morariu Iuliu. "Aspects of Political Theology in the Spiritual Autobiography of Dag Hammarskjöld." *HTS: Theological Studies* 74, no. 4 (2018): 1–5. http://dx.doi.org/10.4102/hts.v74i4.4857.

Marshall, Ellen Ott. *Introduction to Christian Ethics. Conflict, Faith, and Human Life*. Louisville, Kentucky: Westminster John Knox Press, 2018.

Martin, David. "Towards Eliminating the Concept of Secularization." In *Penguin Survey of the Social Sciences*, edited by Julius Gould, 169–182. London: Penguin Books, 1965.

Martinson, Mattias. *Sekularism, Populism, Xenofobi: En Essä Om Religionsdebatten*. Malmö: Eskaton, 2017.

Marty, Martin E. "Two Kinds of Two Kinds of Civil Religion." In *American Civil Religion*, edited by Russell E. Richey and Donald G. Jones, 139–57. New York: Harper & Row, 1974.

Marx, Karl. "'A Contribution to the Critique of Hegel's Philosophy of Right: Introduction'." In *Marx: Early Political Writings*, edited by Joseph J. O'Malley and Karl Marx. Cambridge Texts in the History of Political Thought, 57–70. Cambridge: Cambridge University Press, 1994.

Marx, Karl. "Critique of Hegel's Philosophy of Right." In *Marx on Religion*, edited by J. Raines, 170–181. Philadelphia, PA: Temple University Press, 2002.

Masuzawa, Tomoko. *The Invention of World Religions, or, How European Universalism Was Preserved in the Language of Pluralism*. Chicago: Chicago University Press, 2005.

Matczak, Marcin. "A Theory That Beats the Theory? Lineages, the Growth of Signs, and Dynamic Legal Interpretation." *Social Science Research Network* (2015). http://dx.doi.org/10.2139/ssrn.2595519.

McClendon Jr., James Wm. "Dag Hammarskjöld—Twice Born Servant." In *Biography as Theology: How Life Stories Can Remake Today's Theology*, edited by James Wm. McClendon Jr., 24–46. Eugene, OR: Wipf and Stock Publishers, 2002.

Melloni, Alberto, and Francesca Caddedu. *Religious Literacy, Law and History. Perspectives on European Pluralist Societies.* London and New York: Routledge, 2019.

Moller Okin, Susan. *Is Multiculturalism Bad for Women?* Edited by Joshua Cohen, Matthew Howard and Martha C. Nussbaum. Princeton: Princeton University Press, 1999.

Mouffe, Chantal. *Agonistics: Thinking the World Politically.* London: Verso, 2013.

Mouzakitis, Angelos. "Modernity and the Idea of Progress." Hypothesis and Theory. *Frontiers in Sociology* 2, no. 3 (2017). https://doi.org/10.3389/fsoc.2017.00003.

Moyaert, Marianne. *Christian Imaginations of the Religious Other: A History of Religionization.* Hoboken, NJ and Chichester: Wiley, 2024.

Mudde, Cas. *The Far Right Today.* Cambridge: Polity, 2019.

Mudde, Cas. *Populist Radical Right Parties in Europe.* Cambridge: Cambridge University Press, 2007.

Mudde, Cas, and Cristobal Rovira Kaltwasser. *Populism: A Very Short Introduction.* Oxford: Oxford University Press, 2017.

Mulé, Rosa, and Günter Walzenbach. "Introduction: Two Spaces of Subsidiarity?." *Commonwealth & Comparative Politics* 57, no. 2 (2019): 141–52. https://doi.org/10.1080/14662043.2019.1573991.

Nagel, Alexander-Kenneth, and Mehmet Kalender. "Guestbooks in Multi-faith Spaces as (Inter-)Religious Media." *Religion* 50, no. 3 (2020): 372–91. https://doi.org/10.1080/0048721x.2020.1756068.

Nathan, James A. *Soldiers, Statecraft, and History: Coercive Diplomacy and International Order.* Westport: Praeger Publisher, 2002.

Newman, Melanie. "Muslim Students Continue Street Protest over Closure of Prayer Room." *Times Higher Education*, 16th of March 2010. https://www.timeshighereducation.com/news/muslim-students-continue-street-protest-over-closure-of-prayer-room/410874.article.

Nilsson, Gert. *Socialetik i Svenska Kyrkan under 1900-Talet.* Skellefteå: Artos Norma Bokförlag, 2020.

Noethlichs, K. L. "Revolution from the Top? 'Orthodoxy' and the Persecution of Heretics in Imperial Legislation from Constantine to Justinian." In *Religion and Law in Classical and Christian Rome*, edited by Clifford Ando and J. Riipke, 115–25. Stuttgart: Franz Steiner Verlag, 2006.

Nongbri, Brent. *Before Religion. A History of a Modern Concept.* New Haven and London: Yale University Press, 2013.

North, John. "Religious Toleration in Republican Rome." *The Cambridge Classical Journal* 25 (1979): 85–103. https://doi.org/10.1017/S0068673500004144.

NUS Connect. "Culsu: Right to Pray." 2016, accessed 12th of December, 2021, https://www.nusconnect.org.uk/articles/culsu-right-to-pray.

Nussbaum, Martha. "Reinventing the Civil Religion: Comte, Mill, Tagore." *Victorian Studies* 54, no. 1 (2011): 7–34. https://doi.org/10.2979/victorianstudies.54.1.7.

Odahl, Charles. *Constantine and the Christian Empire.* New York: Routledge, 2010.

Olbrich, Till, and Rudolf Rayle. "Whatever Happened to EU Subsidiarity?" *Project Syndicate*, 8th of December 2015. https://www.project-syndicate.org/commentary/eu-subsidiarity-treaties-important-by-till-olbrich-and-rudolf-rayle-2015-12.

Oliphant, Elayne. *The Privilege of Being Banal: Art, Secularism, and Catholicism in Paris.* Chicago: University of Chicago Press, 2021.

Omer, Atalia. "Religion and the Study of Peace: Practice without Reflection." *Religions* 12, no. 12 (2021): 1069. https://doi.org/10.3390/rel12121069.

Osiander, Andreas. "Sovereignty, International Relations, and the Westphalian Myth." *International Organization* 55, no. 2 (2001): 251–87. https://doi.org/10.1162/00208180151140577.

Oudenampsen, Merijn. *De Conservatieve Revolte—Een Ideeëngeschiedenis Van De Fortuynopstand.* Nijmegen: Uitgeverij Vantilt, 2018.

Pals, Daniel L. *Nine Theories of Religion.* Oxford: Oxford University Press, 2015.

Parsons, Susan Frank. *The Ethics of Gender: New Dimensions to Religious Ethics.* Oxford: Wiley-Blackwell, 2001.

Patton, Steven. "The Peace of Westphalia and It Affects on International Relations, Diplomacy and Foreign Policy." *The Histories* 10, no. 1 (2019): 91–99.

Pely, Doron. "Where East Not Always Meets West: Comparing the Sulha Process to Western-Style Mediation and Arbitration." *Conflict Resolution Quarterly* 28, no. 4 (2011): 427–40. https://doi.org/10.1002/crq.20028.

Petzoldt, Matthias. "Encountering the Other: The Concept of Encounter in Philosophy and Theology." In *Dynamics of Difference: Christianity and Alterity*, edited by Ulrich Schmiedel and James M. Matarazzo Jr., 115–23. London: Bloomsbury T&T Clark, 2016.

Phillips, Gervase. "Deviance, Persecution and the Roman Creation of Christianity." *Journal of Historical Sociology* 29, no. 2 (2016): 250–70. https://doi.org/10.1111/johs.12071.

Pickel, Gert. *Religionssoziologie. Eine Einführung in Zentrale Themenbereiche.* Wiesbaden: VS Verlag, 2011.

Pickel, Gert, and Cemal Öztürk. "Islamophobia without Muslims? The "Contact Hypothesis" as an Explanation for Anti-Muslim Attitudes–Eastern European Societies in Comparative Perspective." *Journal of Nationalism, Memory & Language Politics* 12, no. 2 (2018): 162–91. https://doi.org/10.2478/jnmlp-2018-0009.

Pickel, Gert, and Alexander Yendell. "Islam Als Bedrohung? Beschreibung und Erklärung von Einstellungen zum Islam im Ländervergleich." *Zeitschrift für Vergleichende Politikwissenschaft* 10, no. 3–4/2016 (2016): 273–309. https://doi.org/10.1007/s12286-016-0309-6.

Pius VI. *Breve Quod Aliquantum.* Rome: San Pietro, 1791.

Pius XI. "Quadragesimo Anno." (1931). Accessed 12th of December 2021. https:// www.vatican.va/content/pius-xi/en/encyclicals/documents/hf_p-xi_enc_19310515_quadragesimo-anno.html.

Pollack, Detlef, Olaf Müller, and Gert Pickel. *The Social Significance of Religion in the Enlarged Europe: Secularization, Individualization and Pluralization.* Aldershot: Ashgate, 2012.

Pontifical Council for Justice and Peace. *Compendium of the Social Doctrine of the Church.* Vatican: Libreria Editrice Vaticana, 2005. https://www.vatican.va/roman_curia/pontifical_councils/justpeace/documents/rc_pc_justpeace_doc_20060526_compendio-dott-soc_en.html.

Pope Francis. "For a Culture of Encounter." *L'Osservatore Romano,* 23rd of September, 2016. https://www.vatican.va/content/francesco/en/cotidie/2016/documents/papa-francesco-cotidie_20160913_for-a-culture-of-encounter.html.

Pound, Roscoe. "Law in Books and Law in Action." *American Law Review* 44, no. 1 (1910): 12–36.

Prothero, Stephen. *Religious Literacy: What Every American Needs to Know-and Doesn't.* New York: HarperOne, 2007.

Przeciszewski, Marcin, and Rafał Łączny. *Kościół w Polsce.* Katolicka Agencja Informacyjna (Warszawa: 2021). https://ekai.pl/wp-content/uploads/2021/03/Raport-Kosciol-w-Polsce-2021.pdf.

Puppinck, Grégor. "The Case of Lautsi v. Italy: A Synthesis." BYU *Law Review,* no. 873 (2012): 873–927.

Qurashi, Fahid. "The Prevent Strategy and the Uk 'War on Terror': Embedding Infrastructures of Surveillance in Muslim Communities." *Palgrave Communications* 4, no. 1 (2018): 17. https://doi.org/10.1057/s41599-017-0061-9.

Rajak, Tessa. "Was There a Roman Charter for the Jews." In *The Jewish Dialogue with Greece and Rome,* 301–33. Leiden: Brill, 2001.

Rawls, John. *Political Liberalism.* New York: Columbia University Press, 2005.

Reaves, Dylan. "Peter Berger and the Rise and Fall of the Theory of Secularization." *Denison Journal of Religion* 11, no. 3 (2012): 11–19.

Rémond, René. *Religion and Society in Modern Europe.* The Making of Europe. Edited by Jacques Le Goff. Oxford: Blackwell Publishers, 1999.

Robinson, Mark. "Does Decentralisation Improve Equity and Efficiency in Public Service Delivery Provision?" IDS *Bulletin* 38, no. 1 (2007): 7–17. https://doi.org/10.1111/j.1759-5436.2007.tb00333.x.

Ronchi, Paolo. "Crucifixes, Margin of Appreciation and Consensus: The Grand Chamber Ruling in Lautsi v Italy." *Ecclesiastical Law Journal* 13, no. 3 (2011): 287–97. https://doi.org/10.1017/s0956618x11000421.

Rosa, Hartmut. *Resonance. A Sociology of Our Relationship to the World.* Translated by James C. Wagner. Cambridge: Polity Press, 2019.

Rosa, Hartmut. *The Uncontrollability of the World.* Translated by James C. Wagner. Cambridge: Polity Press, 2021.

Roth, John D., ed. *Constantine Revisited: Leithart, Yoder, and the Constantinian Debate.* Eugene, OR: Pickwick Publications, 2013.

Rüpke, Jorg. "Religious Pluralism." In *The Oxford Handbook of Roman Studies*, 1–15. Oxford: Oxford University Press, 2012.

Sandel, Michael. *Liberalism and the Limits of Justice.* Cambridge: Cambridge University Press, 1982.

Sarat, Austin, and Jonathan Simon. "Beyond Legal Realism: Cultural Analysis, Cultural Studies, and the Situation of Legal Scholarship." *Yale Journal of Law & the Humanities* 13, no. 3 (2001): 3–32.

Scheid, John. "Religions in Contact." In *Ancient Religions*, edited by Sara Iles Johnston, 112–26. Boston, MA: The Belknap Press of Harvard University Press, 2007.

Schmidt, Simon P. *Church and World: Eusebius's, Augustine's, and Yoder's Interpretations of the Constantinian Shift.* Eugene, OR: Pickwick Publications, 2020.

Schmiedel, Ulrich. "The Cracks in the Category of Christianism: A Call for Ambiguity in the Conceptualization of Christianity." In *Contemporary Christian-Cultural Values: Migration Encounters in the Nordic Region*, edited by Cecilia Nahnfeldt and Kaia S. Rønsdal, 164–82. London: Routledge, 2021.

Schmiedel, Ulrich. *Elasticized Ecclesiology. The Concept of Community after Ernst Troeltsch.* New York: Palgrave Macmillan, 2017.

Schmiedel, Ulrich. "The Legacy of Theological Liberalism. A Ghost in Public Theology." In *T&T Clark Handbook of Public Theology*, edited by Christoph Hübenthal and Christiane Alpers, 127–46. London: T&T Clark, 2022.

Schmiedel, Ulrich. "'Take up Your Cross': Public Theology between Populism and Pluralism in the Post-Migrant Context." *International Journal of Public Theology* 13, no. 2 (2019): 140–62. https://doi.org/10.1163/15697320-12341569.

Schmiedel, Ulrich. *Terror Und Theologie: Der Religionstheoretische Diskurs Der 9/11-Dekade.* Tübingen: Mohr Siebeck, 2021.

Schoenfeld, Devorah. "Using Hevruta to Do and Teach Comparative Theology." In *Teaching Interreligious Encounters*, edited by Marc A. Pugliese and Alex Y. Hwang, 163–76. Oxford: Oxford University Press, 2017.

Schulze, Winfried. "Pluralisierung Als Bedrohung: Toleranz Als Lösung." In *Der Westfälische Friede*, edited by Duchhardt Heinz, 115–40: München: Oldenbourg Oldenbourg Wissenschaftsverlag, 1998.

Schweiker, William. "Theology of Culture and Its Future." In *The Cambridge Companion to Paul Tillich*, edited by Russell Re Manning, 138–51. Cambridge: Cambridge University Press, 2009.

Scott, James C. *Domination and the Arts of Resistance. Hidden Transcripts.* New Haven and London: Yale University Press, 1990.

Scott, James C. *Seeing Like a State: How Certain Schemes to Improve the Human Condition Have Failed.* New Haven: Yale University Press, 1999.

Shadid, W. "Muslim Dress in Europe: Debates on the Headscarf." *Journal of Islamic Studies* 16, no. 1 (2005): 35–61. https://doi.org/10.1093/jis/16.1.35.

Shaw, Danny. "Yarl's Wood: Years of Misery and Controversy." *BBC News*, 10th of June 2015. https://www.bbc.com/news/uk-33043395.

Shiner, Larry. "The Concept of Secularization in Empirical Research." *Journal for the Scientific Study of Religion* 6, no. 2 (1967): 207–20. https://doi.org/10.2307/1384047.

Siedentop, Larry. *Inventing the Individual. The Origins of Western Liberalism.* Cambridge, MA: Belknap Press, 2017.

Simonovits, Bori. "The Public Perception of the Migration Crisis from the Hungarian Point of View: Evidence from the Field." In *Geographies of Asylum in Europe and the Role of European Localities*, edited by Birgit Glorius and Jeroen Doomernik. Imiscoe Research Series, 155–76. New York: Springer International Publishing, 2020.

Skinner, Quentin. *Visions of Politics: Regarding Method.* Vol. 1, Cambridge: Cambridge University Press, 2002.

Skov Hansen, Mette. "København Siger Nej Til Neutralt Ceremonirum." *Kristeligt Dagblad*, 14th of September 2016. https://www.kristeligt-dagblad.dk/kirke-tro/koebenhavn-siger-nej-til-neutralt-ceremonirum.

Smith, Graeme. *A Short History of Secularism.* London and New York: I.B. Tauris, 2008.

Smith, Jonathan D. "Multi-Faith Spaces at UK Universities Display Two Very Different Visions of Public Religion." *Religion and Global Society*, 12th of August 2016. https://blogs.lse.ac.uk/religionglobalsociety/2016/08/multi-faith-spaces-at-uk-universities-display-two-very-different-visions-of-public-religion/.

Sofos, Spyros. "Securitizing the "Other" in the European Far-Right Imaginary." *Political Trends & Dynamics in Southeast Europe* 2019, no. 2 (2019): 23–26.

Sommerville, C. John. "Secular Society/Religious Population: Our Tacit Rules for Using the Term 'Secularization'." *Journal for the Scientific Study of Religion* 37, no. 2 (1998): 249–53. https://doi.org/10.2307/1387524.

St. George's University of London. "Protocol for the Multi-Faith and Quiet Contemplation Rooms." 2013, accessed 22nd of April, 2022, https://www.sgul.ac.uk/about/governance/policies/documents/Agreed-Protocol-May-2015-Rochelle-Rowe-1.pdf.

Stanford University Office for Religious & Spiritual Life. "Memorial Church & Companion Spaces." 2021, accessed 12th of December, 2021, https://orsl.stanford.edu/who-we-are/memorial-church-companion-spaces.

Stark, Rodney. "Secularization, R.I.P.". *Sociology of Religion* 60, no. 3 (1999): 249–73. https://doi.org/10.2307/3711936.

Statens Offentliga Utredningar. *Statens Stöd Till Trossamfund i Ett Mångreligiöst Sverige.* Statens Offentliga Utredningar (Stockholm: 2018).

Steinberg, Gerald. "Jewish Sources on Conflict Management: Realism and Human Nature." In *Conflict and Conflict Management in Jewish Sources*, edited by Michal Roness. Tel Aviv: Bar Ilan University, 2017.

Stout, Jeffrey. *Democracy and Tradition.* Princeton: Princeton University Press, 2005.

Stout, Jeffrey. *Ethics after Babel: The Lanuages of Morals and Their Discontents.* Boston: Beacon Press, 1988.

Strømmen, Hannah, and Ulrich Schmiedel. *The Claim to Christianity: Responding to the Far Right.* London: SCM Press, 2020.

Sullivan, Winnifred Fallers. *The Impossibility of Religious Freedom.* New Jersey: Princeton University Press, 2018.

Svendborg Architects. "Ceremony Room in Existing Buildings." Svendborg Architects, 2021, accessed 15th of September, 2021, http://www.svendborgarchitects.dk/Ceremony-Room-Existing-Buildings.

Svenska Dagbladet. "Debatten om Religiösa Friskolor." 2022, accessed 12th of March, 2022, https://www.svd.se/story/debatten-om-religiosa-friskolor.

Svenska Kyrkan Lunds Domkyrkoförsamling. "Studentprästerna i Lund." 2021, accessed 12th of December, 2021, https://lundsdomkyrka.se/larande-motesplatser/studentprasterna/.

Svenungsson, Jayne. *Divining History: Prophetism, Messianism and the Development of the Spirit.* New York: Berghahn Books, 2016.

Svenungsson, Jayne. *Guds Återkomst: En Studie av Gudsbegreppet inom Postmodern Filosofi.* Gothenburg: Glänta, 2004.

Svenungsson, Jayne. "Public Faith and the Common Good a Radical Messianic Proposal." *Political Theology* 14, no. 6 (2015): 744–57. https://doi.org/10.1179/1462317x13z.00000000047.

Svenungsson, Jayne. "The Return of Religion or the End of Religion? On the Need to Rethink Religion as a Category of Social and Political Life." *Philosophy and Social Criticism* 46, no. 7 (2020): 785–809. https://doi.org/10.1177%2F0191453719896384.

Swatos Jr., William H., and Kevin J. Christiano. "Secularization Theory: The Course of a Concept." *Sociology of Religion* 60, no. 3 (1999): 209–28.

Taneja, Poonam. "Prayer Facility Row at University." *BBC News*, 1st of April 2010. http://news.bbc.co.uk/2/hi/8598455.stm. news.bbc.co.uk.

Taylor, Charles. *A Secular Age.* Boston, MA: Belknap Press, 2018.

Taylor, Greg. "Germany: The Subsidiarity Principle." *International Journal of Constitutional Law* 4, no. 1 (2006): 115–30. https://doi.org/10.1093/icon/moi054.

Taylor, Jerome. "Muslim Students Take Legal Advice after City University Shuts Down Friday Prayer Meeting." *Independent*, 22nd of February 2013. https://www.independent.co.uk/news/uk/home-news/muslim-students-take-legal-advice-after-city-university-shuts-down-friday-prayer-meeting-8507166.html.

The President of Hamburg University. "Code of Conduct for Religious Expression." Hamburg University, 2021, accessed 18th of October, 2021, https://www.uni-hamburg.de/en/uhh/profil/leitbild/verhaltenskodex-religionsausuebung.html.

Thurfjell, David. *Det Gudlösa Folket. De Postkristna Svenskarna och Religionen.* Stockholm: Molin & Sorgenfrei Förlag, 2016.

Thurfjell, David, and Erika Willander. "Muslims by Ascription: On Post-Lutheran Secularity and Muslim Immigrants." *Numen* 68, no. 4 (2021): 307–35. https://doi.org/10.1163/15685276-12341626.

Tillich, Paul. *Systematic Theology (in 3 Volumes).* Chicago: University of Chicago Press, 1951–1963.

Tillich, Paul. *Theology of Culture.* New York: Oxford University Press, 1959.

Todd, J. Terry. "The Temple of Religion and the Politics of Religious Pluralism: Judeo-Christian America at the 1939–1940 New York World's Fair." In *After Pluralism: Reimagining Models of Religious Engagement*, edited by Courtney Bender and Pamela Klassen, 201–22. New York: Columbia University Press, 2010.

Torry, Malcolm. *Bridgebuilders: Workplace Chaplaincy—a History.* London: Canterbury Press, 2010.

Tracy, David. "Three Kinds of Publicness in Public Theology." *International Journal of Public Theology* 8, no. 3 (2014): 330–34. https://doi.org/10.1163/15697320-12341354.

Tschannen, Oliver. *Les Theories De La Secularisation.* Geneva: Droz, 1992.

Tucker, William T. "Max Weber's "Verstehen"." *The Sociological Quarterly* 6, no. 2 (1965): 157–65.

Tuininga, Matthew J. *Calvin's Political Theology and the Public Engagement of the Church. Christ's Two Kingdoms.* Cambridge: Cambridge University Press, 2017.

Uddanelses- og Forskningministeriet. *Opgørelse over Antallet af Bederum eller Lignende Faciliteter på de Videregående Uddannelsesinstitutioner.* Copenhagen: Uddanelses- og Forskningministeriet, 2017.

Umeå University. "Multi-Faith Space." 2022, accessed 22nd of April, 2022, https://www.umu.se/en/student/we-can-assist-you/group-rooms-and-other-spaces/multi-faith-space/#:~:text=The%20Multi%2Dfaith%20space%20is,regardless%20of%20faith%20or%20beliefs.

Undervisnings Ministeriet. *Information Vedr. Aktindsigt i Undersøgelse om Bederum på Offentlige Uddannelsesinstitutioner, fra Undervisningsministeren. Bilag 2.* Copenhagen: Undervisnings Ministeriet, 2017.

United Nations. "'A Room of Quiet' the Meditation Room, United Nations Headquarters." 2018, accessed 18th of September, 2021, https://www.un.org/depts/dhl/dag/meditationroom.htm.

Universität Duisburg-Essen. "Erklärung Der Hochschulleitung. Schließung Des Gebetsraums." 2016, accessed 12th of December, 2021, https://www.uni-due.de/de/presse/meldung.php?id=9291.

University of Winchester. "Our Chaplaincies." 2021, accessed 12th of December, 2021, https://www.winchester.ac.uk/accommodation-and-winchester-life/student-life/spirituality/our-chaplaincies/.

University of Winchester. "Spirituality." 2021, accessed 12th of December, 2021, https://www.winchester.ac.uk/accommodation-and-winchester-life/student-life/spirituality/.

University of Winchester. "Your Spiritual Journey." 2021, accessed 12th of December, 2021, https://www.winchester.ac.uk/accommodation-and-winchester-life/student-life/spirituality/spiritual-journey/.

University of York. "Protocol for the Use of Multi-Faith Space at the University of York." 2021, accessed 22nd of April, 2022, https://www.york.ac.uk/media/studenthome/studentsupporthub/Protocol%20for%20the%20Multi-Faith%20Space%20(VS3.0%20Dec%2021).pdf.

Utrecht University. "Meditation, Lactation and First-Aid Rooms." 2021, accessed 25th of September, 2021, https://students.uu.nl/en/meditation-lactation-and-first-aid-rooms.

UWE Faith & Spirituality. "Guidance for Use of Multi-Faith Space." University of the West of England Bristol, 2021, accessed 22nd of April, 2021, https://www.uwe.ac.uk/-/media/uwe/documents/life/health-wellbeing/multi-faith-space-guidance.pdf.

Van Dort, Paul M. "Temple of Religion." 1939 New York World's Fair, 2021, accessed 17th of November, 2021, https://www.1939nyworldsfair.com/worlds_fair/wf_tour/zone-2/temple_of_religion.htm.

Vanoni, Luca Pietro, and Giada Ragone. "From the Secularisation Theory to the Pluralistic Approach: Reconciling Religious Traditions and Modernity in Italian Case-Law." In *Law, Religion, and Tradition*, edited by Jessica Giles, Andrea Pin and Frank S. Ravitch, 1–28. New York: Springer, 2018.

Velasco, Francisco Diez de. *Guía Técnica Para La Implementación Y Gestión De Espacios Multiconfesionales*. Observatorio del Pluralismo Religioso en España (Madrid: 2011).

Velasco, Francisco Díez de. *Multi-Belief/Multi-Faith Spaces: Theoretical Proposals for a Neutral and Operational Design*. RECODE Working Paper Series (Augsburg: 2014). https://www.recode.info/wp-content/uploads/2014/01/FINAL-26-D%C3%ADez-de-Velasco_fin.pdf.

Veranstaltungsgesellschaft 350 Jahre Westfälischer Friede mbH. *1648: Krieg Und Frieden in Europa. Münster/Osnabrück 24.10.1998–17.01.1999* [*Katalog Zur 26. Europaratsausstellung*]. Edited by Klaus Bußmann and Heinz Schilling. Münster: Veranstaltungsgesellschaft 350 Jahre Westfälischer Friede mbH, 1998.

Vincent, James. *Beyond Measure: The Hidden History of Measurement*. London: Faber & Faber, 2023.

Voller, Louise. "Ceremonier Uden Religion Til Folk, Der Lever Uden Gud." *Information*, 2008. https://www.information.dk/kultur/2008/08/ceremonier-uden-religion-folk-lever-uden-gud.

von Brömssen, Kerstin, Heinz Ivkovits, and Graeme Nixon. "Religious Literacy in the Curriculum in Compulsory Education in Austria, Scotland and Sweden - a Three-Country Policy Comparison." *Journal of Beliefs & Values* 41, no. 2 (2020): 132–49. https://doi.org/10.1080/13617672.2020.1737909.

von Brömssen, Kerstin, and Christina Rodell Olgaç. "Intercultural Education in Sweden through the Lenses of the National Minorities and of Religious Education." *Intercultural Education* 21, no. 2 (2010): 121–35. https://doi.org/10.1080/14675981003696263.

von Friedeburg, Robert. "Cuius Regio, Eius Religio: The Ambivalent Meanings of State Building in Protestant Germany, 1555–1655." In *Diversity and Dissent: Negotiating Religious Difference in Central Europe, 1500–1800*, edited by Howard Louthan, Gary B. Cohen and Franz A. J. Szabo. Austrian and Habsburg Studies, 73–91. Oxford, NY: Berghahn Books, 2011.

Vrije Universiteit Amsterdam. "Multi-faith Space." 2021, accessed 12th of December, 2021, https://vu.nl/en/about-vu/more-about/stilteruimte-vu.

Warnke, Raphael. "No Space for Allah as German Unis Close Prayer Rooms." *The Local Germany* , 11th of March 2016. https://www.thelocal.de/20160311/no-place-for-allah-as-german-unis-close-prayer-rooms/.

Weber, Max. "Objectivity in Social Science and Social Policy." In *The Methodology of the Social Sciences*, edited by E. A. Shils and H. A. Finch. New York: Free Press, 1949.

Weber, Max. *The Protestant Ethic and the Spirit of Capitalism.* Translated by Talcott Parsons and R.H. Tawney. New York: Dover Publications, 2003.

Weber, Max. "The Protestant Sects and the Spirit of Capitalism." In *From Max Weber: Essays in Sociology*, edited by H. H. Gerth and C. Wright Mills, 302–22. London: Routledge & Kegan Paul LTD, 1970.

Weber, Max. "Religious Rejections of the World and Their Directions." In *From Max Weber: Essays in Sociology*, edited by H. H. Gerth and C. Wright Mills, 323–59. London: Routledge & Kegan Paul LTD, 1970.

Weber, Max. "Science as Vocation." In *From Max Weber: Essays in Sociology*, edited by H. H. Gerth and C. Wright Mills, 77–128. London: Routledge & Kegan Paul LTD, 1970.

Weber, Max. *The Theory of Social and Economic Organization.* Translated by A. M. Henderson and Talcott Parsons. New York: Oxford University Press, 1947.

Weinberger, Lael Daniel. "The Relationship between Sphere Sovereignty and Subsidiarity." In *Global Perspectives on Subsidiarity*, edited by Michelle Evans and Augusto Zimmermann, 46–63. Dordrecht: Springer, 2014.

Weller, Paul. *Time for a Change: Reconfiguring Religion, State and Society.* London: T&T Clark International, 2005.

Wenman, Mark. *Agonistic Democracy.* Cambridge: Cambridge University Press, 2013.

Whyman, Tom, "Happy Birthday Habermas, Your Philosophy Has Failed Us," *The Outline*, 30th of July, 2019, https://theoutline.com/post/7734/habermas-failure-political-philosophy.

Wilken, Robert Louis. *The First Thousand Years: A Global History of Christianity.* New Haven and London: Yale University Press, 2012.

Williams, Rowan. *Faith in the Public Square.* London: Bloomsbury, 2012.

Williamson, Chilton Jr. "'What Is Paleoconservatism? Man, Know Thyself!" *Chronicles —a Magazine of American Culture.* (January 2001). https://www.chroniclesmagazine.org/what-is-paleoconservatism-2/.

Wohlrab-Sahr, Monika, and Marian Burchardt. "Multiple Secularities. Towards a Cultural Sociology of Secular Modernities." *Comparative Sociology* 11 (2012): 875–909. https://doi.org/10.1163/15691330-12341249.

Wright, K. S. "The Principles of Catholic Social Teaching: A Guide for Decision Making from Daily Clinical Encounters to National Policy-Making." *Linacre Q* 84, no. 1 (Feb 2017): 10–22. https://doi.org/10.1080/00243639.2016.1274629.

Wright, Larry, "Faith in Dention," *This is Church*, 2005, http://www.thisischurch.com/christian_teaching/sermon/faithindentioneaster2005.htm.

Yelle, Robert A., and Lorenz Trein. *Narratives of Disenchantment and Secularization: Critiquing Max Weber's Idea of Modernity.* London: Bloomsbury Academic, 2021.

Yoder, John H. "Is There Such a Thing as Being Ready for Another Millenium?" In *The Future of Theology: Essays in Honor of Jürgen Moltmann*, edited by Miroslav Volf, Carmen Krieg and Thomas Kucharz, 63–72. Grand Rapids, MI and Cambridge, U.K.: William B. Eerdmans Publishing Company, 1996.

Zagorin, Perez. *How the Idea of Religious Toleration Came to the West.* Princeton, NJ: Princeton University Press, 2003.

Zieler, Christoffer. "Parliament Split in Debate over Prayer Rooms." *University Post*, 23rd of February, 2017. https://uniavisen.dk/en/parliament-split-in-debate-over-prayer-rooms/.

Zieler, Christoffer, "UCPH Has an Exceptionally High Number of Prayer Rooms," *University Post*, 2017, https://uniavisen.dk/en/ucph-has-an-exceptionally-high-number-of-prayer-rooms/.

Zubik, Marek. *Prawo Konstytucyjne Współczesnej Polski.* Studia Prawnicze. Warszawa: C.H. Beck, 2021.

Index

Printed in the United States
by Baker & Taylor Publisher Services